Television and the Exceptional Child:

A Forgotten Audience

COMMUNICATION

A series of volumes edited by
Dolf Zillmann and Jennings Bryant

Television and the Exceptional Child:

A Forgotten Audience

Joyce Sprafkin
Kenneth D. Gadow
State University of New York at Stony Brook

Robert Abelman
Cleveland State University

LEA
LAWRENCE ERLBAUM ASSOCIATES, PUBLISHERS
1992   Hillsdale, New Jersey   Hove and London

Lawrence Erlbaum Associates, Inc., Publishers
365 Broadway
Hillsdale, New Jersey 07642

Library of Congress Cataloging-in-Publication Data

Sprafkin, Joyce, 1949-
    Television and the exceptional child : A forgotten audience / Joyce Sprafkin,
Kenneth D. Gadow, and Robert Abelman.
      p. cm.
    Includes bibliographical references and index.
    ISBN 0-8058-0787-X (c) 0788-8 (p)
    1. Television and children—United States. 2. Exceptional children—United
States. I. Gadow, Kenneth D. II. Abelman, Robert. III. Title.
HQ784.T4S73 1992
302.23'45'083—dc20
                                                  92-7974
                                                   CIP

Printed in the United States of America
10 9 8 7 6 5 4 3 2 1

This book is dedicated to

Jay, Bob Blair, Edythe Kahn, and Dalai (JS)

Geneva, Rich, Ron, and Miss Helen Dixon (KDG)

Ryan Austin, Allyson Jacqueline, and the memory of Michele Lynn (RA) ....

special individuals who touched our lives.

Contents

Foreword

James M. Kauffman, Professor of Education
University of Virginia

To the title character in John Irving's *A Prayer for Owen Meany,* television was synonymous with sham. Owen had a pet phrase for describing whatever he perceived as particularly disingenuous: "YOU KNOW WHAT THAT IS? THAT'S MADE FOR TELEVISION—THAT'S WHAT THAT IS." Owen was a particularly bright and sensitive lad, so his characterization of television as the ideal medium for misrepresentation is entirely plausible. Television is not, of course, the exclusive province of misrepresentation, disingenuousness, and sham, nor do all bright and sensitive people view typical commercial television fare with Owen Meany's contempt. Still, the pervasive influence of television in contemporary life and its ability to captivate audiences— especially the more innocent members of any audience—demand special concern for its influence on children. Because exceptional children differ cognitively and socially from their peers, examination of the differing effects television may have on them is long overdue.

This volume is a welcome foil to the television sound bite. It represents the kind of careful review and balanced interpretation of empirical evidence that we virtually never see on screen and too seldom see in print. The authors summarize what we know about how intellectual giftedness, mental retardation, emotional disturbance, and learning disability are related to television viewing and to these exceptional children's interpretation of what they watch. But they go beyond describing the potentially troubling effects of television to suggest how it might be turned to the benefit of these children, including how adults might mediate existing programming and how the medium might be made more appropriately instructive.

The exceptional children about whom the authors write are, indeed, a forgotten audience. Other groups of exceptional children and adults may be seen as long forgotten as well. Only recently has captioning made television dialogue accessible to the deaf, and work on a video descriptive service for the blind is just beginning. However, the children about whom the authors have written are much more numerous than those with hearing or vision impairments, and they are perhaps more easily neglected in the long term. Their special abilities and disabilities cannot be addressed by technological advances that make the medium accessible; the special problems engendered by their exceptionalities are related to the content of television programming.

Television is now a part of nearly every child's earliest experience and a considerable force in shaping the way nearly all children and adults think about the human condition and human relationships. In some respects, television shows promise as a positive influence on viewers' perceptions of people with exceptionalities. Network programming and commercial messages are today breaking some of the old stereotypes of people with special abilities and disabilities, showing them in a more balanced and positive light. More realistic and positive portrayal of exceptional children and adults might promote more humane attitudes that could foster acceptance and inclusion of individuals who are in some way(s) not typical.

Regardless of changes in television programming, including increasing availability of programs designed to stimulate more prosocial behavior in viewers, exceptional children will remain television's forgotten audience until their caretakers exercise their responsibility to control the programs exceptional children watch. Television, like all other mass media, is inherently designed around the modal characteristics of its audience; it is by nature the antithesis of attention to the individual. The authors' concluding suggestions for the adult who may choose to control what an exceptional child watches are therefore of utmost importance.

Preface

Few technological advances of the 20th century have elicited such diverse reactions as television. Almost since its introduction, television has been criticized as a possible contributor to aggressive behavior and attitudes, academic underachievement, racial and sexual stereotypes, and materialism, especially in children. In spite of public outcry over its alleged adverse effects, viewership and sales of televisions and related services (e.g., cable, video cassette recorders [VCRs]) have increased steadily over the years. Along with the criticisms have come the development of some quality programming and the realization of what television could do for enhancing the cognitive and social development of child viewers.

As with most technological advances, social scientists have played a prominent role in examining television's influence on society. To date, literally thousands of studies have been conducted addressing numerous questions about television. Interestingly, this outpouring of research has not generated uniform or clear-cut findings, so the search for answers continues.

The question of what types of children are most influenced by television is a recurrent theme in the scientific literature, particularly since Schramm, Lyle, and Parker's (1961) much cited conclusion that "for *some* children, under some conditions, some television is harmful" (p. 1, italics added). Researchers have known for many years that heavy television viewers are more likely to experience difficulties in their social relationships and to perform poorly in school. Further, studies have shown that children who are more aggressive tend to be the ones most affected by watching violent content. These characteristics—problems with interpersonal relationships, aggressive behavior, and academic underachievement—are common in children who have been labeled by their school districts as emotionally disturbed (ED), learning disabled (LD), or mentally retarded (MR). It is therefore somewhat surprising that with few exceptions, research has focused almost exclusively on "normal" (i.e., nonlabeled, nondisabled) children, with little consideration given to exceptional individuals, that is, those "who require special education and related services if they are to realize their full human potential" (Hallahan & Kauffman, 1991, p. 6).

Similarly, the failure to examine television and children at the other end of the educational continuum, intellectually gifted children, is an oversight. Although one might expect that their advanced cognitive capacities would render them less vulnerable to potential adverse influences of television viewing, this is an empirical question and one that is worth addressing. It is possible that gifted children's need for stimulation results in their watching adult-oriented programs for which they are emotionally or socially unprepared.

Exceptional children have been virtually ignored by television researchers, and they are truly the forgotten audience. Their exclusion may have been defensible in the early days of television research when attention was reasonably devoted to studying the "normal" majority, but television is the great common denominator in contemporary society, the one environmental experience that all children share. Whether television is considered a "magic window" (Dorr, 1986), a "double-edged sword" (Richert, 1981), a "home invader" (Wildmon, 1985), a "vacuous vision" (Emery & Emery, 1980) or a "plug-in drug" (Winn, 1977), an examination of its use by and impact on all children is justifiable. Furthermore, we are not referring to an insignificant segment of the viewing audience when we consider exceptional children. Almost 3 million youngsters in the United States are currently classified as emotionally disturbed, learning disabled, or mentally retarded by their local school district, and an additional 1 million of the school-aged population could be classified as intellectually gifted.

It is somewhat ironic that television researchers ignored exceptional children during a period when the development of educational, vocational, medical, and support services for them skyrocketed. The period from 1960 to 1980 was the most active in the creation of programs and the assurance of rights of individuals with disabilities. Deinstitutionalization, normalization, and the right to both special education and mainstreaming were all important goals of this era. In particular, the passing of the All Handicapped Children Act of 1975 (PL 94-142), along with Section 504 of the Rehabilitation Act of 1973, guaranteed disabled individuals equal access to programs and services. PL 94-142 guaranteed a free, appropriate, public education to every school-aged person identified as disabled in the United States. General support for gifted programs rose dramatically following the 1957 Soviet launching of Sputnik (see Tannenbaum, 1979). Concern for American advancement in science motivated radical changes in public education, and human intellect became a valuable natural resource worthy of nurturance. It is only fitting, therefore, that this book is written in the wake of the Americans with Disabilities Act of 1990, a significant piece of legislation that recognizes exceptional populations and their telecommunications needs (see Brotman, 1990).

This book focuses on ED, LD, MR, and gifted children and how they use, process, and react to television. Our intended audiences are students, educators, and researchers in the fields of communication and special education and the parents and teachers of exceptional children. One reason why television researchers may have ignored these children is their unfamiliarity with this population. For this audience, our goal is to demystify special education and the special needs of exceptional children as television viewers. We also encourage media researchers to examine the degree to which their theories of television use, comprehension, and effects apply to this broader range of children.

Special educators have long recognized the positive potential the medium holds for teaching children who are often unresponsive to traditional methods of instruction. However, their contribution to the television literature has been comprised mostly of speculative or theoretical essays rather than programmatic research designed to answer specific questions. We hope that our book stimulates special educators to conduct research in this area.

Finally, for parents and teachers of exceptional children, we emphasize the importance of their roles in mediating the effects of television viewing. We provide specific suggestions for interventions both at home and in school.

This book describes the research findings on television and exceptional children. Many of the studies in this area have been conducted by the authors and their colleagues over the past decade. Joyce Sprafkin and Ken Gadow developed a program of research in the Department of Psychiatry at the State University of New York at Stony Brook to investigate the role of television viewing in the lives of children with learning and behavior disorders, and Bob Abelman initiated a similar program of research in the Department of Communication at Cleveland State University, which focused primarily on gifted children. Unbeknownst to each other, both groups were studying exceptional children, albeit in different academic disciplines, and the questions addressed by each were remarkably similar. This book represents the integration of our respective efforts.

The topics addressed in this book are organized according to a logical progression of television-oriented topics (e.g., viewing habits, comprehension, behavioral effects). Each chapter offers an overview of the issue being addressed and the relevant literature on nonlabeled children, and then concentrates on research pertaining to exceptional children. Based on the available data, we compare the research findings for the various groups of exceptional children and nonlabeled peers.

Chapter 1 summarizes the four decades of research on children and television and its theoretical perspectives. It shows how early research focused on what television "did to" children and how later research evolved into a more complex framework in which the characteristics of the child and his or her environment functioned as mediators in the viewing process. We also present definitions and descriptions of the various groups of exceptional children examined throughout the book and the settings in which they are educated.

Chapter 2 describes television viewing habits. This topic includes how much and what children watch and the programs and characters that they identify as being their favorites.

Chapter 3 discusses perceptions of the realism of television content. This is important because the perceived reality of television fare has long been recognized as a primary antecedent to the effects of viewing certain material. How and why these perceptions differ among exceptional children and their possible implications are addressed.

Chapter 4 examines comprehension of television programs and commercials. The conceptualization of television viewing as a learned behavior has gained much support in the last decade. Various cognitive abilities and exposure to television are prerequisites for children to recognize, identify, and understand television's unique formats of presenting stories. This chapter examines the comprehension of television techniques and their implications for what is learned.

Chapter 5 describes the behavioral consequences of viewing different types of television programs, specifically anti- and prosocial content. Practically since its inception, television has been identified as contributing to children's aggressive behavior, and this issue has been the focus of extensive scientific inquiry. More recently, scientists have recognized that television also contains positive social models and that children can learn from them as well. In this chapter we examine the degree to which television has been shown to influence both socially desirable and undesirable behaviors in exceptional children.

Chapter 6 introduces environmental variables that influence what children learn from television. Specifically, it examines the extent to which parents consider television to be an influential force in their child's life, the quantity and quality of parental involvement in their child's television viewing, and whether and what type of impact this might have on what children learn from television.

Chapter 7 explores how schools can intervene in influencing what children learn from television. Educators in many schools across the country have become increasingly aware of the role that television plays in society. This has prompted the development of curricula to teach students television viewing skills. This chapter examines the efforts to develop television literacy and critical viewing skills by special educators and discusses the potential of educational institutions in mediating what and how children learn from television.

Perhaps the most exciting potential of television is its applications to teach academic, social, self-help, and vocational skills. Special educators recognize that students' deficits in attention, cognition, or motivation present challenges to traditional teaching methods. Yet virtually all children are attracted to television and seem to absorb at least some of what they view. The degree to which this potential of television has been realized is examined in chapter 8.

In the final chapter we discuss the future directions in research in this area and present the implications of the new television-related technologies (e.g., cable, VCRs) for exceptional children. There is a special section devoted to care providers in which we review the findings for each group of exceptional children and offer suggestions for intervention. In addition, consistent with our goal of stimulating future research in this area, we present our perspective on interesting unanswered questions and research priorities.

ACKNOWLEDGMENTS

We thank Jennings Bryant for his omnipresent and ever-gracious support. Appreciation is extended to the Department of Psychiatry and Behavioral Science at the State University of New York at Stony Brook and the Department of Communication at Cleveland State University, who awarded sabbatical leave to two of the authors and the resultant luxury of uninterrupted time to devote to this project. We acknowledge the following agencies and institutions for their financial support of the investigations whose findings largely comprise the content of this book: the National Institute of Mental Health, the University of Alabama, the Research and Creative Activities Council and Graduate Office (Cleveland State University), the University of Texas–Austin, and the Shell Grant Foundation. We are also indebted to all the children, teachers, school administrators, and parents who participated in our studies and made this book possible. A special thanks goes to the following school administrators whose courageous support of scientific inquiry opened the door to a greater understanding of the needs of special children: James Fogarty, Merrill Zusmer, Irwin Sadetsky, Sherry Leeds, Elizabeth Mulvihill, James Burke, and Doris King.

Joyce Sprafkin
Kenneth D. Gadow
Robert Abelman

1 Introduction and Overview

Television viewing has evolved into the most time-consuming leisure activity of American youth. In fact, by the age of 18 most children will have spent more time watching television than doing anything else except sleeping. As with most other social phenomena, television viewing has been the topic of much scientific inquiry. Literally thousands of studies have examined the content of television programs and the effect that different types of content have on child viewers. Until quite recently, however, virtually all of the research on television and child behavior has focused on average or "normal" children and ignored youngsters with learning or behavioral disabilities or with advanced intellectual capabilities. This book attempts to fill this void by reporting what is known about the programs exceptional children watch on television, how they process the content and how it affects them, and what environmental factors can influence children's reactions to the medium.

Clearly, it would be helpful to have a background in television research as well as in special education to understand many aspects of this book, which is aimed at students and professionals in a variety of disciplines—education, communication, child development, and psychology. However, readers from the education field may not have systematically studied the literature on children and television. Similarly, those from the communication discipline may not be familiar with the prevalence, characteristics, and education of exceptional children. Therefore, in this first chapter we provide the prerequisite knowledge about both television and special education. We begin with a historical perspective of television research to highlight the evolution of thought and theory in this field and to introduce many of the issues that are relevant to this area of research. This is followed by a description of the specific categories of exceptional children that are the primary focus of this book.

HISTORICAL OVERVIEW

With the development of each modern means of storytelling—commercial books, magazines, newspapers, movies, radio, comics, and television—there have been debates about its impact on society. A prominent theme in these debates has been a concern about the adverse influences of specific types of media content on children. This is not, however, a by-product of the technological era. For example, concerns about the possible negative influence of the storyteller on children were expressed in ancient Greece. According to Plato's *Republic:*

> Children cannot distinguish between what is allegory and what isn't, and opinions formed at that age are usually difficult to eradicate or change; it is therefore of the utmost importance that the first stories they hear shall aim at producing the right moral effect.

It was not until the advent of broadcasting, however, that the amount and intensity of criticism and concern reached its height, as can be seen in these comments by a Professor Eisenberg in 1936:

> The popularity of this new pastime (radio) among children has increased rapidly. This new invader of the privacy of the home has brought many a disturbing influence in its wake. Parents have become aware of a puzzling change in the behavior of their children. They are bewildered by a host of new problems, and find themselves unprepared, frightened, resentful, helpless. (cited in Abelman & Ross, 1986, p. 3)

The history of television research can be divided into three global phases. The first, the *medium-orientation phase,* assumed that television had overwhelming power and that young audiences were particularly vulnerable to its influence. During this early stage of scientific inquiry, there was little consideration of developmental or individual differences that influence the power of the medium. During the ensuing *child-orientation phase,* the potential of media effects was thought to reside in the child and not in the medium. In other words, research during this period sought to explain why children processed and reacted to the same program content in demonstrably different ways. This, in turn, has given way to a more *interaction-orientation phase,* in which media effects are treated as an interaction between medium variables (e.g., type of content), child variables (e.g., age), and environmental factors (e.g., parents and teachers).

Medium-Orientation Phase

Although concerns about television initially centered on the disruption and usurpation of children's leisure activities and interactions with peers, the focus rapidly shifted to the impact of viewing portrayals of antisocial behavior, an issue that has been actively pursued by academicians, scientists, political activists, and government agencies for the past four decades. The Kefauver Committee on Juvenile Delinquency (1954), the Dodd Hearings (1961), the Senate Subcommittee on Juvenile Delinquency (1964), and the National Commission on the Causes and Prevention of Violence (1968) all concluded that there was a great deal of violence on television and that such content probably had an adverse effect on children.

According to Liebert and Sprafkin (1988), several issues emerged repeatedly in the scientific and popular literature during this period, including (a) television's instigation of violent, aggressive, or antisocial behavior; (b) stereotyped portrayals and the cultivation of racial and gender stereotyping; (c) commercialism and the questionable practice of selling to children via commercials; and (d) the adverse effect of television on learning processes. Much of this work was initiated by Schramm, Lyle, and Parker's book, *Television in the Lives of Our Children* (1961), which examined the possibility that certain types of television content stimulated the formation of negative attitudes or induced antisocial behavior.

During the 1960s, numerous theories were brought to bear to explain television's adverse effects, particularly those resulting from the viewing of violent content. The most influential perspective was that of social learning theory, developed by Stanford psychologist Albert Bandura (Bandura & Walters, 1963), who proposed that much of what children learn about social interaction results from observing how others behave in various situations. Encompassed in the theory is the assumption that in order for television content to affect a viewer, the viewer must: (a) be exposed to the content, (b) comprehend it to some degree, and (c) accept the message and adopt the behaviors or attitudes portrayed (Liebert, Neale, & Davidson, 1973).

Inspired by his own studies confirming that children can learn novel aggressive behaviors from watching television, Bandura published an article in *Look* magazine in 1963 entitled, "What TV Violence Can Do to Your Child." The article began:

If parents could buy packaged psychological influences to administer in regular doses to their children, I doubt that many would deliberately select Western gun slingers, hopped-up psychopaths, deranged sadists, slap-stick buffoons and the like, unless they entertained rather peculiar ambitions for their growing offspring. Yet such examples of behavior are delivered in quantity, with no direct charge, to millions of households daily. Harried parents can easily turn off demanding children by turning on a television set; as a result, today's youth is being raised on a heavy dosage of televised aggression and violence. (p. 46)

As a result of articles such as this one, studies by Bandura and his colleagues, government hearings, and public outcry, the Surgeon General was directed in 1969 to investigate the effects of television viewing on child development. An advisory committee was appointed, and $1 million was allocated to the National Institute of Mental Health to fund worthwhile research. It was the largest concerted effort to date to examine television's impact on child behavior. Forty projects were conducted, of which the majority examined some aspect of television violence, with individual studies focusing on the amount of violent content, viewing habits, and the influence of aggression-laden content on child viewers.

The results of this research program were published in 1972 as a document that has been referred to as the "Surgeon General's Report." Although each of the studies included in the report had its limitations, researchers consistently found some relationship between viewing television violence and antisocial behavior in children and adolescents. However, it was equally clear that such behavior has many causes. In almost all of the studies, viewing aggression-laden content affected some youngsters more than others. The final report of the Surgeon General's Scientific Advisory Committee on Television and Social Behavior (1972) emphasized the importance of individual differences (e.g., age), predisposing characteristics (e.g., aggressiveness), and other environmental factors (e.g., family) in determining television's impact on children.

The research that immediately followed the Surgeon General's Report remained medium-oriented, albeit broader in scope than earlier efforts. Studies of television violence continued to be conducted, but other topics were also being addressed. This research is summarized in a publication that has come to be called the "10 Year Update" or "NIMH Update," a review of the television literature conducted during the 10 years following the publication of the Surgeon General's Report (Pearl, Bouthilet, & Lazar, 1982a, 1982b). Its conclusions regarding television violence were consistent with the findings of the earlier studies. The major difference between the two reports was that the 1982 publication examined the effects of television on many more areas of functioning (e.g., affective development, educational achievement, imaginative processes, and sexual learning) and recognized the need to identify the myriad factors that influence the impact of the medium.

One of the most significant events that occurred during the medium-orientation phase (which shaped future trends in media research) was the emergence of "Sesame Street" in 1969. This innovative children's series demonstrated that children can learn academic skills from television and that educational messages can be presented in an appealing way. It also suggested that programs could be designed to promote children's social development as well as their cognitive growth. In fact, one of the studies that appeared in the Surgeon Gener-

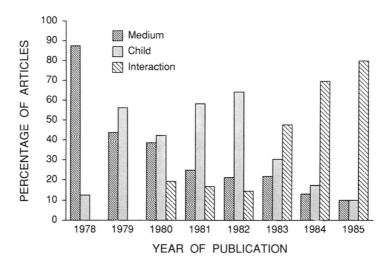

FIG. 1.1.   Percentage of articles reflecting medium, child, and interaction orientations that appeared in *Television and Families* from 1978 to 1985. *Note.* Based on data reported in "Children, Television and Families: An Evolution in Understanding" by R. Abelman and R. Ross, 1986, *Television and Families, 9,* pp. 2–4, 10–13, 26–27, 41–42.

al's Report (Stein & Friedrich, 1972) examined whether the presentation of socially desirable behavior on television could inspire like behavior in child viewers, which opened the door in the mid-to-late 1970s to other investigations of television's positive potential.

The success of "Sesame Street" was largely due to the collaboration of educators, child development specialists, and production professionals. Research on what children attended to and comprehended became the foundation of this influential television series. Consistent with this focus, the primary concern of communication researchers by the late 1970s became the study of the viewing process itself and the wide-ranging cognitive capacities that children bring to television viewing.

Evidence of this shift in perspective can be seen in Fig. 1.1, which presents the findings from a content analysis of articles that appeared in the National Council for Families and Television's (NCFT) quarterly periodical. The NCFT is an organization of professionals from the broadcasting industry, education, and academia. Its periodical, *Television and Families* (formerly *Television and Children*), contains essays by child development specialists, educators, industry regulators, communication researchers, and television professionals, thus providing a barometer of contemporary thought and perspective on television. The content of this periodical clearly reflects a shift in emphasis from a medium to a child orientation during the late 1970s and early 1980s.

This period of television research was reflective of more general developments in our society during which children were made a priority for public awareness and concern. The year 1979, for example, was declared the International Year of the Child by the federal government in an effort to emphasize the importance of children and our investment in their future.

Child-Orientation Phase

During the late 1970s, television research was largely focused on the act of viewing and the processes through which children attend to and comprehend program content. Rather than considering children to be passive recipients of television stimuli, they were now seen as active mediators in the viewing experience. Most researchers adopted a developmental perspective to examine how processing of television changed with maturity and experience. Because children's cognitive abilities change greatly through the course of development, the studies during this phase were strongly influenced by such cognitive theorists as Jean Piaget, John Flavell, Joachim Wohlwill, Jerome Bruner, and Heinz Werner.

During this phase of research, scientists developed sophisticated methodologies for studying what attracted children's attention. For example, Anderson and his colleagues (Anderson & Levin, 1976; Levin & Anderson, 1976) adapted some of the techniques used by "Sesame Street" and showed children television programs in a laboratory/den setting while their attention was being videotaped from behind a one-way window. The videotapes were later analyzed to determine what program characteristics were associated with the onset and termination of attention.

Much of this line of research ultimately focused on the "formal features" of television, "the auditory and visual production and editing techniques characterizing the medium" (Wright & Huston, 1983, p. 836). These features represent the form of television (as opposed to its content) and include such things as action, pacing, and camera cuts. Interestingly, they influence the behavior of child viewers independently of the specific behaviors presented on television. For example, programs that contain high levels of action but no aggressive content can instigate antisocial behavior in child viewers (Huston-Stein, Fox, Greer, Watkins, & Whitaker, 1981). It is the younger child who is most likely to be drawn to programs that contain perceptually salient content such as action and special effects (Wright et al., 1984).

Age has been shown to be an important determinant not only of attention to but also of comprehension of television content. Collins (1982), among others, showed that it is not until about the age of 11 years that most children can really follow a typical prime-time program. Part of the problem is that younger elementary-school children have difficulty discriminating between plot-important and plot-irrelevant content. Furthermore, the older child generally has a greater variety of world experiences to bring to the viewing situation, which help the child to form schemas (or internal models) for encoding, comprehension, and recall of television content.

In more recent years, the specific skills and abilities required to comprehend specific types and forms of television information have been examined in more detail. In particular, studies have explored children's attention to, comprehension of, and ability to organize knowledge about changes in size of televised images (Acker & Tiemens, 1981), velocity and distance of televised events (Acker, 1983; Flessati & Fouts, 1985; Reeves et al., 1984), temporal sequencing (i.e., plot development) and sequential transformations (Collins, Wellman, Keniston, & Westby, 1978), character portrayals (Hoffner & Cantor, 1985; Reeves & Garramone, 1982, 1983), and complexity of visual techniques (Huston & Wright, 1983; Smith, Anderson, & Fischer, 1985; Thorson, Reeves, & Schleuder, 1985; Welch & Watt, 1982), and auditory devices (Calvert & Gersh, 1985; Rolandelli, Wright, & Huston, 1985; Wakshlag, Reitz, & Zillmann, 1982).

Interaction-Orientation Phase

As can be seen in Fig. 1.1, the interaction-orientation phase came into its own in the mid 1980s. What is significant about this phase of television research is that, unlike earlier perspectives, television viewing is perceived to be an interaction between what the child brings to the viewing situation (e.g., skills, psychological characteristics) and what the medium offers (e.g., content, formats, formal features). Some of this research was guided by the symbolic interactionism of Gavriel Salomon (1979a, 1983, 1984), who suggested that "differences in modes of presentation are associated mainly with the differential employment of mental skills" (Salomon, 1979b, p. 55). Also influential was uses and gratification theory (e.g., Rosengren, Wenner, & Palmgren, 1985), which states that children's needs and interests affect how much television is viewed, what content is watched, and how it is interpreted.

The interaction orientation attributes an important role to parents and educators who can influence children's attraction to, use of, and learning from television through the employment of rules, regulations, or instruction. For example, one of the exciting developments in the 1980s has been the formulation of critical viewing skills curricula, school based lessons that teach children how to perceive television more accurately. These programs developed out of the realization that television is an integral part of our culture and that children have to be taught how to use it properly.

One of the motivating factors underlying the critical viewing skills movement has been the gradual deregulation of the broadcasting industry. Both the Federal Communications Commission (FCC) and the Federal Trade Commission (FTC) have been intervening less often than they had in years past to protect child viewers (Kunkel & Watkins, 1986). With regard to the FTC's role in assuring children protection from the abuses of advertising, Choate (1980) wrote, "the handwriting on the wall is clear: Parents must help their children to comprehend the totality of the message in the more than 20,000 commercials per year they view" (p. 336). Making children less vulnerable to the excesses of both commercials and programming (particularly violent content) has been the philosophy underlying the development of critical viewing skills, and both parents and educators have been seen as the purveyors of these skills.

As might be surmised from this brief overview of the major themes addressed in the past four decades of research on children and television, the primary focus of inquiry has been children defined as "normal" or average. But what about children who "require special education and related services if they are to realize their full human potential" (Hallahan & Kauffman, 1991, p. 6), those who have one or more disabilities or unique capabilities? What about exceptional children?

TELEVISION'S FORGOTTEN AUDIENCE

One of the primary reasons for studying exceptional children is that they are at risk for being heavy viewers of television, attracted to violent or adult programs, and more reactive to aggressive content or adult themes. Early communication research showed that children who had major difficulties in their relationships with their peers and/or parents tended to watch a great deal of television (e.g., Himmelweit, Oppenheim, & Vince, 1958; Schramm et al., 1961). Children who behave aggressively have an increased preference for and reactivity to television violence (Dorr & Kovaric, 1980; Surgeon General's Scientific Advisory Committee on Television and Social Behavior, 1972). These characteristics, problems with interpersonal relationships, and aggressive behavior, are particularly prevalent in children who have been identified by their school districts as emotionally disturbed (ED; Hallahan & Kauffman, 1977; Morse, Cutler, & Fink, 1964; Sprafkin & Gadow, 1987; Quay, Morse, & Cutler, 1966), learning disabled (LD; Bryan, 1976; Cunningham & Barkley, 1978; Donahue, Pearl, & Bryan, 1983; Routh, 1979), and mentally retarded (MR; Eyman & Call, 1977; Rutter, Tizard, & Whitmore, 1970).

Intellectually gifted children also warrant attention in the television literature, although some might not ordinarily consider them vulnerable to the adverse effects of the medium in the same sense as disabled youngsters. Indeed, they are not. Yet the combination of natural curiosity (Franks & Dolan, 1982; Sternberg & Davidson, 1986) and the ease and swiftness with which they learn (Davis & Rimm, 1989; Griggs & Dunn, 1984) raises questions regarding their attraction to programming for which they are intellectually but not socially or emotionally prepared.

In addition, parents and special educators have long recognized that television holds unique promise as an educational tool for exceptional children. For children who are frequently deficient in social skills, television offers direct demonstrations of appropriate social interactions that teachers can reinforce with classroom activities. For children who are often unresponsive to traditional learning techniques, television offers stimulating multisensory learning experiences. For children who need frequent repetition to learn new concepts or skills, television provides endless opportunities for repetition through the added technology of videocassette playback. Television has also proven itself to be masterful at capturing the attention of children who cannot sit still and attend to anything else. For gifted children (who generally require enriched learning experiences), television presents programs dealing with exciting and contemporary topics in an accessible format not otherwise available to the classroom teacher. Given the tremendous potential for television to supplement traditional teaching methods, one would expect that there would be scores of studies in the education literature demonstrating the effectiveness of television in enhancing learning in exceptional children. Sadly, this is not the case.

The serious need for more research on television and exceptional children became apparent when researchers examined the studies that were published on this topic between 1966 and 1983. In contrast to the research on nondisabled children, which was plentiful, theory-driven, and often programmatic, studies of disabled children were few in number, largely atheoretical, and essentially nonprogrammatic. Very little research had examined what media production techniques are most effective for teaching disabled children, and what little research existed focused exclusively on mentally retarded individuals. Ironically, although there was a relatively large literature describing various uses of television to teach academic subjects, the efficacy of such efforts could not be determined because most of the authors did not use even the most rudimentary research methods. On a more promising note, several studies found that disabled children could enhance their social skills by watching specially selected or produced programs.

One of the first books about television and disabled children was *Promise and Performance: Children with Special Needs,* edited by Maureen Harmonay (1977). It focused on the portrayal of disabled people on television and pertained to sensory (hearing and vision) impaired and mentally retarded children. Although the goal of our book is different, the foreword of this book, written by Julius B. Richmond (a former surgeon general), reflects the sentiment underlying our endeavor:

> The problems of children with special needs or handicaps have long been neglected by television. Perhaps this is due in part to our problems as a society in dealing with handicapped people in general. As society becomes more sophisticated and adept at doing this, we should be able to better use the mass media—and television in particular—toward this goal. (Harmonay, 1977, pp. xiii–xiv)

Intellectually gifted children have also been virtually ignored by television researchers. Even recent books on children and television (e.g., Dorr, 1986;

Liebert & Sprafkin, 1988; Van Evra, 1990) and exhaustive annotated bibliographies (Murray, 1980) do not contain a single reference to published research directly addressing gifted children. Furthermore, studies specifically seeking to identify developmental differences in children as potential mediators of media effects (e.g., Bryant & Anderson, 1983; Collins, 1982; Hoffner, Cantor, & Thorson, 1988; Wartella, 1979) failed to isolate, recognize, or acknowledge differences associated with gifted intellectual ability.

Although an extensive review of the cognitive and behavioral characteristics of exceptional children and intervention strategies for specific disabilities is beyond the scope of this book, the following is a brief overview of the categorical classification system that applies to exceptional children and the basic terminology in this area. Because exceptional children are educated in a variety of settings, each of which has implications for the impact of television viewing, included in this section is a description of the range of special education settings and services.

CATEGORIES OF EXCEPTIONAL CHILDREN

Because federal law requires that states report to the Office of Special Education Programs the number of children who are receiving special education services, it is possible to obtain fairly accurate figures for the number of school-labeled special education students in the United States. The childhood disabilities that qualify for special education services and the number of children receiving such services according to a recent federal government head count are presented in Table 1.1.

As is clear from the table, the most common disabling conditions in rank order are learning disabilities, speech and language disorders, mental retardation, and emotional disturbance. In a certain sense, these figures should be considered rough estimates of the "true" prevalence of each disability. There are several reasons for this. First, because each child can be counted only once, a student with multiple disabilities (e.g., learning disability *and* mental retardation, emotional disturbance *and* language disorder) is labeled for counting purposes as having only one disability. Second, some of the categories overlap. For example, many of the children who are considered multiply handicapped are mentally retarded. Third, there is considerable variability in the identification and placement criteria between states and even among school districts within a particular state. It should also be noted that federal law does not require school districts to provide special services for intellectually gifted children, who therefore are not represented in these statistics at all.

In addition, learning and behavioral disabilities and intellectual giftedness are not mutually exclusive. Indeed, intellectual giftedness in disabled children has been studied more extensively in recent years by special educators and child

TABLE 1.1
Number of Disabled Children (Ages 3–21 years)
Receiving Special Education During the 1988–1989
School Year

Handicapping Condition	Number	Percentage
Learning disabled	1,998,422	47.7
Speech or language impaired	968,908	32.1
Mentally retarded	581,465	13.9
Emotionally disturbed	377,295	9.0
Multihandicapped	84,870	2.0
Hard of hearing and deaf	57,555	1.4
Orthopedically impaired	47,392	1.1
Other health impaired	50,349	1.2
Visually handicapped	22,743	0.5
Deaf–blind	1,516	0.0
All conditions	4,190,515	100.0

Note. From *Twelfth Annual Report to Congress on the Implementation of the Education of the Handicapped Act,* 1989. Washington, DC: U.S. Department of Education.

development specialists (see Barton & Starnes, 1989, Daniels, 1983; Fox, Brody, & Tobin, 1983; Johnsen & Corn, 1989; Whitmore & Maker, 1985) and represents a genuine interface between the categories of exceptionality addressed by this book. However, because television researchers have yet to enter this area of study, this topic by necessity has been omitted from our review, along with the other lower incidence exceptionalities (e.g., orthopedically impaired, hard of hearing/deaf, visually handicapped). Before beginning our description of exceptional children, it is important to emphasize that the children within each category are extremely heterogeneous with regard to cognitive, behavioral, and social characteristics.

Learning Disabled Children

The term *learning disabled* is generally applied to children who are doing poorly in school despite average or above-average ability level. The latter is generally assessed with an individually administered IQ test. There are, of course, many children who have below-average ability and who are doing poorly in school (sometimes referred to as slow learners). Whether or not an LD child will be placed in a special education program (which means the child will have to be officially labeled learning disabled), receive only remedial help, usually in reading or math (which means the child will not be officially labeled learning disabled), or not be provided with any special services at all is pretty much up to the local school district. Because many parents and school administrators find the terms *emotionally disturbed* and *mentally retarded* unpalatable, children who could be diagnosed as having one or both of these disabilities are sometimes labeled learning disabled. Students who have above-average IQs but who are performing at or only moderately below grade level often do not receive special education at all. At the present time, approximately one half of all children in the United States who are receiving special education services have been labeled learning disabled by their local school district.

Learning disability became a legislative reality in the United States in 1969 with the passage of the Children with Specific Learning Disabilities Act. A slightly modified version of the definition that was formulated for this piece of legislation appears in Public Law 94-142, the Education for All Handicapped Children Act, which states:

> "Specific learning disability" means a disorder in one or more of the basic psychological processes involved in understanding or in using language, spoken or written, which may manifest itself in an imperfect ability to listen, think, speak, read, write, spell, or to do mathematical calculations. The term includes such conditions as perceptual handicaps, brain injury, minimal brain dysfunction, dyslexia, and developmental aphasia. The term does not include children who have learning problems which are primarily the result of visual, hearing, or motor handicaps, of mental retardation, of emotional disturbance, or of environmental, cultural, or economic disadvantage. (U.S. Office of Education, 1977, p. 65083)

The study of learning disabilities is a relatively new area from the standpoint of political (e.g., federal legislation), scientific (e.g., professional journals), and educational (e.g., labeling, teacher training, program development) recognition. Nevertheless, children with the types of problems that are now referred to as learning disabilities have, of course, always been with us, and they have been the subject of study under a legion of labels. As previously noted, the essential characteristic or criterion for a diagnosis of learning disability is a marked discrepancy between ability and school achievement.

The fact that the school-labeled LD population is so heterogeneous makes generalizations about primary causes or cognitive features impossible. With regard to reading disability (the most common academic problem in LD children), a number of researchers have concluded that the primary deficit is in the area of phonological processing, at least for many such children (Vellutino, 1987; Wagner & Torgesen, 1987). Phonemic awareness problems are expressed as difficulty making the connection between a graphic symbol and the speech sound that is associated with that symbol. Children who experience this problem have difficulty storing this information in memory and retrieving it when needed for reading. For some individuals, this deficit is a genetically based disorder (Pennington, 1990). This is but one example of a learning disability and its probable cause and cognitive features. Learning disabled children, as a group, are more likely to encounter problems interacting with other children, resulting in relatively higher rates of social rejection and isolation, and there is growing evidence that LD children are less adept in interpreting social cues (Schumaker & Hazel, 1988; Stone & La Greca, 1990). Other characteristics of the school-labeled LD population that have attracted considerable attention in recent years are problems in attending to relevant task stimuli (Richards, Samuels, Turnure, & Ysseldyke, 1990), language disorders that impair the ability to comprehend incoming information or express ideas (Wiig & Semel, 1984), and memory deficits (Swanson, 1987), to name but a few. As we shall see, some of these disabilities have potential implications for learning from and reacting to television content.

Emotionally Disturbed Children

The term *emotional disturbance* is one of the most ambiguous terms in the special education and child psychology and psychiatry literatures. There is little agreement as to what disorders are subsumed under the rubric of emotional disturbance, and the symptoms of various conditions that are often considered to be manifestations of emotional disturbance are revised and modified on a regular basis. Most of the research on these disorders is conducted by psychologists and psychiatrists, and their diagnostic and classification system is not the same as the one employed by the public school system. In fact, the school's classification system consists only of a vague list of behavioral descriptors. For this and other reasons, ED children differ from one state to the next, primarily with regard to whether or not conduct problems are considered an appropriate reason for requesting special education. With regard to the educational system, for children to be labeled emotionally disturbed in the United States they must meet the criteria specified in the following definition that appears in Public Law 94-142:

> The term (seriously emotionally disturbed) means a condition exhibiting one or more of the following characteristics over a long period of time and to a marked degree, which adversely affects educational performance: (a) an inability to learn which cannot be explained by intellectual, sensory, or health factors; (b) an inability to build or maintain satisfactory interpersonal relationships with peers and teachers; (c) inappropriate types of behavior or feelings under normal circumstances; (d) a general pervasive mood of unhappiness or depression; or (e) a tendency to develop physical symptoms or fears associated with personal or school problems. The term includes children who are schizophrenic or autistic. The term does not include children who are socially maladjusted, unless it is determined that they are seriously emotionally disturbed. (U.S. Office of Education, 1977, p. 42478)

At the present time, 9% of all disabled students are labeled emotionally disturbed, a figure that has remained fairly constant for a number of years.

A major problem with the ED label is that it is offensive and misleading to many people, particularly parents. This is attested to by the fact that many states have adopted the term *behavior disordered* (or some variant) as a substitute for the label emotionally disturbed (see Bricklin & Gallico, 1984). Furthermore, it is unclear exactly whose emotions are disturbed, the child's or his or her caregivers' (see Algozzine, 1977). In other words, although the behavior of school-labeled ED youngsters may disturb our emotional state by making us frustrated and angry, it does not follow that their emotions are necessarily disturbed.

Because few people have ever attempted to examine large samples of school-identified ED children with regard to psychiatric diagnoses, it is extremely difficult to integrate the educational and medical literature on these children. Nevertheless, on the basis of published findings from behavior rating scale studies (e.g., Cullinan, Epstein, & Kauffman, 1984; McCarthy & Paraskevopoulos, 1969; Quay et al., 1966) and clinical experience, it is possible to generate a list of childhood psychiatric disorders that are fairly common in this population of school children. It is important to emphasize that all the disorders described here range in seriousness from mild to severe and that behavioral symptoms are not static. They often improve over the course of time, even during a single school year.

The most common reason for labeling a child ED is a disruptive behavior disorder. At the present time, the American Psychiatric Association (1987) recognizes three types of disruptive behavior disorders: attention-deficit hyperactivity disorder, oppositional defiant disorder, and conduct disorder. Briefly, the primary behavioral features of each disorder are as follows: attention-deficit hyperactivity disorder—inattention, impulsivity, motor restlessness; oppositional defiant disorder—defiance of authority figures, emotional lability; and conduct disorder—confrontational and nonconfrontational aggression, antisocial behavior. These disorders often co-occur, particularly in children who are in self-contained ED classes. In general, children who are diagnosed as having a disruptive behavior disorder exhibit behaviors that meet criteria (b) and (c) in the PL 94-142 definition of emotional disturbance. Much research is currently being conducted on how these three disorders differ, whether or not they are distinct from one another, and the primary basis of the disability (i.e., their biological and environmental antecedents). With regard to the specific features of these disorders that may have special significance for our discussion of television and the exceptional child, most attention has been focused on the relatively high rate of interpersonal conflict experienced by these youngsters, their lack of adequate self-control, and their difficulty sustaining attention.

The federal definition of emotional disturbance also makes reference to anxiety disorders, mood disorders (depression), schizophrenia, and autism. It has been our experience that children are typically not scheduled to receive special education services primarily on the basis of anxiety or depression symptoms. More commonly, these problems are associated with a disruptive behavior disorder. Schizophrenia and autism are rare conditions, and relatively few ED children in any given geographic area have these disorders. It is difficult to comment on the significance of television viewing for any of these children. Given television's ability to arouse emotional state, it is conceivable that viewing certain types of content could either exacerbate or attenuate symptom severity in children with anxiety or depressive disorders. Further, as is discussed later in this book, there is some evidence that the medium can be used to facilitate social development in children with severe social deficits, which are fairly common in schizophrenic and autistic children. Because both of these disorders are associated with misperceptions of or detachment from the real-world environment, their comprehension of television content is likely to be greatly distorted.

Mentally Retarded Children

Historically, mental retardation is one of the oldest disabilities with regard to societal recognition, the provision of special education services, and the development of programmatic research. Mental retardation is formally defined in federal rules and regulations as follows:

> Mentally retarded means significantly subaverage general intellectual functioning concurrently with deficits in adaptive behavior and manifested during the developmental period, which adversely affects a child's educational performance. (U.S Office of Education, 1977)

The degree of mental retardation can range in severity from mild to profound. The approximate IQ cutoffs for each of the four levels of mental retardation are as follows: mild (55 to 69), moderate (40 to 54), severe (25 to 39), and profound (<25). The public school system generally classifies MR children into three categories based on the degree of mental retardation. The highest functioning level is educable mentally retarded (EMR), which refers to children who score between 50–55 and 70–75 on an individually administered IQ test. This category represents the mild to moderate range of mental retardation. The highest academic achievement level for most EMR students is generally between Grades 2 and 6. In other words, by the time they reach high school graduation age, they have mastered the basic academic skills. Elementary school instruction places a lot of emphasis on repetition exercises and information and skills that will allow them to live and function in the community. Secondary education focuses on vocational and life adjustment skills. In general, follow-up studies indicate that EMR individuals can live productive lives within the community.

The number of children who are classified mentally retarded has decreased in recent years, due in part to the undesirability of the label. Many of these youngsters are now labeled LD in many school districts. As a result, the EMR population is now somewhat more severely disabled than in previous decades because only the more impaired are now so classified (MacMillan, 1988; MacMillan &

Bothwick, 1980; Polloway, 1985). Currently, 14% of all children receiving special education have been labeled mentally retarded.

EMR students are generally characterized as developing in much the same way as nonretarded children except that they obtain mastery of cognitive, language, social, and motor skills at a somewhat later age than their peers. This phenomenon is sometimes referred to as a developmental delay. Research on basic skills deficits points to memory deficits and an impaired ability to use mental strategies to use information (Borkowski, Peck, & Damberg, 1983; Justice, 1985; Sternberg & Spear, 1985). Abstract concepts and abstract verbal reasoning pose real challenges for EMR students.

When the level of mental retardation ranges from moderate to severe (30–35 to 50–55), the child is likely to be labeled *trainable mentally retarded* (TMR). With this level of impairment, progress beyond preacademic or beginner level in most academic areas is unlikely. In the elementary school years, instruction focuses on language development (which may include sign language training), self-help skills, and social skills. In the adolescent years, special education consists of training in independent living skills and prevocational skills, designed to facilitate living and working in group homes and sheltered workshops, respectively.

The most debilitating degree of mental impairment is severe and profound mental retardation (SPMR). This label is generally applied to individuals who score below 25–30 on a standardized IQ test. Although the traditional educational setting for SPMR individuals was the institution, there has been a movement toward keeping many of these children in the home (or group homes) and teaching them functional skills in special day schools. Given the level of severity of the cognitive impairment, the implications of television viewing are generally believed to be limited.

Intellectually Gifted Children

In all cultures and historical periods, conventional wisdom has pinpointed some individuals as being gifted because they exhibit aptitudes that are not evident in the majority of people. Despite the widespread recognition of giftedness today, psychologists and special educators have had difficulty reaching a consensus on the precise definition and measurement of gifted ability. Some view giftedness as the top end of a continuum of intellectual ability, which, in turn, is seen as a unitary characteristic heavily influenced by genetic makeup. From this perspective, an assessment of mental ability with an intelligence test is considered a reasonable and sufficient basis for identifying gifted children. The first major investigation of giftedness in the United States, the Terman "genetic studies of genius" (see Terman & Oden, 1947, 1959), used the Stanford-Binet Intelligence Test (IQ score >130) as the primary diagnostic criterion. Other experts see gifted individuals as expressing specific talents that have been nurtured through environmental experiences, the result of being labeled as such with no independent existence in its own right (Becker, 1978), or the product of a combination of internal mechanisms (innate mental abilities), external contextual situations (environmental influences), and a level of experience or familiarity with the tasks employed to measure intelligence (Sternberg, 1985).

A "socially sanctioned" definition was provided by Marland (1972, p. 10), who, as U.S. Commissioner of Education, proposed six areas in which gifted and talented children were to be identified and nurtured: (a) general intellectual ability, (b) specific academic aptitude, (c) creative and productive thinking, (d) leadership ability, (e) visual and performing arts, and (f) psychomotor ability. Within a few years of the release of this definition, however, the community of educators of the gifted succeeded in having the psychomotor category removed on the grounds that athletic talent was already both highly recognized and well funded. The definition in Public Law 97-35, the Education Consolidation and Improvement Act, which was passed by Congress in 1981, characterized the gifted as:

> Children who give evidence of high performance capability in areas such as intellectual, creative, artistic, leadership capacity or specific academic fields and who require services or activities not ordinarily provided by the school in order to fully develop such capabilities. (Sec. 582)

Although this definition includes both intellectually gifted and talented children, this book focuses exclusively on the intellectually gifted due to the paucity of research on television and children who possess special abilities in other areas of development. Because gifted children are not included in Public Law 94-142, states are not required by federal law to provide educational opportunities for their highly intelligent (or talented) students.

The most generally accepted definition of giftedness, and the one most often employed in labelling for special education purposes, falls within the realm of intellectual performance as ascertained by an individually administered IQ test. IQ scores of at least 130 are considered to reflect gifted intellectual ability, which statistically limits the number of gifted children to approximately 2%–3% of the population. Although gifted children are not a homogeneous group, they do share several general characteristics. For instance, in their early years, they learn to speak and develop sophisticated language patterns well in advance of their age-mates (Cohn, 1981). They may teach themselves to read by the time they are 3 or 4 years old without direct supervision, and their verbal and reading fluency and comprehension improve rapidly (Cohn, Cohn, & Kanevsky, 1988; Renzulli et al., 1976). These abilities contribute to a large storehouse of information, facts, concepts, and principles that they are capable of processing at an extraordinary rate. The level of complexity and abstraction found in their questions and responses reflect phenomenal perceptiveness and sensitivity to relationships and patterns of knowledge and in the environment (Barbe & Renzulli, 1981; Roedell, Jackson, & Robinson, 1980).

Despite these strengths, there is a general tendency for gifted children to have fewer friends than their less abled peers. Hollingworth (1929, 1942), for example, found that friendship choices were decreased as IQ scores rose. Similarly, Janos, Kristi, and Robinson (1985) found that 28% of the gifted children sampled had fewer friends than they would like, and about twice the percentage of gifted students as regular students reported experiencing social adjustment difficulties such as loneliness and isolation. Although gifted children generally have a strong self-concept with regard to academic performance (Coleman & Fults, 1982), their sense of "social self" has been rated lower than their nongifted peers (Colangelo & Kelly, 1983; Janos, Fung, & Robinson, 1985; Kelly & Colangelo, 1984).

These features of gifted children have direct consequences with regard to television viewing. For example, their passion for learning and absorbing knowledge often leads them to more sophisticated forms of television content, including programming typically directed at adults (Abelman, 1984, 1986c). Although often capable of comprehending this information and rapidly developing the skills to process television information at an early age, gifted children may be exposed to themes and behaviors that might be particularly disturbing. Their heightened awareness and perceptiveness may leave them vulnerable to influences that may not affect their age-mates. Their response to emotional experiences may be exaggerated (Cohn et al., 1988), which has special significance given their more limited social relationships. As Barbe (1965) suggested, "it is important to realize that although gifted children may be mentally advanced, they are still children, and their advanced mentality does little to help them through the problems of growing up" (p. 175).

Special Education Programs and Services

Special education is provided in a variety of different ways and settings. One of the most important characteristics of special education programs is the opportunities for interaction with nondisabled children during the school day. The extent to which exceptional children are isolated from such interaction is hypothesized to be an important determinant of television's impact on these children. Consequently, this section provides a description of the various types of special education settings and the factors influencing the specific placement of children with special needs.

According to federal law, a child receiving special education should receive these services in the least restrictive setting. Restrictiveness is determined by the extent to which the disabled child can interact with nondisabled peers. The least restrictive setting is the regular classroom. Here, special education consists of

TABLE 1.2
Percentage of Disabled Children and Youth
(Ages 6–21 years) Served in Different Educational
Environments During the 1988–1989 School Year

Environment	Emotionally Disturbed	Learning Disabled	Mentally Retarded
Regular class	12.6	17.6	5.7
Resource room	32.9	59.2	24.0
Separate class	34.6	21.7	57.6
Separate school	14.3	1.4	11.4
Residential facility	3.5	0.1	1.0
Home/hospital	2.2	0.1	0.3

Note. From *Twelfth Annual Report to Congress on the Implementation of the Education of the Handicapped Act,* 1989. Washington, DC: U.S. Department of Education.

modifications in the general school curriculum designed to facilitate academic, social, and emotional development. The most restrictive setting is one that provides little or no opportunity for social interaction with regular classroom students. Examples of such settings are residential programs designed entirely for disabled students, hospital inpatient units, and home-based instruction. In between these two extremes are settings in which the disabled child receives instructional services for a limited amount of time (e.g., 1 hour per day), such as a resource room, half of the school day (part-time special class), or for the entire school day (full-time special class). Full-time special classes that are housed in a regular school are generally considered less restrictive than full-time classes in a school designed entirely for disabled children. The latter are sometimes referred to as *special day schools.* Table 1.2 presents the percentage of ED, LD, and MR children who are educated in each of these settings.

When a child is being considered for special education services, the goal is to provide such services in the least restrictive environment. If the child succeeds well in that setting, the primary objective is to move the child to the next less restrictive environment when he or she has mastered the skills necessary for such a placement. Occasionally, the special education placement committee is too conservative and the child continues to fail in the less restrictive setting and must be moved to a more socially restrictive program. The overall goal of special education is to provide the child with the necessary instructional and support services that will allow him or her to eventually function in the regular classroom.

It is extremely difficult to provide generalizations about specific disabilities and the types of special education services that a child is likely to receive. There are several reasons for this. First, there is considerable variability in the percentage of students with specific disabilities in particular placements from one state to the next. For example, in some states most of the children receiving special education services go to resource rooms for a part of the school day, whereas the general trend in the neighboring state may be placement in self-contained classes. Second, specific disabilities are defined differently from one state to the next. A child considered eligible for special education services in Illinois, for example, may not be considered as a potential candidate in Arkansas. Third, even within the same state, the placement decisions made by individual school districts are highly inconsistent.

With these limitations in mind, the following generalizations about disabilities and special education services are presented. Children who are labeled by our public schools as being learning disabled generally receive special education in a resource room or a part-time special class. The same is true for EMR students. Trainable mentally retarded students are generally placed in self-contained special education classes, which may be housed in a special day school, particularly in rural or thinly populated areas. Even the SPMR population, which in earlier decades was confined almost entirely to institutions, is now being seriously considered for placement in special day schools within the community. Compared with the LD and EMR student population, ED youngsters are more likely to receive their special education in self-contained classes, which is due to their greater propensity for interpersonal conflict or social inadequacies. Within a given school district or special education administrative unit, the more severe the disability, the more restrictive the special education setting.

Terminology

Much consideration has been given to the terminology used to describe exceptional children in this book. It is certainly acknowledged that the language used to refer to individuals with disabilities is often disabling in and of itself. The most flagrant example of this offense is the special education category *emotionally disturbed,* a term that appears in federal legislation and consequently has been adopted by many states' education systems. Although the connotation is unfortunate, the ED label is used in this book because most of the relevant research reviewed was collected in states that use this classification term. In addition to the term *exceptional,* we have used *labeled*—as in school-labeled special education students—to refer to LD, ED, MR, and gifted children. As such, *nonlabeled* refers to children without a labeled ability or disability. The intellectually gifted are also referred to as *exceptionally abled,* whereas children with learning disabilities, behavioral disorders, and mental retardation are collectively referred to as *disabled.* In a parallel fashion, children without school-labeled disabilities are referred to as *nondisabled.*

School-Labeled Samples

Our overviews of disabled and gifted children have highlighted some of the characteristics that define each group, but there is also considerable heterogeneity within each group. Although each special education category has been studied with regard to identifying more homogeneous subgroups of children, the educational system by and large does not make distinctions between subgroups of children for educational purposes. The major problem that sample heterogeneity poses for television researchers is in the selection or identification of research subjects. Ideally, subject selection should be made on the basis of specific behavioral and cognitive criteria. To the best of our knowledge, none of the studies of television and ED, LD, or MR children have approached this level of sophistication. Rather, researchers have been content to study school-labeled samples for several reasons. First, sample heterogeneity is useful in the identification of predictors of reactivity (e.g., IQ, aggressiveness) to specific types of television content. Second, the study of school-labeled samples is ideal in the development of classroom-based interventions such as curricula (see chapter 7). Third, when research is initiated in a new area of study, it is not unusual for scientists to obtain large, heterogeneous samples to identify global differences between groups and to generate hypotheses for future study.

The tendency for researchers to study school-labeled as opposed to criterion-based samples limits the degree to which this book can provide theories to explain the underlying characteristics or processes responsible for differences in the use of or reactions to television among disabled, gifted, and nonlabeled children. More adequate theory development awaits future research on more homogeneous samples of exceptional children, an accomplishment that we hope our book will inspire. Nevertheless, we do integrate several communication theories (e.g., social learning, uses and gratification, cultivation, arousal) as they apply to the various topics covered in this book. Rather than attempting to explain how the research findings in every given area can be explained by each theory, we have made our own interpretation as to which theoretical approach is most relevant to each topic. As such, theory serves more a narrative than an explanatory function.

ORGANIZATION OF THE BOOK

Our examination of television and exceptional children has been influenced both by social learning theory and by the medium, child, and interaction orientations. Consistent with social learning theory, we address exposure (how much television children watch and the kind of content they are exposed to), acquisition (how children process what they view and what they comprehend), and acceptance (the effect specific contents have on their behavior). The exposure and acceptance stages of television viewing are clearly medium oriented in that they explore television as the source of influence. The acquisition stage is more child oriented in perspective, in that it pertains to how children in each of the exceptional categories process television and specific types of content. Two of the chapters are specifically interaction oriented and describe the influence of parents (chapter 6) and schools (chapter 7) on children's use of television. The major goal of this book is to examine the role that television plays in the lives of disabled and gifted children and to explore ways to maximize the positive potential and to minimize the possible adverse influences of the medium on these special children and their families.

SUMMARY

This chapter provided a brief overview of the evolution of the themes addressed by research on children and television. Early efforts focused on the effects of the medium, particularly the viewing of aggression-laden content. There was a gradual shift in interest to the characteristics of the child viewer as an important determinant of media reactivity, which resulted in the discovery that television does not affect all children in the same way. Although most of the research on television pertains to nondisabled children, the trend toward greater specificity in examining child variables has led to the discovery that certain child attributes are associated with seemingly increased vulnerability to adverse media effects. Specific risk factors include problems with academic achievement, interpersonal relationships, and aggressive behavior.

The children that we have identified as representing the most vulnerable segment of the viewing audience are those who have been labeled emotionally disturbed, learning disabled, or mentally retarded by their local school districts. We have noted that these children possess many of the "risk" factors for heavy media use and adverse reactions to certain types of program content. We have also included children who in some ways represent the other end of the risk continuum, the intellectually gifted, to see whether their advanced cognitive abilities serve to reduce their risk of adverse effects compared to children of average intellect. The possibility also existed that the cognitive, social, and emotional characteristics of the gifted could result in adverse reactions to certain types of television content.

It is somewhat ironic that disabled children appear to be the ones most vulnerable to television's adverse effects and at the same time are also the ones who may gain the most from instructional applications of the medium. Television offers an appealing format to teach concepts and skills to children whose education requires more than traditional methods. The degree to which this potential has been realized is discussed later in this book.

2 Television Viewing Habits

All of the areas of concern and criticism regarding children and television are linked to what children watch and for how long. The positive and negative consequences of television viewing effects and all the topics addressed in our text (e.g., reality perceptions, comprehension, parental involvement in television viewing) begin with the simple act of program selection and viewing. Therefore, the study and documentation of viewing habits becomes the necessary first step in the understanding of the effects of television on child behavior.

Several topics are generally subsumed under the rubric of television viewing habits. First is the amount of time that a child actually spends in front of a television set. Researchers often make a distinction between simply being in the same room while the television set is operating and actually observing and attending to its content, which is sometimes difficult to document. A number of different strategies have been developed to determine the amount of television viewing, and they include interviews with the child or care provider, placing video recording equipment in the home, or attaching special devices to the television set. A second topic is program preferences, that is, specific programs or program categories that are viewed. Here, the primary thrust of research is the match between personality and family characteristics and preferred television programs. Using the program category approach, it is possible to calculate the amount of time spent viewing specific types of behaviors (e.g., aggression). A third topic is identification with particular characters that appear in television programs. This is really a type of preference index because television shows are typically identified by the main character or his or her associates. Interest in the child's favorite television character stems from the findings from modeling studies, which indicate that children are more likely to model the behavior of someone they admire (e.g., Bandura & Walters, 1963).

This chapter addresses each of these topics, and, in keeping with the general organization of the book, it begins with an overview of the literature on non-labeled children. This is followed by a more detailed discussion of the research literature pertaining to exceptional children.

In the United States, watching television is the most time-consuming leisure activity. Even 30 years ago, the average television set was on for more than 5 hours a day. Television viewing has increased steadily from that time such that now the average set is on for approximately 7 hours a day. Naturally, the average person does not watch this much television, but the amount of viewing is still considerable, especially for the child audience.

Most children are exposed to television almost from the time they are born. A typical 6-month-old child is in front of a television set almost 1.5 hours per day (Hollenbeck & Slaby, 1979). By the age of 3 years, they are purposeful viewers with favorite programs (Anderson, Alwitt, Lorch, & Levin, 1979). Viewing time increases and peaks at about 2.5 hours per day just before elementary school. At first, the onset of school seems to diminish available viewing time slightly. However, from about the age of 8 years, viewing increases steadily to an average of almost 4 hours per day during early adolescence. Viewing then levels off in the later teens, with the average adolescent watching from 2 to 3 hours a day (Liebert & Sprafkin, 1988).

This pattern of television viewing over the course of a child's development is fairly typical for many other countries as well. The actual number of hours spent watching television depends, to a great extent, on the amount of programming available and the number of hours that television is broadcast. Children in countries such as the United States, the United Kingdom, Japan, Canada, and Australia, which have a wide variety and quantity of television programming, watch from 2 to 3 hours per day. Children in Germany, France, Austria, Italy, Sweden, Holland, and Norway watch only 1–2 hours daily, in part because there are more limited broadcasts in these countries (Gunter & Svennevig, 1985; Murray, 1980).

The time of day that a child is likely to watch television varies as a function of age. For elementary-school children, the peak viewing times are late afternoon and early to mid-evening on weekdays and mornings on weekends. As they grow older, they watch less morning television on the weekends, but evening viewing increases. The highest levels of television viewing by adolescents is mid- and late evening.

Estimates of the average number of hours of television viewing do not reflect the tremendous variation in usage. For example, 25% of the 6th and 10th graders in one survey (Lyle & Hoffman, 1972) watched 8.5 hours on Sunday and 5.5 hours on school days. More than 30% of the first graders watched 4 or more hours on a typical school day, whereas 10% reported no viewing at all. Much of this variability in viewing time is related to family background and various child characteristics. Children from lower socioeconomic or minority backgrounds view more television than White children from middle- and upper-income families. Brighter children tend to watch less television than their intellectually average peers, and youngsters who have major difficulties in their relationships with their peers and/or their parents tend to be particularly heavy users of television (Himmelweit et al., 1958; Schramm et al., 1961). In general, children's viewing habits are quite similar to those of their parents (Comstock, Chaffee, Katzman, McCombs, & Roberts, 1978).

As most parents already know, their child's age and gender determine, to a large extent, what programs he or she prefers. Preschoolers and first graders like cartoons the most, followed by situation comedies, and noncartoon children's programs, in that order. By the second grade, situation comedies are the most popular television shows, and by the end of the elementary school years, in addition to situation comedies, action/adventure, music/variety, and dramatic programs are well liked (Lyle & Hoffman, 1972). Gender differences in program preferences appear quite early and persist throughout adolescence. Aggressive cartoons are more popular with boys than with girls of preschool and early elementary school age. As they grow older, boys' favorite program types become crime and action/adventure programs, whereas girls prefer family situation comedies (Lyle & Hoffman, 1972).

Identification with television characters has been measured by asking children to name the character(s) that is their favorite, most like him or herself, and most desired to be like. Modeling studies have shown that children learn more from models that are perceived as similar to themselves (e.g., Maccoby & Wilson, 1957; Rosenkrans, 1967). More recent research (Huesmann, Lagerspetz, & Eron, 1984) shows that children (especially boys) who identify with aggressive and "all" television characters tend to be aggressive and to be heavy television violence viewers. Furthermore, boys who identified with television characters (both aggressive and overall) and watched television violence frequently exhibited more aggression 2 years later regardless of initial level of aggressiveness. Huesmann et al. (1984) proposed that identification with television characters acts like a "catalyst," increasing the effect of exposure to television violence.

EXCEPTIONAL CHILDREN

As with most areas of research on television and exceptional children, the number of studies of viewing habits is limited. According to Greenberg and Atkin (1979), several variables are antecedent to viewing and learning from television. Each plays a mediatory role in determining what and how much children watch, and they include:

1. Social experience: The range and diversity of the child's real-life experience with representations of social roles and activities influence the level of attractiveness of television representations.

2. Communication: The amount of communication between family members may serve to supplement or replace the amount of television viewing.
3. Attitudes: The child's attitudes toward television and its content influence the amount and type of viewing.
4. Needs: The functional information in television portrayals (e.g., social roles or behaviors) that the child feels is relevant to his or her current situation determines the utilization of the information.
5. Motivation: The gratifications that the child is seeking to obtain from television viewing in order to fulfill instrumental and consummatory needs influence what and how much he or she watches.

Because the very nature of being exceptional is likely to influence each of these variables, it is also likely that exceptional children's television viewing habits will be significantly different from that of nonlabeled children. Indeed, there is some indication that children with learning or behavior problems watch more television than their nonlabeled peers and are more likely to prefer shows with aggression-laden content.

Emotionally Disturbed and Learning Disabled Children

By far the most extensively studied groups of exceptional children with regard to television viewing habits are those receiving special education services under the ED or LD label. Two of the first studies in this area obtained viewing habits information on children and adolescents in residential programs.

Rubinstein, Fracchia, Kochnower, and Sprafkin (1977) surveyed the television viewing habits of 60 ED children and adolescents in a residential treatment facility. The televisions on the ward were reported to be on for an average of 9.5 hours daily (3.7 hours during the day and 5.8 hours at night), with the typical child actually watching about 1 hour during the day and 2.6 hours in the evening. About 90% of the time, the children rather than the staff selected programs, and these selections appeared to be made on the basis of the children's prior knowledge of the program schedule. The five most frequently selected program types were action/adventure shows (especially those with superheroes), cartoons, situation comedies, crime dramas, and monster movies. Ninety-six percent of the ward staff reported having observed behaviors engaged in by patients that seemed related to what they had viewed. The most frequently mentioned types of television-linked imitation included aggressive acts, superhero behaviors, and dance steps.

Another survey (Donahue, 1978) of 53 institutionalized ED children revealed even more television use than was reported by Rubinstein et al. (1977). Based on questions about how many hours they watched television during various periods of the day, it was found that the children viewed an average of 7.7 hours on weekdays and 4.2 hours on Saturday mornings. Of all the favorite programs mentioned, 73% were violent. The two most popular program types were action/adventure and cartoon shows, and the two most frequently mentioned favorite characters were Bugs Bunny and Steve Austin, the "Six Million Dollar Man." Sixty-nine percent of their favorite characters engaged in aggressive behavior either periodically or regularly. Donahue also administered a confrontive situation measure in which the children were asked to describe how they, their favorite television character, parents, best friend, and favorite adult at the institution would handle each of four conflict situations. The children's responses about their own behavior were most similar to what they reported for their favorite television character and best friend, and the projected behaviors for these three item categories were more aggressive than those for parents and favorite adult. These findings suggest that ED children identify with aggressive television characters, who, in turn, may serve as role models.

Sprafkin and Gadow conducted a series of studies on the television viewing habits of ED and LD children who were enrolled in public school programs. In their first study (Sprafkin & Gadow, 1986), they interviewed children in regular and special education classes. The children in the regular classes were separated into two groups: chronological age-matched controls and mental age-matched controls. The special education sample was comprised of children from six self contained special education classes (two EMR classes, two ED classes, two LD classes) from three elementary schools. All children were interviewed for approximately 15 minutes about: (a) their favorite programs and characters, (b) the number of programs viewed during specific time periods, (c) the number of days a week they watched specific types of programs, and (d) how frequently they reacted to television in specified ways. The parents of participating children indicated the number of hours their child viewed television on weekdays, Saturday, and Sunday on a brief questionnaire brought home from school by the child.

As can be seen in Fig. 2.1, the special education group watched significantly more television than did each of the control groups, which did not significantly differ from one another. Descriptively, the ED group watched the most television, followed by the LD group and then the EMR group. The special education youngsters watched both situation comedies and soap operas significantly more often than did the mental age controls; the frequency for the chronological age controls fell in between and did not differ significantly from those of either group. The special education children also watched crime shows on significantly more days than the chronological age or mental age controls. Relevant to the issue of possible behavioral effects is the fact that special education youngsters were more than twice as likely to report that they frequently pretended to be their favorite television character compared with the control group.

Table 2.1 represents the most popular television series for the special education, chronological age match, and mental age match groups. The special education youngsters' preferences contained some of the programs selected by their

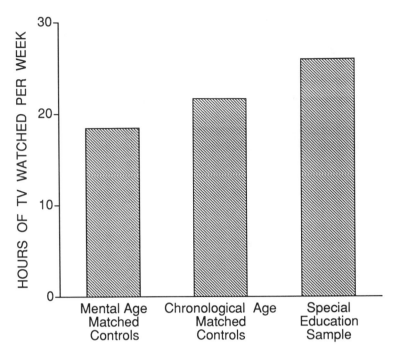

FIG. 2.1. Mean hours of television watched per week for children in special education classes, mental-age matched controls, and chronological-age matched controls. *Note.* From data reported in "Television Viewing Habits of Emotionally Disturbed, Learning Disabled, and Mentally Retarded Children" by J. Sprafkin and K. D. Gadow, 1986. *Journal of Applied Developmental Psychology, 7,* pp. 45–59. Copyright © 1991 by J. Sprafkin and K. D. Gadow.

younger, mental age matches and some of the drama and situation comedies selected by their chronological age matches. The tendency for the special education group to have preferences reflecting both age-matched and younger children is also found in their favorite character responses. For example, a fantasy character (defined as a cartoon, superhuman, or animal character) was selected by 63% of the mental age matches, by 50% of the special education group, and by 25% of the chronological age matches. These findings indicate that the more immature program selections evidenced by some children in special education programs (particularly in self-contained classes) are due, in part, to their generally lower level of intellectual functioning.

Sprafkin and Gadow (1986) focused on ED children in their second study because the findings from the first investigation suggested that they were the most frequent television viewers and the most behaviorally deviant among the groups sampled. The study samples consisted of a group of 42 ED boys from

TABLE 2.1
Favorite Television Series

Special Education	Chronological Age Matches	Mental Age Matches
"Happy Days" (37%)	"Dukes of Hazard" (53%)	"Tom & Jerry" (29%)
"Dukes of Hazard" (24%)	"Greatest American	"Woody Woodpecker"
"Tom & Jerry" (21%)	Hero" (29%)	(18%)
"Woody Woodpecker"	"Happy Days" (24%)	"Bugs Bunny" (18%)
(18%)	"Gilligan's Island" (16%)	"Dukes of Hazard" (13%)
"Dallas" (18%)	"Chips" (16%)	"Enis" (11%)
"Popeye" (16%)	"That's Incredible" (16%)	"Gilligan's Island" (11%)
"Scooby Doo" (16%)	"Dallas" (13%)	
"Flintstones" (16%)	"Different Strokes"	
	(13%)	

Note. Figures in parentheses indicate the percentage of the group selecting that series as one of four favorite programs. Only those series that were named by at least 10% of the children in any group are presented. From "Television Viewing Habits of Emotionally Disturbed, Learning Disabled, and Mentally Retarded Children" by J. Sprafkin and K. D. Gadow, 1986. *Journal of Applied Developmental Psychology, 7,* p. 50. Copyright © 1986 by Ablex Publishing Co. Reprinted by permission.

self-contained special education classes and 42 nonlabeled boys. Instead of an interview, a group-administered Television Diary was used to assess the children's frequency of viewing specific programs aired during the most popular viewing periods. As illustrated in Fig. 2.2, the ED children indicated that they watched more hours of crime dramas and cartoons than their non-special education peers, whereas the latter reported higher rates of viewing situation comedies. ED children also cited crime dramas as being favorite television shows more often than their nonlabeled peers.

Their third study (Kelly, Sprafkin, & Gadow, 1986) of television viewing habits involved 73 elementary-school-age ED and LD students who attended special education schools, and 159 nonspecial education students who attended a regular, public elementary school. Children completed television diaries about the afternoon and evening television shows that they usually watched. Their responses for afternoon and evening viewing are presented in Tables 2.2 and 2.3, respectively. The most notable difference between the two groups of children is the significantly higher rate of viewing crime dramas (in both time slots) and public broadcasting system (PBS) afternoon programs by the ED–LD group. The nonspecial education students reported watching more situation comedies and non-crime dramas in the after-school viewing period. The only statistically significant differences between the ED and LD children were the findings that the latter group engaged in more hours of television viewing overall and more hours of watching news programs. The latter finding suggests that LD children may be somewhat more "passive" viewers (i.e., watching whatever is on at the time).

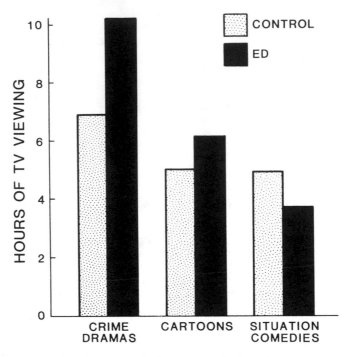

FIG. 2.2. Mean hours watched per week of crime dramas, cartoons, and situation comedies by ED and control boys. *Note.* From data reported in "Television Viewing Habits of Emotionally Disturbed, Learning Disabled, and Mentally Retarded Children" by J. Sprafkin and K. D. Gadow, 1986. *Journal of Applied Developmental Psychology, 7,* pp. 45–59. Copyright © 1991 by J. Sprafkin and K. D. Gadow.

Their fourth study of viewing habits (Sprafkin, Watkins, & Gadow, 1990) compared 81 ED and 86 LD students who were attending a special school for ED and LD children, respectively. The youngsters completed group-administered television viewing diaries such as that presented in Fig. 2.3. In this study, analyses of viewing habits showed that ED and LD children were heavy consumers of television. Similar to the findings of previous studies (Sprafkin & Gadow, 1986), the ED and LD elementary-school-age children were found to watch television almost 4 hours daily. The heaviest viewing period was Saturday morning, with the overall group averages exceeding 3.5 out of 4 possible viewing hours. The next most popular viewing time was after school, with children claiming to watch 13 hours weekly out of 15 possible hours. Both groups of children indicated that they preferred cartoons over all other program types, with weekly viewership of such shows averaging in excess of 11 hours. The two groups of children differed with regard to the type of shows that they preferred to watch. The ED children, as a group, were more likely to watch crime dramas and

TABLE 2.2
Means and (Standard Deviation) for Afternoon
Television Viewing for Special Education
and Regular Classroom Students

Category	Special Education	Regular Class	p <
Crime drama	.68 (0.71)	.47 (0.59)	.05
Non-crime drama	.35 (0.46)	.56 (0.50)	.05
Situation comedy	.55 (0.44)	.80 (0.64)	.05
Cartoons	1.07 (0.51)	1.00 (0.53)	NS
Game shows	.05 (0.25)	.11 (0.28)	NS
Daytime drama	.09 (0.28)	.29 (0.67)	.05
PBS	.22 (0.55)	.07 (0.28)	.05
News	0.00 (0)	.05 (0.21)	NS
Total	3.18 (0.99)	3.35 (1.05)	

Note. From "A Comparative Study of Television Viewing Habits in Special Education and Regular Classroom Students" by E. Kelly, J. Sprafkin, and K. D. Gadow, 1986. Unpublished manuscript.

adventure shows than the LD children, whereas the LD children showed a much greater preference for educational programs than did the ED children. Although the LD students identified more with nonaggressive television characters than the ED children, the latter group did not identify more with aggressive television characters, as we had expected. It was also found that LD children held somewhat more favorable attitudes about television than ED students.

Collectively, the findings from the studies of public school children indicate

TABLE 2.3
Mean and (Standard Deviation) for Evening
Television Viewing by Special Education
and Regular Classroom Students

Category	Special Education	Regular Class	p <
Crime drama	5.55 (1.82)	4.61 (2.48)	.05
Non-crime drama	.93 (.91)	.99 (1.28)	NS
Situation comedy	1.26 (.94)	1.42 (.94)	NS
Talk shows	.39 (.49)	.20 (.40)	NS
Variety shows	.31 (.50)	.43 (.61)	NS
Total	8.57 (2.40)	6.33 (3.62)	.05

Note. From "A Comparative Study of Television Viewing Habits in Special Education and Regular Classroom Students" by E. Kelly, J. Sprafkin, and K. D. Gadow, 1986. Unpublished manuscript.

FIG. 2.3. Sample page from the Saturday Morning Television Diary. *Note.* From the instrument used in "Efficacy of a Television Literacy Curriculum for Emotionally Disturbed and Learning Disabled Children" by J. Sprafkin, L. T. Watkins, and K. D. Gadow, 1990. *Journal of Applied Developmental Psychology, 11,* pp. 225–244. Copyright © 1991 by J. Sprafkin, L. T. Watkins, and K. D. Gadow.

that disabled children receiving special education services (particularly youngsters in self-contained programs) watch more hours of television than students in regular education classes. Even when comparisons are made with mental age controls, the special education groups exceed nondisabled children in the overall level of exposure to television. Several explanations for these findings are possible. First, given their social skills difficulties and associated cognitive deficits and behavioral disturbances, watching television may be a substitute activity for playing with other children. Moreover, this is probably a forced-choice situation given their relatively high rate of social rejection, both active (confrontation) and passive (avoidance). Sadly, their greater propensity to identify with television characters seems to suggest that these electronic phantoms may be providing social acceptance through their passive and nonrejecting presence. This appears to play the most significant role in the lives of ED children. This is highly consistent with the literature on children with disruptive behavior disorders, which shows that aggressive, bossy, and annoying children are frequently avoided by their peers (Milich & Landau, 1982). An alternative but not necessarily conflicting interpretation is that care providers are more inclined to "leave well enough alone" when they encounter their disruptive child watching television. Instead of interrupting their activity with task demands or redirecting them to more socially constructive activities, care providers exploit this opportunity for peace and quiet by leaving the child alone. Third, television viewing is a passive activity that requires very little effort. Given the task demands of psycho-motor activity (e.g., concentration, motor coordination, planning strategies, impulse control, ability to follow directions), watching television offers a wonderful stress-free experience for individuals who are often confronted with the inadequacies resulting from their primary disabilities.

The research on institutionalized ED children suggests a level of television viewing comparable to that of ED children in self-contained special education classes, but the available data are extremely limited. Nevertheless, anecdotal reports suggest that the amount of television viewing in *some* residential programs is relatively large, especially when residential staff actually encourage television viewing because it is an "easy way to manage" the children in their charge (i.e., a substitute for habilitation). In some residential programs, watching television, which is often an activity for times when there is nothing else to do, is a means for escaping the boredom of everyday life.

The preference for and identification with aggressive television characters is certainly consistent with the literature on the temperament of ED children. However, whether aggressive children relate better to aggressive television characters because they themselves are aggressive, their environment rewards or otherwise encourages the viewing of such material, or the viewing of aggression-laden programs makes them more aggressive cannot be inferred simply on the basis that they watch more violence on television than other children.

Mentally Retarded Children

Unfortunately, little information is available on the television viewing habits of MR children. In one study, Baran and Meyer (1975) interviewed 70 TMR children and adolescents from five nonresidential schools about their television viewing habits. Almost three fourths of the youngsters reported watching "a lot of TV." The most popular viewing times were after school, on Saturday, and at night. About half of all favorite programs mentioned contained frequent instances of aggressive behavior. For example, the most popular series included "Gunsmoke," "The Three Stooges," and "Kung Fu." Clear gender differences were found in program favorites, with the violent programs being named by 70% of the boys but by only 37% of the girls. Parallel findings were reported for favorite character choices.

Baran and Meyer also examined the extent to which the youngsters identified with their favorite television characters using a conflict situation method in which children were asked what they would do, what their favorite television character would do, what their parents would want them to do, what their best friend would do, and what the right thing is to do when faced with each of four potentially aggression-provoking situations (e.g., "Suppose you were playing with your favorite toy, and a person you didn't like came up and took it away"). With the responses coded as either violent or nonviolent, the strongest relationships existed between the child's (both boys and girls) report of what he or she would do and both what the favorite television character would do and what the best friend would do. Trainable mentally retarded children saw themselves behaving more similarly to their favorite television characters and best friends than to how their parents would want them to act or what was "right" to do. The identification with television characters and best friends was also found with nonretarded first-, second-, and third-grade children given the same set of conflict situations (Meyer, 1973); however, for the nonretarded children, the relationship between self and what the parents would want done and what is right were both statistically significant, whereas neither was significant for the TMR children. This suggests that television may influence the social behavior of TMR children to a greater degree than their nonretarded peers because the alternative socializing forces seem to be less effective for the former group.

Ahrens (1977) examined the television viewing habits of 250 children and adolescents from a residential facility in New Zealand, most of whom were either moderately or severely mentally retarded. Questionnaires about the children's use of television were completed by the nurses or hostel staff for the inpatients and by the parents for the outpatients. The majority of the children were reported to watch television from 1 to 2 hours daily, but about half of the children under 12 years of age watched from 2 to 3 hours daily. The most popular viewing times were between 5:30 and 7:30 p.m. About half of the children were reported to talk about or act out some of the programs. Based on the children's reports, their favorite programs were the "Flintstones" and "Sing" (a locally produced song-and-dance show). It is interesting to note that a reliability check of the accuracy of caregivers' responses indicated that they were not accurate reporters of child program preferences. The adults reported that the children's favorite series was "Sesame Street."

Intellectually Gifted Children

The level of a child's cognitive sophistication influences social experiences, communication behavior, attitudes, needs, and motivations (see Bryan, 1979; Elliot, 1979; Naremore & Hopper, 1990; Wartella, 1979, 1981; Wolf, Abelman, & Hexamer, 1982; Zigler & Farber, 1985) and may be a critically important determinant of television viewing habits. As a result, intellectually gifted children are very likely to have different patterns of media exposure than intellectually average children.

To determine if this is in fact the case, Abelman (1986b) conducted a study in which he obtained television viewing information (self-reports and parent diaries) on 750 children (ages 4–15 years), who were either nonlabeled or school classified as intellectually gifted. As can be seen in Fig. 2.4, there are clear differences in television viewing habits between the two groups of children. One rather obvious conclusion from these data is that, from elementary school to high

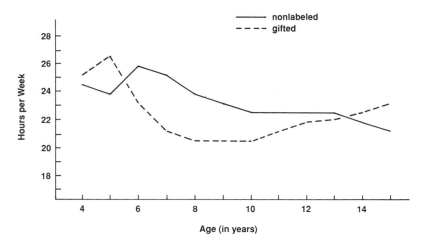

FIG. 2.4. Number of hours of television watched per week for gifted and intellectually average (nonlabeled) children from ages 4 to 14 years. *Note.* From data reported in "Television and the Exceptional Child" by R. Abelman, 1986. *G/T/C, 9*(4), pp. 26–28.

school, gifted children typically watch significantly less television than their intellectually average peers. Generally, gifted children view 2 hours less than average children each day. However, during the preschool years and again during adolescence, gifted children watch more television than their average counterparts.

The overall pattern of television viewing between the two groups of children also differs. The amount of viewing by intellectually average children decreases at a gradual rate from the early school years to adolescence, whereas television viewing by gifted children drops substantially from preschool to early school years.

In addition to differences in the amount of television viewing, Abelman (1986b, 1991a) reported several interesting findings regarding program preferences. First, gifted preschool children were more likely to watch educational programs (e.g., "Sesame Street," "Mr. Rogers' Neighborhood," "Electric Company") than cartoons and other children's programming. They were also more likely to watch these programs with greater regularity than average children. Second, adult-oriented commercial television comedies and action/adventure shows comprised the majority of television programs viewed by all children during the elementary school years and adolescence. However, gifted children turned to these programs at an earlier age than their intellectually average peers. Third, neither news nor educational adult programming was a major part of their television viewing.

Comparison Between Studies

It is difficult to compare the findings generated by the various studies of viewing habits. In addition to differences between studies in the procedures used (e.g., self-report vs. caregiver report, estimates based on typical viewing vs. favorite programs, etc.), program offerings vary both between and within broadcast seasons. For studies to be truly comparable, they would have to be conducted at the same point in time and with identical procedures. Furthermore, the measures of viewing habits have to be evaluated for their reliability and validity (this issue is discussed in greater detail in chapter 9). Nevertheless, despite these problems, considering the fairly consistent pattern of findings between studies, it is likely that the reported differences between disabled, gifted, and nonlabeled students are genuine.

CONCLUSIONS

Studies of television viewing habits suggest that exceptional children in general either watch more television or watch more television at a particularly vulnerable age than nonlabeled children. For example, children with learning and behavioral disabilities (particularly those in self-contained classes) view more television than nondisabled children. It also appears that ED and LD children watch television more frequently than MR youngsters. The favorite programs of disabled children seem to be somewhat more aggressive than those of their nondisabled peers, and this is particularly true for ED children. Cartoon, crime drama, and superhero programs are particularly popular, and all three program types generally contain high levels of aggressive behavior (Poulos, Harvey, & Leibert, 1976; Sprafkin, Rubinstein, & Stone, 1977). Furthermore, children with learning and behavioral disabilities seem more likely to identify with their favorite television characters; that is, they perceive their own behavior to be similar to that of their favorite television characters (Baran & Meyer, 1975; Donahue, 1978), and they report that they frequently pretend to be those characters (Sprafkin & Gadow, 1986). Because some children with learning and behavior problems appear to engage in less social activity than their nondisabled peers, these data suggest that the former may watch television as a substitute for social interaction. Moreover, because physical and nonphysical aggression are frequent components of their preferred shows, ED, LD, and MR children may learn to solve interpersonal conflicts by emulating their television heroes. Well-controlled investigations are needed to clarify this issue.

Intellectually gifted children watch significantly less television than disabled children and, for the most part, less than nonlabeled children as well. Interestingly, two age periods are exceptions to this pattern. The first is during the preschool years (arguably a very vulnerable time in a child's life), when they watch more television than their intellectually average peers. Although the bulk of preschool children's television viewing concentrates on child-oriented, educational programming, research also suggests that their enthusiasm for learning and absorbing knowledge often leads them to more sophisticated forms of television content, including programs typically directed at adults. It has yet to be determined whether intellectually gifted children can comprehend this information at such an early age, whether they are exposed to themes or behaviors that might be particularly disturbing, and whether the learning of this information is dysfunctional.

The second age period for which total viewing time runs contrary to the general trend is early adolescence. Although a relatively high rate of television viewing during adolescence is of little concern in and of itself (particularly among children who have advanced intellectual abilities), it is important to address why increased television viewing occurs at an age when viewing tends to decrease, at least in intellectually average peers. One possible explanation might be found in the social/emotional rather than intellectual realm of giftedness. In addition to experiencing the same physiological and psychological changes that face all adolescents, it has been suggested that the response to emotional and social experiences tends to be exaggerated in intellectually gifted individuals (Cohn, Cohn, & Kanevsky, 1988). This, coupled with the fact that twice as many gifted high school age youths (compared with nonlabeled peers) experience social adjustment difficulties such as loneliness and isolation (Janos, Kristi, & Robinson, 1985), suggests that some gifted adolescents may seek answers or refuge in television viewing. Considering the content of the shows that they are watching (typically aggressive, adult-oriented, entertainment fare), attempts to solve intra- or interpersonal conflicts from information gleaned through watching television may be counterproductive.

Uses and gratification theory hypothesizes that viewers have needs that produce expectations of television, which lead to a particular selection of programs and a gratification of all or some of those needs. Needs include a desire for information, diversion (e.g., relaxation, stimulation), social outlet or contact, and avoidance (e.g., of social contacts or chores). This theory is particularly relevant to the television viewing habits of exceptional children. Given the relative social isolation of ED, LD, and MR children (due to special classes or schools or rejection by peers), one would expect them to turn to television to satisfy social needs and as a way of avoiding frustrating situations (e.g., social rejection, doing academic assignments). Children would not be expected to watch television to seek out information, but the restricted environments of many disabled children may make the information that they do acquire from television more potent because they have fewer alternative life experiences with which to compare it. Considering that many gifted children are provided with numerous enriched academic activities, it is not surprising that they watch less television than their peers during the early school years. However, the relevance and usefulness of television as a source of social and sexual information are heightened for gifted children during their adolescence, when they are immersed in the dramatic physiological and social changes inherent in this stage of development; hence, consistent with uses and gratification theory, their television viewing increases.

Research on children's television viewing habits suggests that children receiving special education services for learning and behavior disorders may be one of television's most vulnerable audiences with regard to the adverse effects of extensive television viewing. As a group they are less able intellectually and more likely to come from lower socioeconomic backgrounds and dysfunctional families and experience interpersonal conflict, all of which are associated with relatively high levels of exposure to television. In the following chapters, we examine the exceptional child's ability to distinguish reality from fantasy in program content, recognize the use of special effects, comprehend the hidden message in television commercials, and learn concepts, skills, and patterns of interpersonal interaction.

3 Reality Perceptions

Any parents of a preschool child could recall a time when they tried to comfort their son or daughter who was frightened by a scary fairy tale or movie with "But it's only a story . . . it's make-believe." This verbal reassurance along with a hug can often calm the disquieted child. Somehow we assume that stories are less frightening to youngsters if they know that they are pretend. This reasoning applies to television as well, and parents generally believe that children are less influenced by what they view if they perceive it as only "make-believe."

The issue is somewhat more complicated than it first appears, however, because television fare can be real in some ways and make-believe in others. Only very young children believe that televised dramas are actual life events occurring in real time inside the television set. Preschoolers can be taught that animated shows are make-believe, and many elementary school students agree that a television crime drama is only a story. But fictional stories about fictional characters can portray life as it is and thus be quite realistic. Further, to truly appreciate many fictional stories, whether they be on television, film, or stage, the audience must temporarily suspend disbelief. Adults can typically process the fiction on two levels: They can react to the story *as if* it were real while at the same time realizing that it is only a story.

Conceptualizations of the ability to distinguish reality from fantasy on television have been influenced by the work of Piaget and his stage theory of cognitive development. In the preoperational stage (ages 2–7), the child makes judgments based on the perceived appearance of objects and events. In the concrete operational stage (ages 7–12), the child develops conceptual skills that are applied to what is perceived; logic and reasoning skills are better developed than in earlier stages, thus making it possible for the child to infer beyond what is visible.

39

The ability to distinguish between make-believe or pretend and reality follows a developmental course through childhood. By age 3 most children have engaged in pretend play, as when they pretend a block is a gun. They are also likely to realize that the people and objects they see on television do not reside in the television set (Flavell, Flavell, Green, & Korfmacher, 1990). Somewhat more difficult to discern, however, is the distinction between appearance and reality. Research by Flavell and his colleagues (Flavell, 1986; Flavell, Flavell, & Green, 1987), for example, demonstrates that preschoolers become quite confused when appearance and reality do not match, as when a stage prop of a rock is held and found to feel like a sponge. By age 7, however, many children can reconcile the inconsistent facts that the object looks like a rock but is really a sponge. Accurate perceptions of television require the ability to distinguish between appearance and reality. For example, although Superman is shown throwing a boulder, people are not that strong, and therefore, the viewer concludes that it must not be a real boulder. Refinements in the ability to distinguish between reality and appearance continue at least to the onset of adolescence.

Children's perceptions of the reality of television content have been identified as an important cognitive mediator of the medium's impact on child behavior. The general assumption is that "to the extent that television content is perceived to be real-to-life, the child's attitudes and behaviors are more likely to be consistent with the content of that exposure" (Greenberg & Reeves, 1976, p. 87). In the case of aggression-laden television content, research has shown a relationship between the viewer's perception of reality and subsequent aggressive behavior. Children are more likely to behave aggressively following exposure to media portrayals of aggression if they believe that the media stimulus is a true event in the real world than if they are told it is a dramatization performed by actors (Atkin, 1983; Feshbach, 1976; Sawin, 1981). In a major meta-analysis of more than 200 studies on television's pro- and antisocial effects, Hearold (1986) concluded that the degree of realism in the televised portrayal was one of the most potent variables affecting the magnitude of antisocial effects.

For example, Atkin (1983) created three versions of a 6-minute television news program, complete with news stories and appropriate commercials, and presented them to 10- to 13-year-old boys and girls in a school setting. The "news program" was identical for all groups except for a critical 15-second scene. The critical scene showed college students arguing and then beginning to physically brawl with each other in a university classroom. In the realistic violence condition the critical scene was presented as an actual bit of news, with an announcer saying the following as the scene appeared on the screen:

Channel Six photographer Bob Ray was on hand this afternoon when young Congressional candidate Bill Tompkins addressed a political science class on university campus, but he didn't plan on this development. . . . The subject of amnesty turned the quiet classroom into a regular pier six brawl—two unidentified students obviously had some opposite views on the issue, and made them forcibly apparent. (p. 618)

The fantasy violence condition presented the identical scene, but the announcer introduced it as an advertisement for a movie rather than as an actual fight scene, saying:

> Saturday night at 11:30 on Cinema Six the focus is on action! Rip Torn, Natalie Wood and Robert Wagner star . . . young Americans on a narcotics trip turn the classroom into a no-holds-barred battle . . . (p. 618)

In the no-violence control condition, the critical scene was a commercial for the movie, which neither mentioned nor displayed any violent behavior.

After the youngsters watched one of the three versions of the program, they completed a response scale that was designed to assess their willingness to behave aggressively in various situations. Those who viewed the fight scene as fictional violence from a movie subsequently responded more aggressively than those who saw no violence at all. Those who thought they were seeing a real fight scene taking place in a college classroom were most willing of all to behave aggressively.

The relation between reality perceptions of television and aggressive behavior has also been examined in longitudinal studies of children's television viewing habits and aggressive behavior. Such studies (e.g., Huesmann et al., 1984) have reported a significant positive relationship between children's aggressiveness and their belief that television violence represents life as it really is. Furthermore, believing that television violence is realistic is correlated with television violence viewing. In other words, children who perceive television violence as realistic are likely to be aggressive youngsters who are heavy consumers of television violence.

Research also suggests that children who perceive television content as realistic and are heavy consumers of the medium are most likely to develop perceptions of the real world that are consistent with television's portrayals. This is an extension of George Gerbner's "cultivation hypothesis" (Gerbner, Gross, Signorielli, Morgan, & Jackson-Beeck, 1979), which proposes that heavy television viewers gradually accept the distortions and stereotypes projected on television and apply them to real-world events. One of the most flagrant distortions in the world of television is the disproportionate number of violent acts. The cultivation hypothesis would predict that heavy versus light viewers would be more likely to overestimate the amount of real crime and their own chances of being victimized. Although the size of this effect is only modest (Hawkins & Pingree, 1982), Potter (1986) showed that the strongest findings apply to children who perceive television as realistic. There are significant correlations between an adolescent's overestimation of a person's risk of being a victim (of murder, robbery, or an automobile accident) and his or her amount of television exposure, but only for youngsters who strongly believe television is an accurate reflection of life.

On a physiological level, it has been shown that, in both children and adults, realistic violence produces stronger emotional responses (e.g., galvanic skin response, palmar sweating) than those produced by fantasy violence (Geen, 1975; Osborn & Endsley, 1971). For example, Osborn and Endsley showed 4- and 5-year-old children four 3-minute film sequences while their galvanic skin reflex (GSR) was being monitored. The GSR (a measure of elecrodermal conductance in the skin) is determined by the amount of sweat produced and is thus an index of emotional response. The children viewed two violent episodes (one containing cartoon characters and one human characters) and two sequences devoid of violence (one animated and the other nonanimated). As measured by GSR, the children responded more emotionally to the violent than to the nonviolent sequences, particularly to the one featuring human characters. They also rated the sequence containing human characters involved in violent action the "scariest," and 1 week later they recalled more details from this film than from any of the other three. Thus, it appears that realistic and aggression-laden material is most influential on child viewers from the standpoint of producing an emotional reaction, being cognitively labeled as scary, and being recalled some time later.

Several studies on children's reality perceptions of television were conducted in the early 1970s, most of which involved asking children to what extent television represented real life. For example, Lyle and Hoffman (1972) asked 1st, 6th, and 10th graders how realistically television portrayed real life and found that about half the 1st graders felt that people on television were like those they knew. The 6th and 10th graders were more skeptical, but a large percentage believed that television characters and real people were alike most of the time. They also found that Mexican American and Black children were less skeptical than Caucasian youngsters.

As may have been gathered from the few studies reported so far, the concept of reality perceptions has tapped several different concepts. Researchers studying reality perceptions of television have included such diverse questions as whether television characters actually live in the television set, the degree to which people on television are like people in real life, and the degree to which events on television really happened or could happen. Hawkins (1977) examined the various dimensions of reality perceptions and discovered that there are, in fact, two independent dimensions. He labeled the first dimension *magic window*, which indicates the degree to which children perceive television characters as real people or actors playing roles. The second dimension, *social expectations*, deals with how similar to real life television characters and events are and how useful they are in guiding the children's own behavior.

What strategies do children use to decide whether a program is real or pretend? Morison, Kelly, and Gardner (1981) identified two categories of criteria for deciding: *TV–real life comparisons,* which involves comparing television events to the real world, and *TV-specific criteria,* which uses one's understanding of how and why television programs are put together. They found that the number of each of these strategies a child uses increases with age. Studying second, fourth, and sixth graders, they found that the youngest children focused on physical features of a program as cues to its nonreality, referring to the presence of techniques such as camera tricks or stunts. Older children were more likely than their younger counterparts to refer to the presentation dimension of whether the program is acted, scripted, rehearsed, or live. Children of all ages considered whether the television content existed in the real world. However, whereas the second graders attended to blatantly unreal or impossible events to explain why programs were unreal, older children were able to use possibility or plausibility to confirm that programs were real. In explaining their findings, the authors noted, "since comparing television to real life is a major component of reality/fantasy evaluation, real world exposure and experience must make necessary contributions by providing the backdrop against which the television world is compared" (p. 241).

These studies and others indicate that certain characteristics and conditions diminish the viewer's capacity to make reality/fantasy distinctions. Children who have lower IQs, are frequent television viewers, and are from minority or lower socioeconomic backgrounds tend to perceive entertainment television programs as presenting life as it is (Greenberg, 1972; Greenberg & Dominick, 1970; Greenberg & Reeves, 1976; McLeod, Atkin, & Chaffee, 1972; Potter, 1988). The ability to make reality/fantasy distinctions also changes with age, whether the material is pictures (Taylor & Howell, 1973), stories (Lottan, 1967), or brief television episodes (Skeen, Brown, & Osborn, 1982). In general, limited cognitive abilities and restricted exposure to the majority culture, coupled with concentrated exposure to television, produce a viewer who has difficulty discriminating reality from fantasy on broadcast television. One would expect that ED, LD, and MR children, given their social restrictiveness, cognitive disabilities, and heavy exposure to television, would be more apt to perceive television portrayals as real. Conversely, gifted children would be less apt to perceive television content as real, given their advanced cognitive abilities, potential for diversified social experiences, and comparatively less frequent use of television.

EXCEPTIONAL CHILDREN

Most of what we know about how children perceive the realism of television content is from global questionnaires. One of the problems with such instruments is that the majority of disabled children have reading and academic deficits and may therefore have problems understanding what is asked of them. One way to eliminate this problem is to create a test that can be easily understood by disabled children. One such test, called the Perceptions of Reality on Television (PORT), was developed by Sprafkin, Gadow, and Dussault (1986). It was constructed to assess, with minimal reliance on the test taker's reading ability, children's knowledge about the realism of people and situations shown on television. The PORT consists of a series of videotaped excerpts, each about 1 minute long, from television programs. After each excerpt, children are asked several true–false questions about the excerpt and circle either "yes" or "no" (for true and false, respectively) on an answer sheet. The PORT questions are based on five concept categories identified as being relevant for media literacy (Singer, Singer, & Zuckerman, 1981):

1. Judging the realism of aggressive content.
2. Judging the realism of nonaggressive content.
3. Judging the realism of superhuman feats.
4. Differentiating between the actor and the role played.
5. Differentiating between cartoons and nonanimated programs.

Filler items, which focus on explicitly presented factual content, are included to determine the degree to which the children are paying attention to the test and complying with the instructions. If the children being tested are watching the segments, they should get most of the filler questions correct. The regular items on the PORT measure whether television characters are perceived as real people or as actors playing roles (magic window) and how similar to real life television characters and events are perceived (social expectation; Hawkins, 1977). The PORT has been found to be a reliable and valid measure of children's perceptions of reality on television (Kelly, 1986; Sprafkin, Kelly, & Gadow, 1987).

Emotionally Disturbed Children

Sprafkin and Gadow conducted two studies in which the PORT was used to evaluate the reality perceptions of ED children. In the first study (Sprafkin, Gadow, & Dussault, 1986), the PORT was administered to 41 ED boys (IQ: $M = 86$) and 41 nondisabled boys (IQ: $M = 112$) from a neighboring school. All participants were between the ages of 7 and 13 years old. The regular class boys performed significantly better than the ED boys (88% vs. 63% correct, respectively). Even when the difference in IQ was statistically controlled, the nondisabled group's perceptions of television reality were more accurate than those of the ED sample. When each item on the test was analyzed separately, although the two groups performed comparably on the filler items, the regular class students were more aware of the unreality of television violence, better able to discriminate the actor from the role played, and more knowledgeable about cartoon animation. These findings strongly suggest that ED children have many more misconceptions about important reality/fantasy aspects of television than students in regular classes.

Their second study (Sprafkin, Kelly, & Gadow, 1987) involved 73 children receiving special education (N: ED = 38, LD = 35) and 159 nondisabled children in regular classes, between 5 and 9 years old. All children were administered the PORT in their classrooms. Similar to the findings of the earlier study, the nondisabled group responded more accurately on the PORT than did the ED children, and this difference was maintained even after initial IQ differences were controlled statistically (covaried). As one would expect, the older ED children (69% correct) performed better than the younger ones (57% correct). Across the ED, LD, and nondisabled groups, boys and girls performed comparably on the PORT.

Table 3.1 presents a sample of questions from the PORT, the percentage of ED, LD, and nondisabled children who answered each item correctly, and the significance level of the statistical tests (chi square) to evaluate the differences between the three groups. The responses to the questions regarding the technique of animation ("Bugs Bunny" cartoon segment) indicate that about half the nondisabled children answered them correctly. However, an even smaller percentage of the ED and LD children seemed to know that the characters in cartoons are not actors but a series of drawings. Similarly, they showed confusion about the existence of Bugs Bunny.

The degree to which the youngsters realized that actors are not really hurt in fictional scenes of violence was assessed in several excerpts (e.g., "Dukes of Hazard," "Wonder Woman"). In all cases, regular classroom students were far more likely to understand the staged nature of television violence. For example, in response to a fist-fight scene from the "Dukes of Hazard," about half of the ED children thought that the actors needed to see a doctor before they could continue making the show.

The children's perception of superhuman feats was assessed with excerpts from "Wonder Woman" and "Mr. Merlin" (a sorcerer). An alarming proportion of ED children seemed to perceive superhuman feats that were portrayed on television such as flying and making a telephone booth disappear as realistic and possible. For example, almost 40% of the ED children witnessed Wonder Woman jump over trees and then responded that ordinary people could do that if they wore her shoes.

The ability to discriminate between actors and the roles they play was evaluated with several excerpts. Again, the ED and LD children were far less likely than their nondisabled peers to realize that the actor's role does not continue off the set. For example, a large percentage of the ED children thought that television family characters are related in real life (e.g., "Dukes of Hazard," "Land of the Lost").

Finally, television portrayals of unlikely or unrealistic situations were more likely to be seen as representative of the real world by the ED and LD children

TABLE 3.1
Sample Questions from the PORT and the Percentage of ED, LD,
and Nondisabled Children Who Correctly Answered Each Question

Test Questions[a]	ED	LD	Nondisabled	p < [b]
"Bugs Bunny"				
Cartoon sequence in which we see Bugs Bunny fighting with a Knight.				
1. The actors wore special costumes for this program. (No)	19	18	47	.001
2. Bugs Bunny lives in Hollywood where they make TV shows. (No)	36	24	55	.01
"The Dukes of Hazard"				
The Duke boys have a fist fight with two other males. Next, there is a car chase scene in which a police car flies over a gully and lands safely.				
1. The two boys who were knocked out saw a doctor before they could make the rest of the show. (No)	56	67	88	.001
2. When the show is over, the Duke boys go home to the same house. (No)	44	21	61	.001
3. Most cars can do what these cars did. (No)	46	50	83	.001
4. Police have to drive that way almost everyday. (No)	43	31	65	.001
"Mr. Merlin"				
Introduction to the situation comedy in which Mr. Merlin, a sorcerer, makes people and things disappear.				
1. A good magician can do all the tricks that Mr. Merlin does. (No)	31	27	57	.001
2. After the show, Mr. Merlin is like any other person. (Yes)	64	67	86	.01
"Wonder Woman"				
A man tries to hurt Wonder Woman and she defends herself by throwing a large stereo speaker and pushing the man through a wall. In the next scene she jumps over tree tops.				
1. If a woman practices real hard, she can do everything Wonder Woman can do. (No)	60	30	83	.001
2. When Wonder Woman is not on TV, she wears regular clothes. (Yes)	81	75	95	.01

TABLE 3.1
(*Continued*)

Test Questions[a]	ED	LD	Nondisabled	p <[b]
3. After this show, the man who fought with Wonder Woman probably went home with a headache. (No)	30	31	57	.01
4. If you wore Wonder Woman's shoes, you could jump over the trees like she did. (No)	62	53	89	.001
"Land of the Lost"				
A man and his two sons are chased by a dinosaur.				
1. The boy and the man were brave to be in this show because they could have gotten hurt by the monster. (No)	54	25	65	.001
2. They probably had to go to a far away place like Africa to get the dinosaur for this show. (No)	46	31	7	.001
3. When this show isn't on TV, the man and the two kids live together because they are a family. (No)	35	9	71	.001
4. People made the dinosaur in this show. (Yes)	76	72	89	.05

[a]The correct answer for each question appears in parentheses.

[b]Chi square test was performed on each item to determine whether the percentage correct score varied significantly by educational placement (ED, LD, nondisabled).

Note. From data reported in "Reality Perceptions of Television: A Comparison of Emotionally Disturbed, Learning Disabled, and Nonhandicapped Children" by J. Sprafkin, E. Kelly, and K. D. Gadow, 1987. *Journal of Developmental and Behavioral Pediatrics, 8,* pp. 149–153.

than by the regular classroom students. For example, after watching a car chase scene involving a sheriff and "bad guy," in which the cars literally fly over a gully and land safely, more than half the ED group responded that most cars can do such a stunt and that police have to drive that way almost every day.

Learning Disabled Children

Little is known about how LD youngsters perceive television. This is unfortunate given the large number of school-labeled LD children in the country and the fact that LD children are less able intellectually and have poorer social interaction skills, both of which are risk factors for misperceiving the unreality of television fiction. LD students in self-contained special education classes may be at greatest risk for the adverse effects of media viewing because they are isolated from the mainstream of the educational experience.

After gaining the cooperation of a school for LD elementary children, Gadow, Sprafkin, Kelly, and Ficarrotto (1988) administered the PORT to all students (N = 104) between the ages of 6 and 12 years old (IQ: M = 82). From the same township, they enlisted the cooperation of a regular elementary school to serve as a comparison group. Students (N = 229) from two classes from each grade level from first to sixth participated in the study. The children in each school were divided into three age groups: 7-, 9-, and 11-year-olds.

As expected, Gadow et al. (1988) found that the non-LD students performed significantly better than the LD group (76% vs. 52% correct, respectively). This difference remained even after initial IQ differences were statistically controlled. Within the LD group there were significant differences in the accuracy scores for the three age groups: 11-year-olds (63%), 9-year-olds (52%), and 7-year-olds (42%). As would be expected, children become more sophisticated in their understanding of reality/fantasy discriminations and special effects with increasing age. (Gender did not influence the scores in either group.)

Why LD children know less about the unreality of television (even when the effects of intellectual ability is partialed out statistically) is difficult to explain. It is interesting to speculate that the same information-processing deficits that contribute to the cognitive and social skills deficits in this population may also be implicated in more general misunderstandings of reality. For example, there is some evidence that LD children are less able to interpret verbal cues (Donahue et al., 1983) and nonverbal cues (e.g., Bryan, 1977) during social interchanges and may be less knowledgeable about socially relevant behaviors such as emotions (e.g., Bachara, 1976).

Mentally Retarded Children

There are no studies of the television reality perceptions of MR children, although this would seem to be a likely group to study based on the fact that lower intellectual ability is associated with the belief in the reality of television. It is reasonable to hypothesize that MR students encounter greater difficulty making reality/fantasy distinctions in their processing of television content than intellectually average peers.

Intellectually Gifted Children

According to Janos and Robinson (1985), most parents and educators of gifted children tend to believe that the association between cognitive maturity and any form of advanced psychosocial development (including interpersonal problem solving, perspective taking, making social judgments, and play interests) is highly doubtful:

Remarks such as "he's bright, but he's still a little child" or "skipping grades is harmful because children can't handle the social demands" reflect an assumption that psychosocial status corresponds much more closely to chronological than to mental age. However, this assumption is far from proven. In fact, the inference that intellectually precocious children show no advancement in psychosocial domains appears to be untenable. (pp. 150–151)

Indeed, the literature on psychosocial development suggests that gifted students are superior to intellectually average peers in social problem solving (Roedell, 1978), perceptual, conceptual, and affective perspective taking (Abroms & Gollin, 1980), and social knowledge (Scott & Bryant, 1978).

Unfortunately, assessments of social cognition have employed conceptual tasks with social content akin to items that are included in intelligence tests. Therefore, it is not surprising that bright children do well with them. It should be noted, however, that social cognitive skills do not reliably manifest themselves in actual social behavior any more consistently in gifted than average children. In other words, although gifted children appear to have the capacity for engaging in more sophisticated perspective taking, they may not actually demonstrate this skill in social situations.

Clearly, this poses an interesting question about gifted children's perceptions of reality of television characters and situations. Do gifted children engage in advanced social perspective-taking abilities when watching television? Although limited cognitive abilities coupled with concentrated exposure to television produces a viewer who has difficulty discriminating reality from fantasy on commercial television, do advanced cognitive abilities generate different results?

Abelman (1982; Abelman & Courtright, 1983) addressed these questions in a study of intellectually average ($N = 156$) and gifted ($N = 137$) fourth-grade children that examined reality perceptions of television character portrayals. The TV Character Index employed in these investigations contained 10 items that tested the children's perceptions of the disparity between television characters and people in the real world. The items pertained to several highly rated child- and adult-oriented programs, program types, and characters, the selection of which was based on those "favorites" most commonly suggested by approximately 250 fourth-grade students. Each program and program type was familiar to approximately 97% of the sample. All items asked children whether the specific characters in the programs were "real" or "made up." The items were as follows:

1. Is there really a man named J. R. Ewing living in Dallas, or is he made up?
2. Is there really a family named Duke living in Hazard County, or are they made up?

3. Are those real people doing incredible things [on "That's Incredible"], or are they made up?

4. Is David Banner [on "Incredible Hulk"] a real or made-up person?

5. Is the Hulk a real or made-up person?

6. Are the people playing the games [on TV sports] real or made up?

7. Are the people in cartoons real or made up?

8. Are the animals in cartoons real or made up?

9. Are the people reading the news real or made up?

10. Are the people being talked about in the news real or made up?

Several interesting findings emerge when looking at the characters in adult-oriented programming (see Table 3.2). First, in several instances gifted children demonstrated a significantly more accurate perception of reality than their intellectually average peers. For example, the gifted children were significantly more likely than the average children to perceive J. R. Ewing (from "Dallas") as "made up" [$\chi^2(2) = 7.10, p < .03$]. Interestingly, approximately 12% and 7% of intellectually average and gifted children, respectively, believed that J. R. Ewing was a real person. There was also a significant difference in children's perception of the reality of the Duke family from "Dukes of Hazard" [$\chi^2(2) = 6.87, p <$

TABLE 3.2
Perceived Reality of Television Characters by Average
and Gifted Children

	Average			Gifted		
Character	Real	Made Up	Don't Know	Real	Made Up	Don't Know
J. R. Ewing	12.2	39.0	48.8	7.3	68.3	24.4
Duke	4.9	61.0	34.2	0.0	85.4	14.6
That's Incredible	74.4	7.7	17.9	69.9	7.7	22.4
Dave	31.4	51.9	16.7	26.9	57.1	16.0
Hulk	12.8	80.1	7.0	6.4	87.8	5.8
Game	98.1	0.0	1.9	96.8	1.9	1.3
Cartoon people	1.9	96.2	1.9	0.6	96.8	2.6
Cartoon animals	6.8	93.2	0.0	1.9	95.6	2.6
News anchor	96.2	0.0	3.9	97.2	0.0	2.8
News story	93.6	0.6	5.8	91.7	2.8	5.6

Note. Percentage of children selecting each response option (real, made up, don't know). From data reported in "Television Literacy: Amplifying the Cognitive Level Effects of Television's Prosocial Fare Through Curriculum Intervention" by R. Abelman and J. Courtright, 1983. Journal of Research and Development in Education, 17, pp. 46–57.

.04], with the gifted children being more likely than those in the average group to accurately perceive them as "made up."

Although there was not an overall significant group difference in the children's perceptions of the Hulk from "The Incredible Hulk" program, significantly fewer gifted children perceived the Hulk to be real compared with average children. Table 3.2 also shows that both groups were confused by several characters. David Banner from "The Incredible Hulk," for example, was perceived as real by more than one fourth of the children in each sample. Conversely, less than three fourths of the children in each group perceived the people depicted on "That's Incredible" (who were real) as real.

One possible explanation for the children's misperceptions of the reality of some of these characters (e.g., the Hulk, J. R. Ewing) is that the adult-oriented programs in which they are featured contain more "reality-based" content than other program types, with the exception of news and documentaries (Newcomb, 1979). This misperception was enhanced further by the similarity in the program titles of two series that differed markedly in their degree of realism: "The Incredible Hulk" (a fantasy) and "That's Incredible" (an informational entertainment program).

Comparisons Among Exceptional Children

What has been presented so far has described the differences between exceptional and typical children in their reality perceptions of television content. It is also interesting to compare the different categories of exceptional children with regard to such perceptions. One of the aforementioned studies (Sprafkin, Kelly, & Gadow, 1987) examined how the ED, LD, and nondisabled children's reality perceptions differed relative to one another. The nondisabled group outperformed both the ED and LD groups, and the ED children responded slightly more accurately than the LD children. The percent correct scores were as follows: ED (52%), LD (47%), and nondisabled (71%). The performance of the three groups on the filler items was much better and more comparable to one another (ED: 83%, LD: 89%, and nondisabled: 90%), which suggests that the disabled children were attending to the television excerpts and comprehending the explicit features but were much more naive about the unreality of television content than their peers in regular classes. With IQ statistically controlled (covaried), the ED and LD children's PORT scores were now comparable, although the difference between the disabled and nondisabled groups were maintained.

In the only study that compared ED and gifted children's perceptions of television, Donahue and Donahue (1977) asked 11- to 16-year-old children from each category to rate the degree of reality of television role stereotypes (e.g., mothers, fathers, teachers), general television situations (e.g., marriage, dating, families), and specific television characters (e.g., Archie Bunker, John Boy

Walton) on a 7-point scale ranging from "very real" to "extremely unreal." The ED children rated the general television situations and specific television characters as more real than the gifted group, whereas there were no group differences on the role stereotype items.

CONCLUSIONS

Clearly, the degree of realism attributed to television portrayals of fictional characters is highest for disabled children and lowest for gifted children. Considering the previously discussed strategies (Morison et al., 1981) that children use to decide whether a program is real or pretend, it is likely that disabled children lack the fundamental skills inherent in these strategies. One of the more elemental strategies used by children is to employ TV-specific criteria such as the physical features of a program (e.g., camera tricks or animation) as a cue to its realism. Most nondisabled children have some knowledge of animation; therefore, it is not surprising that more than 90% of gifted and intellectually average children correctly label cartoon characters such as Bugs Bunny as "made up." However, only a minority of ED and LD children in self-contained classes know how cartoons are made, and thus most are unaware that cartoon characters and events are unreal.

Research findings strongly suggest that ED and LD children also lack the more advanced strategies for deciding whether a program is real or pretend. Such strategies include making TV–real life comparisons, applying information about how programs are made (e.g., actors follow scripts), and assessing the plausibility of the people and events portrayed (Morison et al., 1981). Most intellectually average (and gifted) elementary-school children appear to understand the staged nature of aggressive behavior in fictional programs and realize that the actors do not really hurt each other or continue in their roles after filming the program. In contrast, most ED and LD age-mates appear to be unaware of all of these features of program production and thus lack the more advanced strategies for determining the realism of a program.

Nondisabled children seem to rely heavily on the strategy of assessing the plausibility of situations and people in determining a program's realism, whereas this is not evident in disabled children. For example, they do not seem to see the implausibility of people performing superhuman feats. However, it is interesting to note that significantly more average (13%) than gifted (6%) children thought that the Incredible Hulk is real. Gifted children's superior talents in determining plausibility are also reflected in their responses to questions about more realistic television characters. Far more gifted (than average) children perceived J. R. Ewing and the Duke family as "made up," suggesting that the gifted group was tuning in to more subtle differences between real life and the television portrayals than were their peers. The fact that gifted children have more accurate reality perceptions of television characters also attests to their ability to engage in more sophisticated perspective taking than average children.

In spite of the fact that ED and LD children differ with regard to the nature of their social interactions, particularly in structured classroom settings (Sprafkin & Gadow, 1987), these children appear to share the problem of believing that television content is more realistic than it is. Several explanations are possible. First, both groups of disabled children are less likely to participate in the kinds of social interactions that lead to a more realistic world view. Children in self-contained special education classes (especially youngsters in special schools) are isolated to some extent from their nondisabled age-mates during the school day and engage in fewer social out-of-school activities (McConaughty & Ritter, 1985; Sprafkin & Gadow, 1986). For some of these children, watching television may serve as a substitute for social interaction and as a purveyor of a distorted reality. Second, it is also possible that the cognitive mechanisms that induce or exacerbate the child's primary disability are in some way involved in the misperception of the reality of television content. Third, the parents of disabled children may spend less time explaining to their children the nature of television (see chapter 6).

Regardless of the reason, ED and LD children spend much of their leisure time watching television, and they tend to perceive many of the fictional portrayals as real. Research has yet to determine the combined effects of these two factors. However, cultivation theory (discussed earlier in this chapter) and research on aggressive children suggest that the outcome may be particularly deleterious for ED, LD, and MR children. Cultivation theory predicts that the heavy viewer is exposed to frequent portrayals of violence and develops a "mean world" outlook on life, cynical and suspicious attitudes of people, and overconcerns about one's chances of being a victim of aggression. This influence is most applicable to children who perceive television as realistic (Potter, 1986). Emotionally disturbed children in particular are often aggressive, and Dodge (1980; Dodge & Newman, 1981) has shown that aggressive children are especially sensitive to the motivations of other people (i.e., if they perceive the other person to have antisocial motivations, they are more likely to respond aggressively themselves). If heavy exposure to television violence makes it more likely that they will view the intentions of others as antisocial, this could result in heightened aggressive behavior, clearly a negative outcome. In that behavior problems are also prevalent in groups of LD and MR children, this cultivation effect could have adverse influences on them as well. If television exposure is only a modest determiner of the social behavior of disabled children, misperceptions of its reality may only compound an existing social deficit.

4 Comprehension of Television Information

In the early 1960s, the most widely accepted summary evaluation of research concerning television's impact on children was provided by Schramm et al. (1961), and read: "For some children, under some conditions, some television is harmful. For other children under the same conditions, or for some children under other conditions, it may be beneficial" (p. 1). Since this statement was first issued, well over 3,000 scientific research articles and governmental reports have been published examining media effects (see Liebert & Sprafkin, 1988), with special emphasis on the impact of television on young children. The literature continues to be far more definitive regarding how and why media effects occur, and the consideration of differences among children and the unique conditions under which viewing occurs continue to be viable intervening variables.

Indeed, the conceptualization of television viewing as a learned activity and a skill acquired at a different rate by different children under diverse conditions has gained much support in the last decade. Compared with the traditional "medium-oriented" literature that examined television's disruption and usurption of children's leisure-time activities and peer interactions (see chapter 1, this volume, as well as Himmelweit et al., 1958; Klapper, 1960) and the direct impact of televised portrayals (Baker & Ball, 1969; Comstock & Rubinstein, 1971; Gerbner, 1972), this new body of communication research has embraced a more "child-specific" orientation. According to Bryant and Anderson (1983):

> In the 1970s and 1980s public and research interest in television has been increasingly directed at the act of television viewing itself. This interest has taken several forms . . . [including] the belief that an elucidation of the fundamental psychological processes underlying television viewing is essential for any full understanding

of its impact. As a result, researchers in psychology and communication have begun to study systematically children's attention to and comprehension of television. (pp. xii–xiv)

These contemporary investigations "caught up in the rising tide of cognitive explanations . . . to communicative behaviors" (Greene & Sparks, 1983, p. 349) have focused largely on differences among children that are assumed to mediate media effects. Salomon (1979a, 1981, 1983), for example, initiated much of the formative work in this area by suggesting that the amount of invested mental effort (AIME) children apply to the televiewing experience influences their program recall and comprehension, and the resultant inference making and effects. Child-specific factors influencing AIME include one's perceptions of what the material is, how much effort it deserves, the worthwhileness of effort expenditure, and one's belief in one's own efficacy. The orientation reflected in these and other investigations (see Van Evra, 1990) recasts the general question that guides research from how television impacts on children, to how children differentially respond to television information. In other words, how do individual and developmental differences influence children's attention to and comprehension of various forms of television content?

Clearly, this body of research represents an important progression in our understanding of children's learning from television. However, like the investigations before it, it too offers a rather unidimensional view of the child in that there has been little consideration of exceptional children and the cognitive skills and abilities they may or may not possess for accurate comprehension of television information. For instance, Salomon (1984) observed that "the strongest debilitating effects of television are observed with high ability children. They have the most negative views of the medium, expend the least mental effort in processing a presented program, and show the poorest inference-making performance" (p. 62). Nevertheless, he failed to take into account the differences between exceptional children and their nonlabeled counterparts, as well as differences among children with divergent exceptionalities.

This chapter addresses these issues. We begin with an examination of children's attention to and comprehension of production techniques, special effects, and persuasive strategies used in television programs and commercials. This is followed by a discussion of the cognitive processes presumed to underlie children's comprehension of television information.

DEVELOPMENTAL DIFFERENCES

Research assessing developmental differences in nonlabeled children's attention to and comprehension of television information has typically considered chronological age (as opposed to social age or specific cognitive capabilities) as the most appropriate indicator of developmental distinctions. More than 20 years ago, the formative work on the creation of "Sesame Street" and "3-2-1 Contact" by the Children's Television Workshop (CTW, 1990; Mielke, 1990) initiated the model for studying how children at different ages attended to television. Borrowing from this model, Anderson and Levin (1976; Levin & Anderson, 1976) showed preschoolers program excerpts in a setting with natural distractors such as toys while their attention was being monitored. Findings suggested that preschoolers attended to the presence of women, children, puppets, peculiar voices, auditory changes, animation, camera cuts, lively music, laughing, applause, rhyming, repetition, and alliteration. They were less likely to attend to the presence of men, extended zooms and pans, animals, inactivity, and still drawings.

Attention to television content has also been found to be greater for visually presented information than for similar material presented verbally, and this difference is more pronounced in younger (kindergarten age) than in older (later elementary school age) children (Calvert, Watkins, Wright, & Huston-Stein, 1979; Hackett, 1977; Hackett & Sprafkin, 1982). Another related finding is that younger children's attention to television is more influenced than that of older children by perceptual salience; that is, the young child is more likely to be drawn to television content that is high in movement, intensity, change, and contrast (Rice, Huston, & Wright, 1982).

A developmental perspective has also been used to understand how children comprehend what they attend to on television. Much of this research has been spearheaded by W. Andrew Collins (1979, 1982, 1983), who has shown that preschool children understand and retain surprisingly little information about plots of the stories they have seen on television. Part of the problem, suggests Collins, is that preschool and early elementary-school children have difficulty discriminating between plot-important (central) and plot-irrelevant (peripheral) content. As children grow older, central content accounts for an increasing proportion of what they recall.

This has also been found to be the case with regard to children's comprehension of various formal features and specific visual and auditory techniques employed in television production. In general, it has been found that older children are better able to comprehend size (Abelman, 1989; Acker & Tiemens, 1981) and velocity transformations (Acker, 1983; Flessati & Fouts, 1985; Reeves et al., 1984) of televised images (i.e., changes in the size of televised objects represent changes in distance), temporal sequencing (i.e., plot development) and sequential transformations (Abelman, 1990b; Collins et al., 1978), character portrayals (Hoffner & Cantor, 1985; Reeves & Garramone, 1982, 1983), complexity of visual techniques (Hoffner, Cantor, & Thorson, 1988, 1989; Huston & Wright, 1983; Smith et al., 1985; Thorson et al., 1985; Welch & Watt, 1982), and complexity of auditory devices (Badzinski, 1991; Calvert & Gersh, 1985; Rolandelli et al., 1985; Wakshlag et al., 1982).

EXCEPTIONAL CHILDREN

That divergent levels of attention to and comprehension of television's visual and auditory techniques may indeed exist among exceptional children was first identified by Abelman and Sparks while conducting preliminary interviews with 7-year-old MR, LD, and intellectually gifted (IG) children in preparation for a future investigation (e.g., Abelman, 1984; Abelman & Sparks, 1985; Sparks & Abelman, 1985). During the interviews, 50 children were shown brief excerpts of representational techniques from popular off-air television programming and were asked to describe what had just happened. The following quotations typify the responses to the questions and offer descriptive insight into identifiable differences of comprehension among exceptional children.

Zoom in to closeup (The camera brings the viewer into closer proximity with object of focus):

MR: "The person is losing his face. He got nothing but eyes and his skin is covering the rest of his head."

LD: "The guy's face is getting bigger and bigger and you think it's going to pop. His nose is as big as my dad's truck. Like I once saw a movie when a guy took some juice and grew bigger and bigger. He was real mad and stepped on houses. It was a good thing there were big trees and mountains, because he was running around naked. He didn't have no clothes on."

IG: "We are getting closer to him. And it always makes me scared, because I know that something bad is going to happen when we get close. It's always bad. Going from close to far away usually means something good, like a happy ending when you see hillsides and rainbows."

Background music (Music is introduced to complement the visual activity and/or set the mood for forthcoming action):

MR: "The girl has a radio in her pocket."

LD: "Someone's window is open and you can hear someone playing the piano or some instrument. It don't have nothing to do with what's going on, we just hear music."

IG: "It's TV's way of telling you something without using the words, because maybe the people in the show don't even know what's happening. The guys in the show can't hear it."

Time continuity (The post-production manipulation of temporal sequencing to advance or delay action):

MR: "I think maybe I don't watch carefully. He's swimming in a pool and then he's driving a car. He's all dry. I think that I miss something and I don't pay attention enough."

LD: "He's magic."

IG: "That's just TV. If you watched them do everything that other people do, the show would be on all day and it would be boring. They really do all those other things, but they don't show it. They take it out. Maybe they make another TV show with it."

Program types   (The different genres of television programming):
MR: "Don't know. There's channels."
LD: "There's cartoons. And funny shows and scary shows. Oh, and there's shows for children and shows for adults. Oh, and there's shows my sister can't watch because she's four and there's shows I can't watch 'cause I'm seven."
IG: "Action shows, and comedy shows, and science shows, and news shows. We have cable and there's movies and 'Disney' and 'Playboy' and sports and music shows and theatre. My dad watches sports, my mom likes soaps, [my sister] watches 'Fraggle Rock' and I like 'Playboy.' No. I really don't."

With the goal of assessing how exceptional children process television programs and commercials, Sprafkin and Gadow created several paper-and-pencil instruments for use with disabled children. One instrument was the Knowledge About Television Techniques (KATT), which was designed and employed to assess nondisabled, ED, and LD children's awareness of the special effects and production techniques typically used in television programming. The KATT contained 40 items that applied to 12 television excerpts depicting a variety of narrative devices and special effects[1] such as disappearances, superhuman strength, dangerous and aggressive acts, and animation.

Another instrument was the Perceptions of Commercials (POC). It assessed the degree to which disabled children understood the selling techniques used in television commercials, including the promise of enhanced personal appeal, exaggerated product size and performance, irrelevant attributes of the product (e.g., the prize inside), jargon, personality endorsements, and disclaimers regarding nutritional value, required assembly, and accessories sold separately. The instrument entailed the viewing of brief excerpts that exemplified nine actual 30-second television ads and response to 27 POC items that asked a series of true–false or yes–no questions, requiring children merely to circle their response on an answer sheet.[2]

Knowledge About Television Techniques

Sprafkin, Kelly, and Gadow (1987) used the KATT to study 159 nondisabled, 38 ED, and 35 LD children. Nondisabled children scored significantly higher than both ED and LD children, with the latter two groups performing comparably to each other. The percentage of correct scores for the three groups were 74%, 52%, and 51%, respectively. Because of the moderate correlation between

---

[1]KATT is an internally consistent measure for ED and LD children, as indexed by the split-half correlation coefficient (.91), and is stable over short time intervals such as 6 weeks ($r = .54$). Scores on the KATT were significantly related to those obtained on an interview version of the test.

[2]The POC test proved to be internally consistent (.71) and relatively stable over 6 weeks ($r = .65$) with ED and LD children.

KATT scores and IQ ($r = .56$), it was important to determine how the groups would differ if IQ were statistically controlled. After equating for IQ, the non-disabled children still outperformed the ED and LD children, and the ED and LD children still performed at a comparable level to each other. Consistent with the literature examining nondisabled children, the older youngsters (7.5–9.4 years) demonstrated a greater knowledge of television techniques than the younger ones (5.5–7.4 years). Boys and girls performed comparably on the KATT.

The findings for LD youngsters were replicated in a larger scale investigation comparing the KATT performance of 104 LD and 229 nondisabled children (Gadow et al., 1988). The nondisabled children outperformed their LD counterparts (78% vs. 54% correct, respectively), and the significant difference remained even after IQ was statistically controlled. For both the LD and nondisabled children, the 9- and 11-year-olds attained significantly higher scores than the 7-year-olds, but the two older groups did not differ significantly from each other.

Emotionally Disturbed Children.   To determine what specific techniques were most troublesome to the ED children, individual items on the KATT scores were examined (see Table 4.1). Compared with the nondisabled sample, the ED children had greater difficulties comprehending how scenes involving violence were accomplished. For example, only slightly more than half the ED children realized that the bullets in a gunfight scene were not real, whereas 86% of their nondisabled counterparts knew that. In another excerpt, a fistfight scene was shown and only 50% of the ED children realized that the actors remained unharmed, whereas more than 75% of the nondisabled children correctly interpreted this. For another item, the children saw a fight in which a man hit another man over the head with a chair and the impact shattered the chair. When asked how the chair broke, half of the ED sample attributed it to the man's head being very hard whereas 80% of the nondisabled children knew that this was not the reason.

The ED children also had difficulty with the televised presentation of special effects that make superhuman feats appear real. An example of this involved a scene from the "Six Million Dollar Man," in which Steve Austin broke out of a cement entrapment. A far smaller proportion of the ED children realized that real cement was not used when compared to nondisabled children. Similarly, a "Wonder Woman" excerpt showed her jumping over treetops, and the nondisabled youngsters were far more likely than the ED children to realize that it was a television technique rather than her special powers.

The technique of animation was also relatively misunderstood by the ED children. For example, the ED children were more likely than those who were nondisabled to endorse items indicating that the cartoon characters in "Tom and Jerry" were actors dressed up in costumes and less likely to respond to the item stating that the characters were drawings.

TABLE 4.1
Sample Questions from the KATT and the Percentage of ED, LD,
and Nondisabled Children Who Correctly Answered Each Question

Test Questions[a]	ED	LD	Nondisabled	$p <$[b]
"The Rookies"				
Excerpt from a crime drama showing an exchange of gunfire between policemen and a criminal.				
What was really happening when everyone was shooting?				
1. Real bullets were coming out of real guns. (No)	53	42	86	.001
2. The bullets really went up into the air. (No)	47	58	80	.001
3. The bullets were fake. (Yes)	56	42	86	.001
"The Six Million Dollar Man"				
Scene in which the bionic man's legs are encased in cement and then he breaks free.				
The man broke out of the cement because:				
1. He was very strong. (No)	41	26	84	.001
2. It was not real cement, it just looked like it. (Yes)	62	81	90	.001
"Wonder Woman"				
We see Wonder Woman jump over the treetops.				
How did Wonder Woman jump so high?				
1. She's able to do it because she has special powers. (No)	47	25	81	.001
2. It just looked like she jumped high, the camera tricked us. (Yes)	65	72	84	.05
"Tom and Jerry"				
A cartoon sequence in which we see Tom and Jerry torturing each other and we hear Tom screaming in pain.				
How did the cat scream "ooooooooooow"?				
1. The cat was specially trained and could scream "oooooow" just like a person. (No)	55	53	93	.001
2. The cat really didn't scream "oooooow" because it's not a cat, but just a picture of a cat. (Yes)	67	56	80	.05

[a]The correct answer for each question appears in parentheses.

[b]Chi square test was performed on each item to determine whether the percentage correct score varied significantly by educational placement (ED, LD, nondisabled).

Note. From data reported in "Reality Perceptions of Television: A Comparison of Emotionally Disturbed, Learning Disabled, and Nonhandicapped Children" by J. Sprafkin, E. Kelly, and K. D. Gadow, 1987. *Journal of Developmental and Behavioral Pediatrics, 8,* pp. 149–153.

Learning Disabled Children.   Compared with the nondisabled group, the LD sample also had difficulties comprehending how scenes involving violence were accomplished; only 42% of the LD children realized that the bullets in the gunfight scene were not real, compared to 86% of their nondisabled counterparts. In addition, much like the ED group, the LD children were not aware of the methods used to protect actors from getting hurt in scenes of aggressive activities or to enable actors to look as if they can do superhuman feats. For instance, a smaller proportion of the LD children realized that real cement was not used in the excerpt from the "Six Million Dollar Man" and that Wonder Woman could not jump over treetops than did their nondisabled counterparts. In addition, as with ED children, LD children show evidence of a lack of knowledge about the process of animation, specifically the use of drawings to create the action. Only half of the LD children realized that the "Tom and Jerry" cartoon was based on a series of drawings to create the action, compared to over three-quarters of the nondisabled same-age children.

Intellectually Gifted Children.   Although gifted children were not administered the KATT instrument, investigations examining similar areas of inquiry have been conducted by Abelman (1982, 1986a) and allow for further comparisons among groups. The author created an Awareness of Prosocial and Antisocial Behavior Index that was operationalized at two levels: (a) the situational level, which assessed perceived motives behind prosocial and antisocial acts from a series of 10 off-air program excerpts; and (b) the character level, which assessed perceived rationale for those prosocial and antisocial acts.

Findings reveal that significantly more fourth grade gifted children (30%) could identify the prosocial motives behind aggressive behaviors depicted by "good guys" on commercial television than their intellectually average counterparts (16%). Nonlabeled sixth-grade children correctly identified 31% of the motives compared to 47% of gifted sixth graders. In addition, when asked why people in television shows fight with or yell at each other, approximately 46% of the nonlabeled fourth graders provided "fantasy" (e.g., "they don't like each other") rather than "reality" (e.g., "it's in the script") response, compared with only 25% of gifted fourth graders; there was no difference among sixth graders. Finally, approximately 47% of gifted fourth graders were able to predict a form of conflict resolution for their favorite television character in an aggressive situation, compared with 25% of the nonlabeled group. This suggests that gifted children have a better comprehension of character portrayals and plot development than their nonlabeled counterparts.

Perceptions of Commercials

How ED, LD, and nondisabled groups compared on their perceptions of commercials and the selling techniques contained within these ads was also addressed by Sprafkin, Kelly, and Gadow (1987). Nondisabled children were found to be more perceptive than the disabled children in recognizing the distortions and other selling techniques used in television ads. The nondisabled children attained higher scores on the POC than the ED and LD groups, and the ED children performed better than their LD peers. The POC scores were 70%, 52%, and 46%, respectively. As with the KATT instrument, POC scores were highly associated with IQ, so scores were reanalyzed controlling for IQ. The results remained essentially the same, with the nondisabled children attaining higher POC scores than those of the two exceptional children groups; however, when IQ was equated, the ED and LD groups were about even with respect to their performance on the POC. In all three groups of children, the older age group (7.5–9.4 years old) demonstrated a better knowledge of commercial techniques than the younger group (5.5–7.4 years old). In addition, gender did not significantly impact on the POC scores for any of the groups.

It should be added that the finding that nondisabled children perform significantly better on the POC than do ED children was also found in another study that compared POC performance of 41 ED and 41 nondisabled elementary school boys (Sprafkin, Gadow, & Dussault, 1986). Furthermore, the results for LD children were similar to those obtained in the large-scale study on 104 LD and 229 nondisabled children described earlier (Gadow et al., 1988).

Emotionally Disturbed Children.   Various advertising techniques were misperceived by the ED children. For instance, ED children were more likely to be impressed by the advertised products on the basis of jargon (i.e., "MFP" in toothpaste) and endorsements by children and appealing adults in the ads (i.e., those good at karate), and to lack an awareness of the nutritional disclaimers contained in the ads. As can be seen in Table 4.2, 44% of the ED youngsters (compared to only 14% of the nondisabled children) thought that a cereal that had an ad portraying karate pros could actually make you stronger than other cereals could. Across the many commercials presented in the POC, the ED children displayed a naivete regarding the more popular disclaimers contained in the children's ads such as those stating that "partial assembly is required," "accessories are sold separately," or the food product presented is only "part of a balanced breakfast." They also tended to see advertised products as larger, more powerful, and more able to impress others than did the nonexceptional children.

Learning Disabled Children.   These children were found to be just as limited in their comprehension and recognition of disclaimers, product endorsements, and exaggerated performance and presentation of products in commercials as ED children. When questioned about the cereal commercial portraying karate pros, more than half of the LD group thought that the advertised cereal could make you stronger than could other cereals, and 71% thought that people who were involved in karate prefer that cereal. In response to a toothpaste ad, almost 75% of

TABLE 4.2
Sample Questions from the POC and the Percentage of ED, LD,
and Nondisabled Children Who Correctly Answered Each Question

Test Questions[a]	ED	LD	Nondisabled	p <[b]
"Colgate Gel"				
A commercial featuring children who proclaim how good the toothpaste tastes. Included is the jargon phrase, "MFP" for Maximum Fluoride Protection.				
1. Colgate gel works better than other toothpastes because it tastes good. (No)	63	28	86	.001
2. Other toothpastes also have MFP. (Yes)	63	55	78	.05
3. The children in this commercial may like another toothpaste better. (Yes)	57	55	86	.001
"Honeycomb"				
A cereal commercial that takes place at a karate school. Included is the disclaimer, "Part of a balanced breakfast."				
1. Honeycomb can make you stronger than other cereals can. (No)	56	46	86	.001
2. People who do karate like Honeycomb cereal. (No)	38	29	84	.001
3. For a good breakfast, you need more than Honeycomb cereal. (Yes)	59	75	79	.05

[a]The correct answer for each question appears in parentheses.

[b]Chi square test was performed on each item to determine whether the percentage correct score varied significantly by educational placement (ED, LD, nondisabled).

Note. From data reported in "Reality Perceptions of Television: A Comparison of Emotionally Disturbed, Learning Disabled, and Nonhandicapped Children" by J. Sprafkin, E. Kelly, and K. D. Gadow, 1987. *Journal of Developmental and Behavioral Pediatrics, 8,* pp. 149–153.

the LD children (compared with only 14% of nondisabled children) responded that the advertised toothpaste works better than other toothpastes because it tastes good.

Summary

In general, the same age-related discrepancies in attention to and comprehension of television information identified in the literature examining nonlabeled children were also found to exist among exceptional children. Interestingly, it was also found that older ED and LD children processed television more like a younger nondisabled child than a same-age peer. In particular, they recalled significantly less information, were relatively indiscriminant in their recall of what Collins labeled as central versus peripheral content, had difficulty in making correct inferences about story line, and were rather naive about special effects. Gifted children, however, possessed a greater ability to comprehend than their nonlabeled same-age peers. Indeed, younger gifted children performed at a level comparable to older nonlabeled children.

Although the aforementioned studies employing the KATT and POC provide information about children's comprehension of television content at different ages and with different learning abilities and disabilities, they provide little insight into the nature of the specific skills necessary for comprehension. Similarly, the research cited above describes differences in levels of comprehension among ED, LD, and gifted children, but fails to take into account the specific cognitive skills that might be more or less prevalent or accessible among these children. This is addressed in the following section.

COGNITIVE PROCESSES AND CHILDREN'S TELEVISION VIEWING

In his review of the children and television literature, Collins (1983) noted that at least three specific cognitive tasks were believed to be involved in the comprehension of dramatic presentation on television. They are (a) selective attention to and perception of central program events (see also Anderson & Lorch, 1983; Howitt & Cumberbatch, 1976; Krull & Husson, 1979); (b) temporal integration, involving inferences about implicit relations among explicit scenes (see also Collins, 1979; Collins et al., 1978); and (c) orderly organization of the program events (see also Calvert & Gersh, 1985; Huston & Wright, 1983). Research on exceptional children suggests that there are significant differences in their ability to perform each of these tasks, and this, in turn, might affect their comprehension of television content.

Attention and Perception

According to Weener and Senf (1982), "attention and memory are the two most commonly measured variables showing consistent deficits in the learning disabled group" (p. 1962). When disabled children do attend, they may be prone to direct their perception to the unimportant aspects of the situation rather than to its most relevant features (Krupski, 1986). Ross (1976) suggested that disabled children show a delay in the development of selective attention abilities; these children are slower to learn how to focus their attention upon relevant dimensions of the learning task. In addition, like younger nonlabeled children, the attending behavior of disabled children is more influenced by perceptual salience (i.e., high in movement, intensity, change, and contrast) and these children are less able to integrate stimuli from different (i.e., visual vs. auditory) modalities (Beery, 1967; Birch & Belmont, 1964, 1965; Vande Voort, Senf, & Benton, 1972; Zendel & Pihl, 1983).

Conversely, intellectually gifted children possess the ability to be exceptionally selective in their attention and perception—often to a fault. They are able to attend to and assimilate information from various modalities with relative ease and speed (Scruggs & Cohn, 1983).

The application of children's perceptual skills and visual attention capabilities to television viewing has been a recent development. It has taken the form of assessments of children's comprehension of one of the most common and prevalent narrative devices employed in broadcast and narrowcast programming (Newcomb & Alley, 1983), which is thus among the most rudimentary techniques requiring attention and comprehension—projective size. Projective size entails changes in object size as a way of relaying our getting "closer to" and "farther away from" an object (Abelman, 1989; Acker & Tiemens, 1983).

Beginning with Piaget and Inhelder (1956), the ability to infer how changes in location alter the appearance of an object or array has been a traditional concern in the perspective-taking literature and has been believed to be an accurate assessment of perceptual skills. Findings from this and other studies (e.g., Piaget, 1969; Vurpillot, 1964) suggest that children under the age of 7 years— that is, those children that are perceptually bound and unable to conserve— neither are aware of nor understand projective phenomena in vision. Recent efforts by Flavell and his colleagues (Flavell, 1978; Flavell, Everett, Croft, & Flavell, 1981; Flavell, Flavell, Green, & Wilcox, 1980; Pillow & Flavell, 1986) and other neo-Piagetian researchers (e.g., Case, 1984), however, have identified certain perceptual differences in children ("Level 1" and "Level 2" knowledge of visual perception) within early levels of Piagetian-based assessments of cognitive development that show traces of perceptual understanding well before the age of 7 years. Results suggest that children begin to notice changes in projective size and shape, and to understand the visual consequences for projective size and shape of certain spatial transformations, during the preschool years.

Basically, at Level 1, children can attend to specific objects and infer what objects can or cannot be seen from another person's viewpoint. At Level 2, children also know that an object or array may present different appearances to viewers at different locations. That is, Level 2 knowledge enables children to infer the nature, as well as the content, of another person's visual experience. Flavell and his colleagues found that although children between the ages of 2 and 6 are typically classified as "preoperational" and incapable of perspective-taking, Level 1 knowledge is often acquired during the third year, whereas Level 2 knowledge is often acquired during the fourth.

Acker and Tiemens' (1983) investigation into children's perceptions of changes in size of televised images corresponded with Piaget's results. It was found that young nonlabeled children who failed the traditional conservation task perceived changes in image size from a medium shot to a close-up shot as changes in the object itself. By the fourth grade, a more accurate perception existed. However, employing the methodology developed by Flavell et al. (1981), Abelman (1989) found that of the nonconserving 3-year-olds in his sample, 53% were capable of Level 1 knowledge and 1% were capable of Level 2 knowledge. Similarly, 90% of his sample of 4-year-olds were identified as nonconservers, but 25% were capable of Level 1 thought and 73% were capable of Level 2 thought.

These children were then subjected to a series of assessments of their ability to comprehend projective size of objects depicted on television. Sixteen videotape presentations were extracted from old episodes of off-air programming that attracted a large child audience. Four presentations depicted a steady "zoom in" on a stationary object (e.g., mountain, car, house, swimming pool) from a single, stationary camera, showing the object getting bigger as the zoom progressed; four presentations were the reverse, depicting a "zoom out" on the object from a single camera. Four other presentations depicted an edited compilation of multiple camera angles of an object, showing the object getting closer with each edit; four presentations were the reverse, depicting the object getting farther away with each edit. The action shown in each presentation lasted 25 seconds, with the first 5 seconds consisting of a shot of the object prior to transformation and the last 5 seconds consisting of a shot of the object after the complete transformation. The videotape was stopped every 5 seconds and the subject was asked if the object was getting "closer," or "farther away," or "staying the same."

In general, regardless of age, children at Level 0 demonstrated a very low level of understanding of projective size. Children at Level 1 demonstrated a significantly higher understanding of the "zooming," but their knowledge did not sufficiently contribute to their comprehension of the edited version. Those possessing Level 2 knowledge of visual perception demonstrated a significantly higher level of understanding of "zooming" and an increased comprehension of the edited presentations. The direction of the "zoom" was found to be inconsequential. Interestingly, the amount of children's television consumption impacted on their comprehension of the edited technique at both Level 1 and Level 2; those children that traditionally watched more television had higher levels of comprehension.

Exceptional Children

Abelman (1992b) replicated his study of zoom techniques with a sample of 5-year-old children who had been identified by their schools as intellectually gifted ($N = 73$), LD ($N = 62$), and nonlabeled ($N = 89$). The relationship between subject category and divergent performance on the traditional liquid conservation task was not significant, with the vast majority of all children being classified as

TABLE 4.3
Performance on Conservation Task
by Exceptionality

	Nonconserver		Conserver	
Exceptionality	N	%	N	%
Nonlabeled	87	97.8	2	2.2
Gifted	66	90.4	7	9.6
Learning disabled	61	98.4	1	1.6

Note. Based on data reported in "Exceptional Children's Understanding of Projective Size on Television" by R. Abelman, 1992. Paper presented at the Speech Communication Association Conference, Chicago, IL.

nonconservers (see Table 4.3). However, the correspondence between classification of visual knowledge and subject category (see Table 4.4) reveals a significant difference ($p < .0007$) in level classification. No gifted children were classified at Level 0, while 15% of the LD and 2% of the nonlabeled children were so classified. Table 4.4 also reveals that significantly more gifted children were classified at Level 2 (86%) when compared with nonlabeled children (73%). No LD children were found to possess Level 2 knowledge of visual perception at this age.

Learning Disabled Children. Findings revealed that children at Level 0 demonstrated a very low level of understanding of projective size, as was found in the original investigation, with LD children performing especially poorly at this level of classification. All children at Level 1, however, demonstrated a significantly higher understanding of zooming, with no significant differences identified between LD, gifted, or nonlabeled children at this level of classification. Level 1 LD children also demonstrated a very low level of comprehension

TABLE 4.4
Level of Visual Perception Classification by Exceptionality

	Level 0		Level 1		Level 2	
Exceptionality	N	%	N	%	N	%
Nonlabeled	2	2.2	22	24.7	65	73.1
Gifted	—	0.0	10	13.7	63	86.3
Learning disabled	9	14.5	53	85.6	—	0.0

Note. Based on data reported in "Exceptional Children's Understanding of Projective Size on Television" by R. Abelman, 1992. Paper presented at the Speech Communication Association Conference, Chicago, IL.

of the edited presentation of changes in projective size. Comprehension of the zooming and edited presentations did not improve with higher amounts of television consumption for Level 1 LD children.

Intellectually Gifted Children. In addition to significantly higher understanding of zooming at Level 1, as was demonstrated by all children at this level, it was also found that gifted and nonlabeled Level 1 children demonstrated higher comprehension of the edited version of project size when they were moderate- or high-level television consumers. Comprehension of the edited presentation was significantly higher for gifted moderate and high consumers than for nonlabeled children with the same amount of television consumption.

Nonlabeled and gifted children possessing Level 2 knowledge of visual perception also demonstrated a significantly higher level of understanding of zooming and edited content than Level 1 children, with the mean score performance of gifted children being well above that of nonlabeled children at this level of classification. Once again, those children who consumed a greater amount of television demonstrated a greater degree of understanding of the edited presentation than individuals who watched less television.

Temporal Integration and Organization

The accurate comprehension of television requires viewers, at the very least, to temporally integrate and coordinate program material. In typical dramatic programming, story line, plot progression, and character development are all relayed through a series of discrete scenes from which coherence must be inferred (Krull, 1983). The child development literature suggests that children generally begin to use temporal order as an organizing principle in their social interactions no later than their third year (Bretherton, O'Connell, Shore, & Bates, 1984; Nelson, 1978; O'Connell & Gerard, 1985). By children's fourth year, "content-free" sequential understanding evolves (Case & Khanna, 1981; Nelson & Gruendel, 1981), which allows them to generalize ordering principles to unfamiliar events.

Research has also found that temporal sequencing abilities are strongly associated with the development of linguistic competence and performance (Conti-Ramsden & Snow, 1990; Naremore & Hopper, 1990; Wales, 1979). The association between linguistic competence and television literacy in general has been given much consideration in recent years (see Davis & Walton, 1983; Hall, 1980; Harris, 1988; Rice, 1983, 1984, 1990; Smith et al., 1985). According to Huston and Wright (1983), television's visual and aural displays:

> are analogous to punctuation, capitalization, paragraphing, and chapter headings in print. . . . Language is used to organize, segment, and otherwise structure television content [and] children can decode the meaning . . . using the same linguistic

processing strategies and constraints that they draw upon in the presence of live speakers. (p. 46)

Luke (1985) also believes that how knowledge is "acquired, structured, and used to process everyday linguistic and non-linguistic information is a critical factor in accounting for children's abilities (or inabilities) to deal with TV's context and symbol system" (p. 92). She further noted that:

> A fundamental aspect of the "meaning" accessible to the viewer is the reliance of this symbol system, no matter how visually and technically complex, upon spoken language and the cultural conventions governing language and action. As with text, the viewer calls into play a variety of linguistic and perceptual skills to make sense of, and actively interpret, the given program. (pp. 92–93)

Evidence suggests that the processing and organization of information presented via television are more complex tasks for young children. According to Collins (1983), simply following normal activity on television is a difficult task for children because "temporal integration [of mediated messages] involves inferences about implicit relations among explicit scenes" (p. 131). Similarly, Simon (1976) characterized programs as "ill-structured problems" that require considerable attention and organizational and inferential activity by the viewer. Most 3- and 4-year-olds have been found to experience difficulty in tasks that require the reverse or scrambling of causal sequences in pictorial presentations (Brown, 1976; Gelman, Bullock, & Meck, 1980), and even 5- and 6-year-olds have some difficulty reconstructing sequences of pictures presented in modified (i.e., reversed or scrambled) order (Brown & Murphy, 1975; Fivush & Mandler, 1984). Calvert and Gersh (1985) and Abelman (1990b) found that many non-labeled 4-year-olds who were able to coordinate two or more real-world events in a normal sequence failed to show reliable ordering of two or more televised events linked by editing or other visual techniques.

Exceptional Children

With regard to exceptional children, it has been found that intellectually gifted children are particularly able to recognize the nature of problems, to select strategies that are appropriate for problem solving, to map higher order relations, and to distinguish between relevant and irrelevant information (Scruggs & Cohn, 1983). Sternberg and Davidson (1985) suggested:

> The gifted individual is less likely to attempt to assimilate information that needs to be accommodated and is less likely to see accommodation as necessary when new information can be assimilated, perhaps in a nonobvious way, to an existing schematic structure. (p. 48)

With regard to language competence and performance, gifted children learn to speak and develop sophisticated language patterns well in advance of their age-mates. They may teach themselves to read by age 3 or 4 without direct supervision, and their verbal and reading fluency and comprehension improve rapidly (see Cohn, Cohn, & Kanevsky, 1988). The level of complexity and abstraction found in their probes and responses reflects phenomenal perceptiveness and sensitivity to relationships and patterns in knowledge (Glasser, 1985). Thus, they may be extremely competent when it comes to piecing together televised events.

Learning disabled children, however, have been found to be particularly poor at the aforementioned skills (see Lynch & Lewis, 1988b; Sternberg, 1982). Ross (1976) suggested that LD children show a delay in the development of selective attention abilities; these children are slower to learn how to focus their attention on relevant dimensions or cues of a problem and to establish necessary cognitive scheme for problem solving than their nonlabeled peers (Zeaman & House, 1979). As was noted earlier, like younger nondisabled children, the attending behavior of LD children is more influenced by perceptual salience, and these children are less able to integrate stimuli from different modalities or make inferences about implied relationships (Beery, 1967; Vande Voort et al., 1972; Zendel & Pihl, 1983).

In language, young LD children may experience delays in the development of listening and speaking skills, and in the acquisition of knowledge about linguistic structures. LD children tend to lack a sensitivity to various patterns of textual organization and to the relative importance of major and minor ideas (Nodine, Barenbaum, & Newcomer, 1985; Scardamalia & Bereiter, 1984; Vallecorsa & Garriss, 1990). According to Adelman and Taylor (1986), "if there is a learning disability, the trouble is likely to have affected . . . perception and psycholinguistic abilities" (p. 72). Longitudinal studies conducted by McKinney and Feagans (1984) have also found that LD children fall progressively further behind their nonlabeled peers in reading comprehension and text processing. Communication problems may result from disorders of language processing and language production (Lewis, 1988; Wiig & Semel, 1976). It is expected, therefore, that young LD children will be less able to engage in temporal sequencing of televised events than their nonlabeled counterparts.

To assess children's ability to comprehend temporal sequencing of television programming, Abelman (1992a) employed a sample of 5-year-old children who were nonlabeled ($N = 71$), gifted ($N = 82$), or learning disabled ($N = 73$). Two versions of an unaired scene from the highly popular "The Cosby Show," which included seven distinctive, logically flowing actions, were used for the experimental stimuli. The first version, taped in real time (length = 63 seconds), depicted Cliff Huxtable answering a ringing telephone in his living room (10 seconds), talking on the phone to a pregnant patient (12 seconds), informing her that he will meet her in his office in a few minutes and hanging up (7 seconds), informing his wife and youngest daughter that he is meeting a patient and walking to his downstairs office (21 seconds), entering his office and walking to his desk (4 seconds), sitting in his desk chair (4 seconds), and greeting the patient as she enters the door (5 seconds).

The second version depicted the same action as the original, but without the three actions showing Cliff informing his wife of his departure and walking to and entering into his office. Instead, there was a postproduction "time-leap" edit immediately upon Cliff hanging up the phone, where he next appears sitting in his chair in his office and welcoming his patient (length = 34 seconds), thereby implying his departure from the living room and entrance into his office and reducing action to four distinct scenes.

Seven pictures depicting a moment representative of each of the scenes from the video stimuli were used in a Picture Sequence Task. The task required the children to put the pictures in the right order, from the first thing that would happen in this program to the last, in a way that best tells the story. A picture sequence score was calculated for each subject by comparing the child's picture order to its correct absolute position and to the number of correctly sequenced adjacent picture pairs.

Learning Disabled Children.   As can be seen in Table 4.5, LD children demonstrated a lower level of comprehension of the normal, or "canonical," mode of presentation of temporal sequencing when compared with nonlabeled and gifted children. This is also true with regard to their comprehension of the "time-leap" technique, although the differences here were not statistically significant. The lower portion of the table provides insight into the role of television viewing habits on the comprehension of temporal sequencing on television. It suggests that the amount of television viewing significantly contributes to, but does not necessarily completely explain, their comprehension of temporal sequencing. In particular, data analysis suggests that LD children who watch more television are not more likely to accurately comprehend time leaps than LD children with lesser amounts of viewing time.

Intellectually Gifted Children.   Gifted children demonstrated a higher level of comprehension of the normal, or canonical, mode of presentation than nonlabeled children, and nonlabeled children demonstrated a higher level of comprehension of this mode of presentation than those with learning disabilities. No such increase in comprehension of the time-leap technique was evident. However, gifted children with higher levels of television consumption had a higher level of comprehension than gifted children with more moderate levels of consumption. Similarly, nonlabeled children who watched a lot of television had a higher level of comprehension of time leaps than nonlabeled children who viewed less television. Interestingly, nonlabeled high consumers still had a lower level of comprehension of time leaps than did gifted low consumers.

TABLE 4.5
Mean Comprehension as a Function
of Capability and Consumption

Parameter	Mode of Presentation	
	Canonical	Time Leap
Capability		
Learning disabled	4.2$_a$	2.7$_a$
Nonlabeled	9.6$_b$	5.2$_a$
Gifted	12.8$_c$	5.7$_a$
Mean difference	8.4$_B$	3.0$_A$
Consumption level		
Low	8.3$_b$	3.8$_a$
Moderate	8.7$_b$	5.2$_a$
High	9.5$_b$	7.9$_b$
Mean difference	1.2$_A$	4.1$_A$

Note. The greater the mean, the higher the comprehension level of the presentation. Scores range from 0 (very low comprehension) to 13 (very high comprehension). Means having no letter in their lower-case subscripts in common differ significantly at $p < .05$ by the Scheffe method. Means differences having no uppercase letter in their subscript in common differ at $p < .05$. From "Putting the Cart Before the Horse: Exceptional Children's Comprehension of Temporal Sequencing on Television," by R. Abelman, 1992a. Paper presented at the International Communication Association Conference, Miami, FL.

Summary

Cognitive skills associated with the ability to engage in liquid conservation transformations have, in turn, been found to be associated with children's ability to comprehend changes in projective size as depicted on television. Interestingly, differences in visual perception skills were found to exist among children identified as nonconservers, with profound differences existing among nonconserving children identified as nonlabeled, learning disabled, and intellectually gifted. Higher levels of visual perception capabilities were evident among nonlabeled children when compared with same-age LD children, and among gifted children when compared with same-age nonlabeled children. Higher levels of visual perception capabilities were found to contribute to the comprehension of television information.

Differences in the comprehension of temporal sequencing on television were also found among gifted, nonlabeled, and LD children. In particular, greater comprehension of temporal sequencing was evident among gifted children when compared with same-age nonlabeled children. These children, in turn, possessed greater comprehension than LD children.

It was also found that the amount of children's television viewing, coupled with developed perceptual skills and linguistic abilities, facilitates comprehension of projective size and temporal sequencing, particularly when presented in a mode unique to television. Interestingly, despite the fact that LD children consume more television than their nonlabeled and gifted counterparts (see chapter 2), this was not sufficient to make up for deficits in perceptual or linguistic abilities as they apply to the comprehension of specific forms of television information.

CONCLUSIONS

The research reported throughout this chapter is in line with Schramm, Lyle, and Parker's (1961) observation that differences among children and the unique conditions under which viewing occurs influence what children take from television. Clearly, fundamental differences exist regarding young children's ability to attend to and comprehend television information. Numerous studies report that many of these differences are attributable to chronological factors, suggesting that children eventually mature as media consumers; their comprehension of television evolves in accordance with the natural development of basic social skills and intellectual abilities. For instance, it was reported that children capable of liquid conservation are competent at comprehending rudimentary forms of television narrative, while younger nonconservers are not (Acker & Tiemens, 1981; Fivush & Mandler, 1984). However, as Sprafkin, Gadow, and their colleagues demonstrated, when age and IQ are controlled for, differences in comprehension capabilities still exist among same-age children who have been identified as exceptional. In other words, there are clear, developmental differences among children classified as mentally retarded, emotionally disturbed, learning disabled, and intellectually gifted. Thus, the literature cited here points to the futility of classifying children by age without accounting for the highly divergent capacities of same-age children to learn from their environment.

This chapter reinforces the conceptualization of television viewing as a learned activity, but it also highlights the interrelatedness of linguistic, cognitive, and perceptual skills for accurate television comprehension. It further demonstrates that these abilities are impaired or enhanced by factors associated with being intellectually gifted or disabled, which, in turn, have been found to influence children's understanding of television content. In addition, differences in comprehension are most profound with more complex forms of media presentation. For example, visual perceptual skills, which have been linked to the ability to understand projective size, are required at a higher order to accurately comprehend the more complex "telegeneric" mode of projective size. Learning disabled children were found not to possess this higher order (Level 2) knowledge of visual perception. Similarly, linguistic abilities, which have been linked to the ability to follow temporal sequencing of televised events, are required for the comprehension of time leaps. Gifted children demonstrated a higher comprehension of this technique when compared with same-age nonlabeled and LD children. The research reported here also suggests that the comprehension of some of television's most commonly used visual techniques requires skills that cannot be obtained through daily real-world interaction. Even children who are intellectually advanced and possess exceptional perceptual and linguistic capabilities require media experience for higher levels of comprehension. Conversely, heavy consumption by children who do not possess fundamental perceptual and linguistic abilities does not facilitate comprehension of these techniques.

This chapter discussed three specific cognitive tasks—temporal integration, organization of program events, and selective attention and perception—involved in the comprehension of only a handful of specific forms of dramatic presentation on television. Because television is an "interaction, an active engagement between viewer and program representational forms" (Barker, 1988, p. 53), there is little doubt that other forms of television narrative require the application of other cognitive skills and perceptual abilities for accurate comprehension. These require careful consideration and further research. Indeed, the cognitive processes that contribute to the creation of learning and behavioral abilities and disabilities need further exploration with regard to their relationship to the comprehension of television content.

5 Media Effects: Antisocial and Prosocial Behavior

The scientific literature in child development provides overwhelming support for the conclusion that child behavior is determined in large part by interactions with other people. Just observing others interact is an important source of learning new behaviors. Given that the content of most television programming involves social interactions, the relatively high rate of children's television viewing suggests that the medium may play an important role in shaping their social behavior. Of greatest concern have been the potential adverse effects of television viewing because interpersonal aggression has been a dominant theme in many television programs for a number of years. From the year 1967, George Gerbner has charted the amount of violence on prime-time and Saturday morning television. His annual "violence index" has revealed that despite the public criticism and government hearings, the percentage of programs containing violence and the rate of violent acts has remained remarkably consistent during the last 18 years. The most alarming finding is that cartoons (obviously intended for children) are far more violent than prime-time fare (Gerbner, Gross, Signorielli, & Morgan, 1986). Television may also have beneficial consequences for the development of social skills, particularly programs that emphasize altruistic social interactions. Although much less attention has been focused on prosocial content, this area may have important implications for exceptional children with social skills deficits.

In this chapter, we examine the research on both prosocial and antisocial content. Each topic is treated separately, given the highly divergent nature of their social implications, which, ironically, are not always supported by research. In keeping with the general format of the text, an overview of the literature on nondisabled children is presented first, followed by a discussion of specific studies of exceptional children. Regrettably, the absence of any research on gifted children precludes them from consideration in our discussion of the media and social behavior.

VIEWING ANTISOCIAL BEHAVIOR

Almost as soon as television had found a niche in our daily lives, people were expressing concerns about its possible adverse effects on children. Aggression-laden content was the target of the majority of the early criticisms. The behavioral psychologist Albert Bandura (1963) popularized the term *TV violence* in an article he wrote for *Look* magazine in 1963 titled, "What TV Violence Can Do to Your Child." His early "Bobo doll" studies (e.g., Bandura, 1965; Bandura, Ross, & Ross, 1963) showed that children would imitate aggressive acts they saw on simulated television programs. However, the largest effort to examine the effects of viewing aggressive television content on child behavior was the program of research that came out of the Surgeon General's Report on Television and Social Behavior in 1972.

Public criticism was eventually translated into political pressures, and in 1970 the National Institute of Mental Health funded $1 million worth of research to address the question of television's effects on children. The 23 funded projects dealt with a variety of aspects of television, but the emphasis was on aggression-laden content. Laboratory studies showed that children exposed to aggressive content were subsequently less sensitive to aggression (Rabinovitch, McLean, Markham, & Talbott, 1972), more willing to hurt an unseen child in a game context (Liebert & Baron, 1972), and more likely to handle hypothetical situations in an aggressive manner (Leifer & Roberts, 1972) than children who viewed control programs. Correlational studies showed that children who watched large amounts of television (aggressive content in particular) were also more aggressive and approving of aggressive behavior (Dominick & Greenberg, 1972; Lefkowitz, Eron, Walder, & Huesmann, 1972; McIntyre & Teevan, 1972; McLeod, Atkin, & Chaffee, 1972; Robinson & Bachman, 1972). The conclusions of the report were somewhat guarded and replete with qualifiers, and, not surprisingly, a summary of the report was misinterpreted by the press (Gould, 1972), which then stirred angry rebuttals by the scientists who felt that their studies were misrepresented.

Ten years later television researchers (many of whom were involved in the Surgeon General's Report) organized a project to update the research on television in our society. Unlike the earlier endeavor, this enterprise was a review of the research that had been conducted in the interim rather than a program of new research. The update addressed the television violence issue, but it covered a much wider breadth of topics than its predecessor. With regard to television violence, the update concluded:

Most of the researchers look at the totality of evidence and conclude, as did the Surgeon General's advisory committee, that the convergence of findings supports the conclusion of a causal relationship between televised violence and later aggressive behavior. (Pearl et al., 1982a, p. 37)

In the history of research on the effects of viewing television violence, there has been controversy concerning how to interpret the findings of the individual studies, as well as the entire body of research (Freedman, 1984, 1986; Friedrich-Cofer & Huston, 1986; Gadow & Sprafkin, 1989; Kaplan & Singer, 1976). In order to better understand the basis for this controversy, we present an overview of research methodology in this area and theories of reactivity to television.

Research Methodologies

Many of the issues associated with this area of research pertain to the strengths and weaknesses of the various research methodologies and their respective findings. Three different research methods have been used to investigate the effects of viewing television violence (laboratory experiments, correlational studies, and field experiments), each of which is briefly described here.

Laboratory experiments afford the researcher the highest degree of control. The prototypic design involves randomly assigning subjects to two viewing conditions. One group is exposed to a television excerpt containing violence, and the other group views a nonviolent excerpt. Then participants are put in a situation in which they are given the opportunity to behave aggressively (or not). The behavioral test situation varies substantially and has included such measures as preference for aggressive versus nonaggressive toys (Lovaas, 1961), expressed desire to pop a balloon (Mussen & Rutherford, 1961), noxious stimuli ostensibly administered to others (Feshbach, 1972; Hartmann, 1969; Liebert & Baron, 1972), and paper-and-pencil responses to hypothetical situations (Leifer & Roberts, 1972). These studies have found that exposure to aggressive television excerpts produces more aggressive responding than nonaggressive excerpts during the time interval immediately following the viewing of the media material. Although these findings suggest that viewing television violence can increase the likelihood of aggressive behavior, the laboratory method is somewhat weak in allowing researchers to generalize to real-life situations. First, the form of aggressive behavior in most studies is far removed from real-life aggression. Second, the laboratory setting contains no deterrents to behaving aggressively, whereas the child's natural environment generally produces consequences for such actions (e.g., retaliation by the aggressee, getting into trouble with care providers). Third, the television condition is usually an edited excerpt from a full-length program selected on the basis of its probable aggression-inducing effect, whereas in the real environment a child usually sees a whole program, not just the aggression-laden part. Fourth, in the laboratory the child is usually left alone in a sterile room with just the television to entertain him or her, but home television viewing is accompanied by many other activities and people coming and going from the viewing situation. All of these variables may influence a child's response to watching television violence.

The second major method of determining the effects of viewing television violence on children's aggressive behavior is to examine the correlation between the amount of exposure to television violence (e.g., hours of viewing) and the level of aggressive behavior. A number of investigators have used this technique (e.g., McIntyre & Teevan, 1972; Robinson & Bachman, 1972) and found a significant association between these two variables. The major criticism of this approach is that a significant correlation does not necessarily imply that television violence viewing *causes* aggressive behavior. For example, a third variable related to both television viewing habits and aggressive behavior may account for the association, thereby invalidating the causative claim. Alternatively, the direction of the effect may be opposite to that proposed. In other words, aggressive children may simply like to watch violence on television. A number of studies have reduced the possibility of competing hypotheses by controlling for possible third variables (e.g., McLeod et al., 1972) and by exploring the feasibility of alternative causative chains (e.g., Chaffee & McLeod, 1971). However, although these refinements are improvements over simple bivariate correlations, they cannot transform the basic technique from a correlational method (which precludes causative statements).

The final method, the field experiment, is similar to a laboratory study in that causative inferences can be made because media conditions are systematically manipulated. It is also similar to the correlational method in that measurements are made in the child's natural environment. In a typical field experiment, the investigator selects real television programs and shows them in a setting such as a school or camp. One group watches aggressive programs, and the other group views nonaggressive shows. Then both groups are observed following the media exposure, in a naturalistic setting such as a free-play period on the playground. Interestingly, the results of these studies are mixed. Some field experiments have demonstrated that exposure to violent media material increases the rate of aggressive behaviors (e.g., Leyens, Camino, Parke, & Berkowitz, 1975). Other studies have failed to find that aggressive programs produce any more aggression-instigating effect than more neutral fare (e.g., De Koning, Conradie, & Nel, 1980, 1990), and several show that neutral programs can produce *higher* levels of aggression than aggressive programs (e.g., De Koning et al., 1980, 1990; Sawin, 1975, 1990). In a recent review of the field experiments, Gadow and Sprafkin (1989) concluded that just watching television is stimulating in that both aggressive and nonaggressive content can produce elevated levels of aggressive behavior. Unfortunately, despite the advantages of the field experimental method, these contradictory findings have sparked heated scientific debates (e.g.,

Freedman, 1984; Friedrich-Cofer & Huston, 1986) that leave the issue unresolved.

Theories of Reactivity to Television

Various theories have been promulgated to explain these divergent findings. One of the most popular theories is *social learning theory,* which was developed by the psychologist Albert Bandura. As was stated in chapter 1, it proposes that children learn from seeing how others behave in specific situations, and the conditions under which this learning is most likely to take place is described in his theory of modeling.

One aspect of Bandura's (1965) research shows that children can learn novel forms of aggression from televisionlike films. If a male aggressor in the film is rewarded, children are more likely to imitate him than if he is punished; however, when children are given incentives to demonstrate what they saw, both types of vicarious consequences produce the same amount of recall. Bandura thus discovered the important acquisition–performance distinction. His studies often involved Bobo dolls as the "victim," but other researchers used more lifelike victims such as an adult dressed as a clown (e.g., Hanratty, Liebert, Morris, & Fernandez, 1969). In general, the assessment period is the time interval immediately following the viewing of the media stimuli.

Aside from direct imitation, social learning theory also predicts that observation of a model can disinhibit other behaviors in the same response class. In other words, after exposure to an aggressive model, the child may act more aggressively without directly imitating the specific aggressive acts just witnessed. Studies have shown, in fact, that children play more aggressively following exposure to aggressive media material (Bandura, Ross, & Ross, 1961; Hartmann & Gelfand, 1969; Nelson, Gelfand, & Hartmann, 1969; Rosenkrans & Hartup, 1967).

Arousal theory contends that communication messages can evoke varying degrees of generalized emotional arousal and that this can influence any behavior an individual is engaged in while the state of arousal persists. Increased aggression following the viewing of television would be interpreted as a result of the level of arousal elicited by the story, rather than modeling. One of the propositions of the theory is that nonaggressive but arousing television content can instigate increased levels of aggressive behavior. This proposition has been supported by experiments showing that an erotic film that was more arousing than an aggressive film produced more aggressive responses in viewers (Tannenbaum, 1971; Zillmann, 1969).

The basic assumption of the *catharsis hypothesis* is that frustration produces an increase in aggressive drive. This state is unpleasant, causing the individual to seek to reduce it by engaging in either aggressive acts or fantasy aggression. One way to induce aggressive fantasy is by exposing someone to fictional aggression, such as the sort often found in action/adventure television programs. Catharsis theory predicts that exposure to television violence reduces aggression in the observer (Feshbach, 1955). The catharsis hypothesis has generally failed to receive support in studies with children; however, notable exceptions are two studies of adolescents, which found that viewing low-aggression television shows was more aggression inducing that high-aggression fare (Feshbach & Singer, 1971; Wells, 1973).

Some social scientists have argued that focusing attention on television as a cause of violence in society is unfortunate because it detracts from addressing more pressing and insidious causes such as poverty, racial prejudice, and the ease of obtaining guns and alcohol (Kaplan & Singer, 1976). The debate among scientists concerning the social significance of television violence has not abated, as indicated by recent journal articles on this topic. In 1984 *Psychological Bulletin* published an article by Jonathan Freedman that reviewed the studies on television violence and concluded that, "there is little convincing evidence that in natural settings viewing television violence causes people to be more aggressive" (p. 227). This was followed by a rejoinder by Friedrich-Cofer and Huston (1986) and a reply by Freedman (1986).

We believe that the majority of scientists agree that laboratory studies show that children can learn aggressive behaviors from television and that portrayals of violence can disinhibit aggressive responding in viewers. However, laboratory studies are not ecologically valid (i.e., the situations studied are far removed from the conditions present in the child's natural environment), and we must therefore consider the findings from field experimental studies that are much closer to real life. Interestingly, these studies do not provide compelling evidence that aggressive content per se produces increased aggressive responding in children (Cook, Kendzierski, & Thomas, 1983; Freedman, 1984; Gadow & Sprafkin, 1989). A meta-analysis of 230 television studies showed that the size of the effect diminished substantially as one progressed from highly contrived studies to ecologically valid field experiments (Hearold, 1986).

Exceptional Children

The research on nonlabeled children suggests that certain individuals are more susceptible to adverse reactions from viewing television violence. Dorr and Kovaric (1980), for example, concluded from their literature review that one of the most important determinants of reactivity to television violence is baseline level of aggressiveness—that is, children who are naturally aggressive are more likely to be reactive to televised violence. Second, youngsters who are heavy viewers of television violence tend to be low academic achievers (Chaffee & McLeod, 1972; Eron, 1982), aggressive (Chaffee & McLeod, 1972; Lyle, 1972), socially incompetent with peers and parents (Himmelweit et al., 1958; Schramm et al., 1961), and heavy overall television viewers (Chaffee & McLeod, 1972; Greenberg, Ericson, & Vlahos, 1972; Lyle & Hoffman, 1972). Recall the discussion from chapter 2 about research on viewing habits, which suggests that special education children (ED, LD, and MR) watch more television overall and more crime-oriented dramas. Furthermore, they preferred aggressive superhero characters and, according to self-reports, were more apt to imitate the behavior of their favorite television character.

Emotionally Disturbed Children.   As previously noted, numerous studies have shown that school children who are labeled emotionally disturbed or behavior disordered by their public school systems exhibit significantly higher rates of interpersonal conflict than their nonlabeled peers. Given this fact, it seems reasonable to speculate that ED youngsters may be at greater risk for the ill effects of viewing television violence than nondisabled children.

One of the first studies in this area was a modeling experiment by Walters and Willows (1968). They compared the behavior of institutionalized ED and non-disturbed children following their exposure to a 4-minute aggressive or nonaggressive videotaped model. Twenty-four ED and 24 nondisturbed children between 7 and 12 years of age saw one of two videotapes (a woman behaving aggressively toward toys or a woman treating toys in a nonaggressive manner). Twelve additional nondisturbed children observed a tape that featured toys but no humans. Relative to the nonaggressive videotape, exposure to the aggressive tape produced more aggressive behavior toward the toys shown in the videotape by both the disturbed and nondisturbed children. The amount of aggression did not differ between the ED and nondisturbed groups. However, because the critical comparison was based on such a small sample (the 12 ED and 12 nondisturbed children who saw the aggressive tape), the finding of no difference should be regarded cautiously.

Because there were no laboratory studies of television aggression on non-institutionalized samples of ED children, Sprafkin and Gadow (1988; Gadow, Sprafkin, & Grayson, 1990) conducted two studies in an attempt to replicate prior research (Collins & Getz, 1976; Liebert & Baron, 1972; Liss, Reinhardt, & Fredriksen, 1983), which showed that nondisabled children who viewed an aggression-laden excerpt behaved more aggressively when playing the Help–Hurt game than youngsters who watched a nonaggressive excerpt. The Help–Hurt game consists of an apparatus that allows the subject to either "help" or "hurt" another child, who is hidden from view, usually by depressing a button. The subject is told that the child who is hidden from view is playing a game or doing a task, and the subject, depending on the button that he or she pushes, can either help or hurt the performance of the hidden child.

In their first study, 60 ED children (average age was 10 years) played the Help–Hurt game, viewed either an aggressive or prosocial television excerpt, and then played the game again (Gadow et al., 1990). The media presentation was an episode of the "Six Million Dollar Man" that was edited to form a highly aggressive story and a prosocial story. Each edited segment was approximately 25 minutes in length. Unexpectedly, there were no significant treatment effects. In other words, children who watched the aggression-laden episode pressed the Hurt button equally as long as the group who viewed the prosocial episode. One possible explanation for this odd outcome was the procedure that was employed. In this study, the Help–Hurt game was played twice, once before media exposure and a second time after viewing the "Six Million Dollar Man." It is possible that the premedia exposure altered the game's sensitivity to detect media effects by somehow changing the subject's perception of or reactivity to the game. To examine this possibility, Sprafkin and Gadow conducted a second study involving the Help–Hurt game.

In their second study (Sprafkin & Gadow, 1988), 38 ED and LD children (M = 7 years old) viewed either an aggressive ("Tom & Jerry") or nonaggressive ("Lassie's Rescue Rangers") cartoon and then played the Help–Hurt game. The children who watched the aggressive cartoon pressed the Hurt button for significantly more time than those who were exposed to the nonaggressive cartoon (see Fig. 5.1). The findings from the second study are consistent with prior research on nondisabled youngsters.

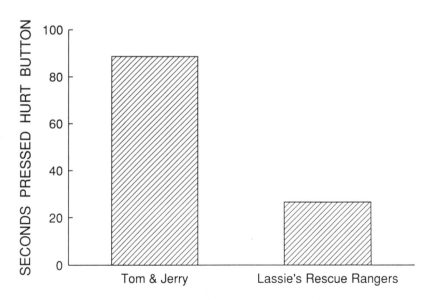

FIG. 5.1.   Duration of time pressing the Hurt button of the Help–Hurt game. *Note.* From data presented in "The Help–Hurt Game as a Measure of Aggression in Children with Learning and Behavior Disorders" by K. D. Gadow, J. Sprafkin, and P. Grayson, 1990, *Learning and Individual Differences, 2,* pp. 75–89. Copyright © 1991 by K. D. Gadow and J. Sprafkin.

To help clarify the clinical relevance of viewing television aggression for ED youngsters, Sprafkin and Gadow conducted three field experiments using cartoons as media stimuli. Although the studies varied with regard to specific details, they all followed the same general protocol. Prior to and following the media exposure periods were baseline conditions that allowed them to evaluate the children's normal level of social interaction. During the media exposure period, children watched either aggressive or nonaggressive cartoons prior to going to lunch. A within-subject design was employed (all subjects saw both media conditions, but obviously on different days), and the cartoon viewing sequence was counterbalanced. Direct observations of social interactions during lunch and recess were completed by trained observers who were "blind" to the treatment conditions. The data were analyzed by comparing baseline and aggressive and control cartoon conditions.

In their first field experiment, Gadow and Sprafkin (1987) examined two classes of ED children, one younger (average age 6.6 years) and one older (average age 10.1 years). The findings indicated that the older ED class exhibited a significant increase in physical aggression and appropriate social interaction following the aggressive cartoons compared with baseline levels, with a similar trend for nonphysical aggression. The increased level of aggression was evident during both lunch and recess. The younger group, however, showed a different pattern of reactivity. Their level of physical and nonphysical aggression decreased following the control cartoons. They did, however, become more noncompliant following exposure to the aggressive cartoons. The younger ED class exhibited this reaction pattern during lunch only. Given the unexpected nature of these findings, additional field experiments were conducted in which the age of the children and the nature of their disability varied.

Their second field experiment (Sprafkin, Gadow, & Grayson, 1988) involved four classes of ED children (average age 8.1 years). During a 3-week period, each class observed six cartoons with primarily aggressive content ("Tom and Jerry," "Bugs Bunny," "Woody Woodpecker") and six cartoons in which the characters engaged in high rates of appropriate social and prosocial interaction ("Lassie's Rescue Rangers"). An analysis of the content of these cartoons appears in Table 5.1. The results revealed a significant media effect for two behavioral categories, nonphysical and physical aggression (see Fig. 5.2). There were more instances of nonphysical aggression on days that the children were shown either aggressive or control cartoons than on baseline days, and more acts of physical aggression (especially on the playground) in the control than in the aggressive cartoon or baseline conditions.

Their third field experiment (Gadow, Sprafkin, & Ficarrotto, 1987) involved ED preschoolers, an age group that is at potentially greater risk for the ill effects of viewing television violence because of their lesser capacity for differentiating reality from fantasy. The preschooler study consisted of two substudies, each of which was conducted during a summer school program in two consecutive years.

TABLE 5.1
Social Content and Activity Level
in Cartoon Conditions

Parameter	Aggressive	Control
Social content[a]		
Physical aggression	58.5	3.6
Nonphysical aggression	23.0	5.1
Altruism	3.3	69.9
Appropriate social interaction	19.3	96.7
Activity level[b]	3.1	2.5

[a]Percentage of 15-sec. intervals containing behavior (average over two raters).
[b]Average activity level (1-to-4 scale) rated the last 5 sec. of every 15-sec. interval (averaged over two raters).
Note. From "Effects of Viewing Aggressive Cartoons on the Behavior of Learning Disabled Children" by J. Sprafkin, K. D. Gadow, and P. Grayson, 1987, *Journal of Child Psychology and Psychiatry, 28,* p. 390. Reprinted by permission.

The media presentations consisted of aggression- and non-aggression-content cartoons similar to those that were shown in the previous field experiment. The effects of media viewing were assessed during a free-play period that immediately followed the television viewing. The findings from the first substudy with one class of 10 preschool-aged ED youngsters failed to confirm the existence of media effects (Fig. 5.3). The two classes in the second substudy, however, showed a clear pattern of media reactivity. The preschoolers' level of nonphysical aggression increased following both aggressive and control cartoons, with the highest levels of antisocial behavior after the control cartoons (Fig. 5.3). These findings are similar to Sawin's (1975, 1990) earlier research on preschoolers in an inner-city day-care center. Contrary to expectation, the preschool-aged ED children became less noncompliant and engaged in less play aggression following exposure to the high-aggression cartoons. Both ED classes exhibited this same reaction pattern.

The findings from these field experiments with ED children are difficult to summarize because they are somewhat inconsistent with regard to *specific* behavioral categories. In general, they show that both aggressive *and* nonaggressive cartoons are capable of inducing antisocial behavior (compared with baseline levels). Moreover, the control cartoons generally produced the highest levels of postviewing aggression. Although these findings are counterintuitive and at odds with our research on viewing habits, comprehension, and laboratory manipulations, they are not inconsistent with other field experiments of prepubertal children. In fact, almost all of these field experiments have demonstrated the existence of a media effect, and several found the control material to be more

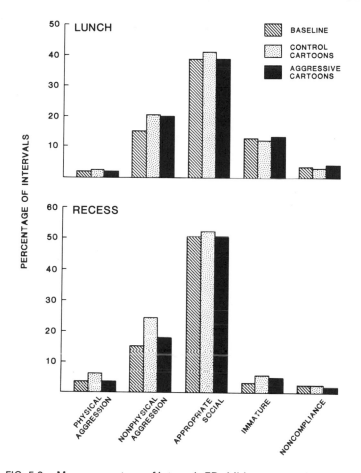

FIG. 5.2.   Mean percentage of intervals ED children engaged in specif-
ic categories of behavior. *Note.* From data presented in "Effects of
Cartoons on Emotionally Disturbed Children's Social Behavior in
School Settings" by J. Sprafkin, K. D. Gadow, and P. Grayson, 1988,
Journal of Child Psychology and Psychiatry, 29, pp. 91–99. Copyright
© 1991 by J. Sprafkin and K. D. Gadow.

aggression-inducing than the aggressive material (Gadow & Sprafkin, 1989).
Why this should be the case is unknown. Popular laboratory-based theories are of
little help, and only continued research can ever hope to shed light on this
apparent paradox.

Learning Disabled Children.   Research on the LD child's reaction to television portrayals of aggressive behavior is limited to one study conducted by
Sprafkin, Gadow, and Grayson (1987). In this study, five classes of LD children

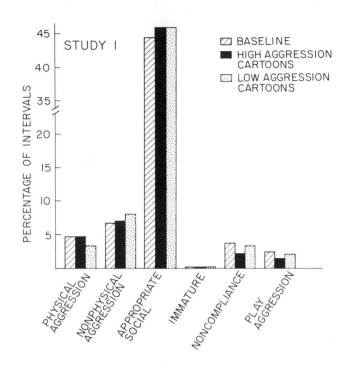

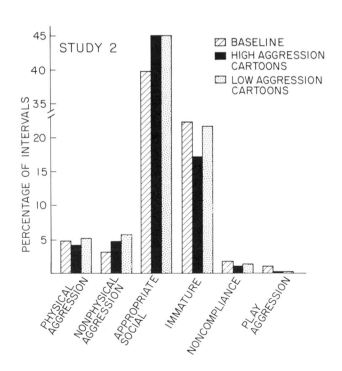

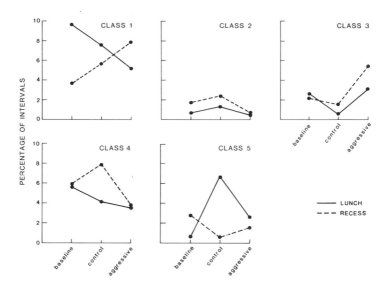

FIG. 5.4.   Mean percentage of intervals five classes of LD children engaged in physical aggression. *Note.* From data reported in "Effects of Viewing Aggressive Cartoons on the Behavior of Learning Disabled Children" by J. Sprafkin, K. D. Gadow, and P. Grayson, 1987, *Journal of Child Psychology and Psychiatry, 28,* pp. 387–398. Copyright © 1991 by J. Sprafkin and K. D. Gadow.

(N = 54) who were between 6 and 10 years old viewed either high- or low-aggression cartoons on 12 consecutive days (6 days for each type of cartoon) before going to lunch. Observations of child behavior were conducted in the lunchroom and on the playground. The only media effect that emerged from the analyses was the finding that LD children of lower intellectual ability became more physically aggressive following the low- compared with the high-aggression cartoons. The varied pattern of media reactivity is presented in Fig. 5.4. The only classroom response pattern that is supportive of the aggression-induction hypothesis is Class 3. However, as indicated in Fig. 5.5, viewing the high-aggression cartoons also resulted in markedly elevated levels of appropriate social interaction as well. Gender and initial level of aggressiveness were unrelated to media reactivity.

FIG. 5.3.   Mean percentage of intervals preschool-aged ED children engaged in specific categories of behavior. *Note.* From data presented in "Effects of Viewing Aggression-Laden Cartoons on Preschool-Aged Emotionally Disturbed Children" by K. D. Gadow, J. Sprafkin, and T. Ficarrotto, 1987, *Child Psychiatry and Human Development, 17,* pp. 257–274. Copyright © 1991 by K. D. Gadow and J. Sprafkin.

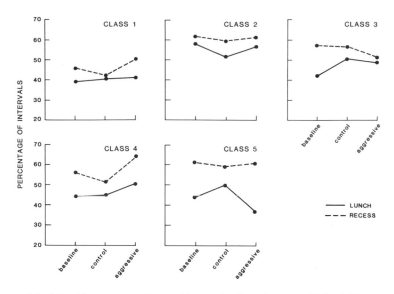

FIG. 5.5.   Mean percentage of intervals five classes of LD children engaged in appropriate social interaction. *Note.* From data reported in "Effects of Viewing Aggressive Cartoons on the Behavior of Learning Disabled Children" by J. Sprafkin, K. D. Gadow, and P. Grayson, 1987, *Journal of Child Psychology and Psychiatry, 28,* pp. 387–398. Copyright © 1991 by J. Sprafkin and K. D. Gadow.

Mentally Retarded People.   There is relatively little research on the effects of viewing televised antisocial behavior on MR people. Moreover, the few studies that have been conducted are laboratory modeling experiments.

Fechter (1971) conducted one of the first studies of mentally retarded children's reactions to an aggressive model. Subjects ($N = 36$) were exposed to a 5-minute videotape of a 12-year-old nonretarded female playing in either an aggressive or a friendly manner with an inflatable Donald Duck doll. Based on observations of the children on the ward after the television presentation, Fechter found a significant media effect, with aggressive responses increasing after viewing the aggressive tape and decreasing following the friendly tape.

Talkington and Altman (1973) compared the subsequent playroom behavior of 144 MR males (IQ: $M = 49$) after exposing them either to: (a) a 3-minute silent film of a model hitting, kicking, and throwing a Bobo doll; (b) an equivalent film of the same model kissing, cuddling, and petting Bobo doll; or (c) no film. The subjects who viewed the aggressive model exhibited significantly more aggressive behaviors and significantly less affectionate behaviors toward a Bobo doll than those who viewed either no film or the affectionate film model. The group that watched the affectionate model did not respond less aggressively or more affectionately than the no-film group. Hence, MR individuals are not equally likely to imitate aggressive and affectionate behaviors.

Summary. Despite the fact that ED, LD, and MR children share many characteristics that put them at risk to be both frequent viewers of and potential reactors to television violence (e.g., aggressive behavior, poor social relations with peers and caregivers, low academic achievement, heavy television use, identification with aggressive television characters, preference for aggression-laden shows), field experiments conducted to date do not show that they are more reactive to high- than low-aggression material. These findings are, for the most part, in accordance with those of other researchers who use field experiment procedures to study media effects in nondisabled children (Gadow & Sprafkin, 1989). Further, evidence supporting the conclusion that individuals who are more aggressive prior to the onset of the study are more reactive to aggression-laden content than children whose initial levels of interpersonal aggression are low is inconsistent. As is the case with nondisabled students, youngsters receiving special education do show increased levels of antisocial behavior (compared with baseline) after watching television cartoons, regardless of content. This effect appears to be greater in ED than LD children in self-contained special education classes.

An adequate theoretical explanation for the finding that both aggressive and nonaggressive cartoons can induce antisocial behavior in the postviewing interval is wanting. Social learning theory cannot be used to explain the increase in aggression following the viewing of the nonaggressive programs. However, the authors speculate that the nonaggressive cartoons were somewhat more realistic and suspenseful than the aggressive cartoons and that these factors may have contributed in some way to the observed findings. Although physiological measures were not collected during or after the children viewed the television programs, arousal theory offers a possible explanation for the findings and suggests an exciting avenue for future research.

The findings from laboratory studies show a very different pattern of findings. Here, as is the case with nondisabled students, ED, LD, and MR children react more aggressively to an aggression-laden media presentation than to low-aggression material. Numerous hypotheses have been put forward to explain these findings, but, regardless of the causal mechanism, the two experimental procedures (laboratory vs. field) appear to assess different or only partially overlapping behavioral phenomena.

VIEWING PROSOCIAL BEHAVIOR

The possibility that television could be used to inculcate positive social or "prosocial" values has always been an appealing idea to parents, educators, and mental health professionals. As early as 1969, when the Surgeon General's Scientific Advisory Committee was getting under way to investigate the adverse effects of television, Surgeon General William Stewart declared to Congress:

> The knowledge that should emerge from this kind of scientific endeavor will be knowledge aimed to understanding. If television can have a negative effect on children, it can also be a positive stimulus. . . . We must learn more about how to promote this latter capacity while we learn how to avoid the hazards of the former. (U.S. Senate, Subcommittee on Communication, 1969, p. 339)

The Ten-Year Update to the Surgeon General's Report voiced the same idea and went on to say that "research on television's influence on prosocial behavior burgeoned into one of the most significant developments in the decade after the report of the Surgeon General's committee" (Pearl et al., 1982a, p. 48).

Prosocial has been defined as "that which is socially desirable and which in some way benefits another person or society at large" (Rushton, 1979, p. 323), and includes such behaviors as generosity, helping, cooperating, resisting temptation, and delaying gratification. Content analyses of regular entertainment television indicate that there is a fair amount of prosocial behavior in programs that children watch, especially situation comedies (Greenberg, Edison, Korzenny, Fernandez-Collado, & Atkin, 1980; Harvey, Sprafkin, & Rubinstein, 1979). Even Saturday morning children's programs present a high rate of altruistic acts, one estimate reporting a rate of close to 20 such behaviors hourly (Greenberg et al., 1980).

As one would expect, programs on educational television such as "Mister Rogers' Neighborhood" contain high rates of prosocial behavior and have been shown to increase positive interpersonal behavior in nondisabled preschool and kindergarten-age children (Stein & Friedrich, 1972). This is especially true if the viewing is supplemented with reinforcement activities such as role playing or relevant play materials (Friedrich & Stein, 1975; Friedrich-Cofer, Huston-Stein, Kipnis, Susman, & Clewett, 1979).

The more exciting area for enhancing social skills development is commercial television because the viewership is much greater than that for educational television, and hence the potential reach of prosocial effects is expanded enormously. The earliest study of entertainment television's potential to enhance prosocial behavior in nondisabled children examined children's willingness to help puppies in distress after they had seen either a "Lassie" program containing a highly dramatic scene in which the lead child character risks his life to save a puppy, another "Lassie" program without such an altruistic display, or a situation comedy devoid of animals (Sprafkin, Liebert, & Poulos, 1975). As shown in Fig. 5.6, the first graders who saw the prosocial "Lassie" program were more willing to sacrifice good prizes to help animals ostensibly in distress than were those who saw one of the control programs.

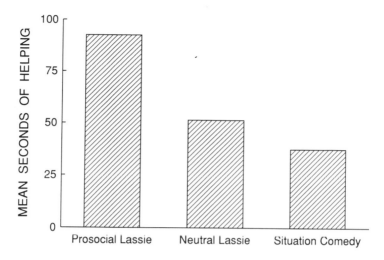

FIG. 5.6.   Duration of time pressing the Help button of the Help–Hurt game. *Note.* From data reported in "Effects of a Prosocial Televised Example of Children's Helping" by J. Sprafkin, R. M. Liebert, and R. W. Poulos, 1975, *Journal of Experimental Child Psychology, 20* pp. 119–126.

Researchers have also used variants of the Help–Hurt game to study prosocial behavior. Using such diverse television series as "Mod Squad," "Waltons," and "Superfriends," research shows that nondisabled children exposed to the prosocial version subsequently help the hidden child more than subjects who view the control program (Baran, Chase, & Courtright, 1979; Collins & Getz, 1976; Liss et al., 1983).

Hearold (1986) used a statistical procedure (meta-analysis) as a way to summarize the results of numerous studies on the effects of viewing prosocial television on prosocial behavior. She found that 190 tests of the effect of viewing prosocial television had appeared in the scientific literature since 1978. Interestingly, the magnitude of the media effect (average effect size) for prosocial television on prosocial behavior was far higher (ES = .63) than that for the effect of aggression-laden television on antisocial behavior (ES = .30). Hearold interpreted her findings as having policy implications by stating that rather than removing antisocial content from television:

I would recommend accentuating the positive: apply money and effort to creating new entertainment programs with prosocial themes, especially for children. . . . Although fewer studies exist on prosocial effects, the effect size is so much larger, holds up better under more stringent experimental conditions, and is consistently higher for boys and girls, that the potential for prosocial effects overrides the smaller but persistent negative effects of antisocial programs. (p. 116)

Exceptional Children

Research indicating that viewing prosocial behavior is an effective strategy for teaching social skills in children is exciting because it suggests that media-assisted instruction may be an effective strategy for students receiving special education. As previously noted, numerous studies show that children with learning and behavior disorders, as a group, are less effective in social situations than their nondisabled peers. In fact, social skills deficits are such a common problem for LD children that some experts have proposed a new definition of learning disabilities that recognizes the need to remediate these deficits (Kavanagh & Truss, 1988).

Interest in media applications for the teaching of social skills has focused on three categories of disability: ED, LD, and MR. However, the little research that does exist pertains almost entirely to institutionalized populations.

Baran (1973) argued that MR children are highly susceptible to social learning from commercial television and that there is great potential for using instructional media to teach positive social skills. After reviewing the observational learning literature, he highlighted several relevant characteristics of the MR population that support his hypotheses. First, social isolation increases responsiveness to social reinforcement, which in turn facilitates observational learning. This is important because the MR label and certainly institutionalization promotes social isolation. Second, high dependence, a history of prior failure experiences, and low self-esteem increase imitation, and these are all characteristics of MR children. Third, because MR children are often deprived of social contacts and are left with commercial television as their only source of companionship, the characters in television programs probably become potent socializing agents.

As for ED children, Elias (1983) noted several reasons why the medium is an excellent educational tool for the acquisition of social skills. First, television captures their attention and interest. Second, it can be used to graphically present somewhat complex social situations that can be analyzed for problem-solving strategies. Third, the dialogue in much commercial television is easy to understand, generally consistent across programs, and, because it is so similar to everyday interpersonal interactions, is easy to learn. Fourth, television has considerable potential to influence behavior. To this we would only add that creating media materials for social skills training is relatively easy (especially when compared with print): one need only to videorecord social sequences from commercial television programs.

Emotionally Disturbed Children.   Modeling studies show that ED children can learn social skills using this procedure. For example, Kassier (1979) assigned severely withdrawn ED children (age 9–14 years) to one of two treatment conditions: a videotape depicting two children engaged in interactive play with a marble raceway toy or a videotape of two models playing the same game independently. There were 10 dyads in each condition. Kassier found highly significant differences between the two groups: The children who saw the interactive version engaged in more cooperative play than the controls.

Elias (1979, 1983; Salvador, 1982) conducted what is certainly the most ambitious media-assisted social skills curriculum assessment study. The subjects ($N = 109$) were ED children and adolescents who were receiving special education services in a residential facility. One group of youngsters experienced a special media-plus-discussion intervention, whereas a comparison group, picked at random from the remaining residents, received the standard school program. The intervention consisted of ten 30-minute sessions in which a videotape was shown followed by a teacher-led class discussion that highlighted appropriate problem-solving strategies. The media consisted of 10 episodes of the series "Inside/Out" (Agency for Instructional Television, 1973), which featured 8- to 12-year-old children coping with common social problems such as teasing, peer pressure, and bullying. Afterward, teachers and aides stimulated group discussion and emphasized the coping strategies employed. The immediate program effects included teacher-rated increases in self-control and peer-rated increases in popularity and decreases in social isolation. Two months later, child-care workers rated the experimental group youngsters as significantly less emotionally detached and socially isolated, significantly more capable of delaying gratification, and having fewer personality problems than those in the control group. The latter finding was particularly satisfying because it suggests that the behavioral improvement exhibited by the treatment group was maintained over time and across settings. Elias (1983) cited the following anecdote as an indication of the power of media intervention.

> When this author (Elias) returned to Children's Village 14 months after the initial study began, a class was viewing the "Inside/Out" program "Bully." One boy, whose treatment team had consistently labeled him as hyperactive, severely learning disabled, and brain damaged with memory impairment, was able to sit attentively and anticipate all of the action and much of the dialogue in the story. Subsequent checking confirmed that he had only seen this 15-minute program once previously, over a full year earlier. (p. 70)

Elias described in some detail the rationale for his intervention as well as its instructional components (see Elias, 1982; Elias & Maher, 1983) and has prepared a list of television and film media (by grade level) for teaching social skills and the agencies to be contacted with regard to their acquisition (Elias, 1982). He also prepared a curriculum or discussion guide for the "Inside/Out" intervention (Elias & Salvador, 1980). Elias (1982) currently identified his intervention with the acronym TVDRP, which refers to television (TV), discussion groups (D), and role playing (RP). He noted that the literature suggests that media and discussion groups interact synergistically (Salomon, 1979a) and that role playing increases the probability that skills learned in instructional settings will generalize to real-world situations.

Sprafkin and Rubinstein (1982) studied 132 children and adolescents in a state residential facility for ED youngsters. The researchers constructed a prosocial television diet containing 10 programs with frequent instances of prosocial behavior and assessed its influence relative to a control television diet. The study also compared the effect of the two viewing regimens with and without a postviewing discussion, which evaluated the pro- and antisocial behaviors contained in the programs, encouraging the former and discouraging the latter. The four treatments (prosocial with and without discussion, control television diet with and without discussion) were rotated through the four wards over a period of approximately 1 year. Each treatment phase involved: (a) 1 week of observing the youngsters' social behavior, (b) 2 weeks of watching the 10 programs (either prosocial or control) with or without discussion, and (c) 1 week of follow-up behavioral observations. The programs in the prosocial diet were previously broadcast on commercial television and dealt with the benefits of helping others, compromising when there is conflict, considering other peoples' feelings, cooperating with teachers, and the disadvantages of stealing and playing practical jokes. They included situation comedies ("Brady Bunch"), dramas ("Room 222"), and cartoons ("Fat Albert and the Cosby Kids"). The control programs were composed of the children's 10 most popular series, which included cartoons ("The Flintstones") and situation comedies ("Sanford and Son").

The results indicated that altruistic behaviors increased for children exposed to the prosocial television relative to those who saw the standard fare (see Table 5.2). This facilitation of altruism was more pronounced for those youngsters who were above average on baseline measures of physical aggression. Verbal aggression (e.g., threats, teases, name calling) and aggression toward objects decreased for youngsters exposed to the prosocial shows without group discussion, whereas both behaviors increased if the television show was followed by a discussion (see

TABLE 5.2

Mean Altruism and Symbolic Aggression at Pre (and Post) Phases
for Low and High Aggressive Youngsters Exposed to Two TV Diets

Behavior	Prosocial TV Diet		Control TV Diet	
	Low Aggression	High Aggression	Low Aggression	High Aggression
Altruistic behavior	1.07 (1.00)	1.01 (1.49)	1.16 (1.23)	1.70 (0.36)
Symbolic aggression	0.03 (0.10)	0.37 (0.08)	0.05 (0.03)	0.28 (0.25)

Note. From data reported in "Television and Persons in Institutions" by E. A. Rubinstein and J. Sprafkin, 1982, in *Television and Behavior: Ten Years of Scientific Progress and Implications for the 1980s* (Vol. 2, pp. 322–330), edited by D. Pearl, L. Bouthilet, and J. Lazar. Washington, DC: U.S. Government Printing Office.

TABLE 5.3
Mean Verbal and Object-Aggression at Pre (and Post) Phases
for Youngsters Exposed to Two TV Diets With and Without Discussion

| | Prosocial TV Diet | | Control TV Diet | |
Type of Aggression	Discussion	No Discussion	Discussion	No Discussion
Verbal aggression	0.15 (0.25)	0.21 (0.13)	0.20 (0.09)	0.10 (0.28)
Object aggression	0.01 (2.79)	0.09 (0.02)	0.08 (0.06)	0.03 (0.06)

Note. Based on data reported in "Television and Persons in Institutions" by E. A. Rubinstein and J. Sprafkin, 1982, in *Television and Behavior: Ten Years of Scientific Progress and Implications for the 1980s* (Vol. 2, pp. 322–330), edited by D. Pearl, L. Bouthilet, and J. Lazar. Washington, DC: U.S. Government Printing Office.

Table 5.3). Symbolic aggression (use of noncontact and nonverbal aggressive behaviors, including chasing and threatening gestures) decreased in the physically aggressive children who were exposed to the prosocial programming compared with the other groups (see Table 5.2). For reasons perhaps unique to this population, discussion following prosocial viewing appears to be at best ineffective and at worst detrimental in facilitating prosocial and reducing antisocial behavior. Sprafkin and Rubinstein (1982) reasoned that these "tough-image" youths reacted against the moralistic tone of the prosocial discussion. Nevertheless, the study showed that prosocial commercial television can be used as a therapeutic tool for shaping positive social behavior in the institutionalized ED child.

Learning Disabled Children. In an effort to improve the social interaction skills of LD students, Grayson, Gadow, and Sprafkin (1989) conducted a study to examine the efficacy of a media-based social skills training program. Ninety-two LD children, ranging in age from 5 to 13 years old, participated in an evaluation of the efficacy of a television-based social problem-solving curriculum. The curriculum consisted of ten 30-min lessons administered over a 5-week period. Children in the curriculum group viewed a 15-minute episode from the "Inside/Out" series and participated in a teacher-led discussion. Prior to and following the administration of the curriculum, children were tested using the Teacher Blaming and Peer Inclusion subtests of the Social Problem Analysis Situation Measure (Elias, Larcen, Zlottow, & Chinsky, 1978). Peer ratings of popularity and aggression, as well as unbiased ratings of behavior, completed by the children's art, gym, and library teachers were also collected at pre- and posttesting. Children's behavior and problem-solving ability during a structured arts and crafts activity at posttesting were coded by raters unaware of each child's treatment status.

In spite of the teachers' intensive efforts, the "Inside/Out" curriculum was not found to be an effective means of changing LD children's social problem-solving knowledge, peer relations, or behavior. Grayson et al. (1989) offered several suggestions for improving the curriculum, two of which are noted here. First, primary consideration in the development of future curricula should be given to remediating the LD child's problem in interpreting social events and the emotions associated with them. It is likely that these problems are significant contributors to the LD child's difficulty in developing and maintaining friendships. These same problems may also interfere with the LD child's ability to learn from television portrayals of social interactions. For example, one study comparing LD and nondisabled sixth, seventh, and eighth graders' comprehension of social interactions in television soap operas found that the LD group made more comprehension errors than their nonlabeled peers (Pearl & Cosden, 1982). Second, to be more successful, a curriculum should contain several lessons focusing on each skill in order for the skill to become integrated into the child's repertoire of social behaviors.

Mentally Retarded People.   As previously noted, Fechter (1971) conducted one of the earliest studies of modeling and social behavior (aggressive and prosocial) in mentally retarded people. In this study, Fechter found that viewing a tape of friendly doll play resulted in more friendly doll play in the postviewing setting and more prosocial behavior. He also noted that the friendly subjects were more friendly following the aggressive tape than were the aggressive subjects following the friendly tape.

Gadberry, Barroni, and Brown (1981) also demonstrated that institutionalized MR adults were influenced by prosocial media. Subjects who watched a videotape that encouraged helping behavior were later more likely to help another adult in a situation similar, but not identical, to the ones presented in the videotape.

Kysela (1973) investigated the use of videotape models to increase interactive play in socially isolated MR children attending a special education school. Two videotapes were prepared for the study: The control tape depicted nonretarded children engaged in four different play activities (similar activities occurred in the special school), and the experimental tape, which used the same activities, depicted an isolate child who was encouraged to join in the fun by a playmate. Kysela found that the experimental tape had a marked effect on isolate children by increasing the degree of social interaction to a level equivalent to that of their nonisolate peers. The control condition did not alter the degree of social interaction.

Nelson, Gibson, and Cutting (1973) taught three social responses (using grammatically correct questions, smiling, and talking about appropriate topics) to a 7-year-old educable mentally retarded boy using videotape modeling. Three treatment practices were used in a modified multiple baseline design: modeling, instructions plus social reinforcement, and modeling plus instructions plus social reinforcement. The researchers found that all three interventions (compared with baseline) produced significant increases in each target behavior.

In one of the few studies to actually use broadcast television, Baran (1977) made four half-hour television dramas with trainable mentally retarded individuals as actors. The shows depicted MR people attending a dance and a sheltered workshop, preparing for the Special Olympics, taking a trip downtown, and participating in a day at school. The programs were aired on four consecutive weekday mornings. The investigator randomly assigned 160 parent–child dyads to one of four conditions: (a) parent and child watched show and discussed content using specially prepared workbook; (b) parent and child watched show with parent responding only to questions asked by child; (c) child watched alone; and (d) neither parent nor child viewed the shows. Immediately following the last broadcast, interviewers went to each house to assess the effectiveness of the project. Unfortunately, Baran selected as his dependent measures a self-esteem scale and a self-perception ability questionnaire based on the skills presented in the television shows. Although comparisons between groups on a few items were statistically significant, supporting the efficacy of such programming, the author noted that a direct test of modeling might have produced more compelling results.

Summary.   To summarize, in spite of the enormous interest in the media and its potential to facilitate interactive play and the acquisition of social skills in exceptional children, relatively few empirical demonstrations support this claim. The majority of the studies have sought to show a modeling effect with short-term (less than 10 min) media presentations. Examples of more curriculum- or intervention-oriented projects are few in number (Baran, 1977; Elias, 1979, 1983; Grayson et al., 1989; Sprafkin & Rubinstein, 1982). Most of the research has involved institutionalized and/or severely disabled MR and ED children, and little attention has been given to media material prepared for broadcast television. Collectively, the research on prosocial media strongly suggests a modeling effect with exceptional children. Adult, peer, and disabled models all appear to be effective. Nevertheless, it must be emphasized that there is no evidence of a programmatic approach to empirical issues or predictors of television reactivity. Long-term treatment effects and the generalization of acquired skills also need to be assessed, as does the individual contribution of media to complex treatment packages.

CONCLUSIONS

For the past several decades, researchers, care providers, and policymakers have been enormously interested in the consequences of television viewing for the social development of children. Most of the attention has been focused on the behavior of television characters (much of which is antisocial) and to a lesser degree the substitution of television viewing for more "wholesome" or productive childhood activities. Ironically, some researchers (e.g., Hearold, 1986) have concluded that although television's effect on prosocial behavior is more profound than its impact on aggression, little use has been made of either broadcast television or specially prepared videotapes for teaching social skills development. At the present time, this remains a fertile area for future study. Unfortunately, research involving ED and LD children (e.g., Sprafkin, Gadow, & Grayson, 1987, 1988) who viewed highly prosocial cartoons has *not* found socially significant increases in appropriate social interaction compared with baseline levels. Further, treatment gains from social skills intervention programs that use media portrayals of social interactions have not been particularly robust, but research on this topic is very limited. Sadly, studies of television violence are so contradictory that they offer little insight into its implications for disabled students. Much more effort will be required to determine the short- and long-term effects of viewing aggression-laden content on ED, LD, and MR children in naturalistic social settings and the behavioral, cognitive, and environmental correlates of their reactivity to the media.

In spite of the mixed results from the field experiments, there are compelling reasons to discourage children from watching television that is heavily saturated with realistic violence. First, there are dramatic and tragic real-life incidents that suggest that television may have played a role in instigating antisocial and sometimes fatal acts (see Liebert & Sprafkin, 1988). Second, other effects of exposure to such content are possible. Research by Drabman and Thomas (1974, 1976) indicated that children shown aggressive programs (compared with nonaggressive ones) were more apathetic to displays of aggression by other children (which was reflected in their slow response to give help to younger aggressive children). Another possible adverse influence was discussed in chapter 3, namely, a cultivation effect. George Gerbner and his colleagues (e.g., Gerbner et al., 1979) have shown that children and teenagers (as well as adults) who watch a lot of television come to perceive reality in ways that are similar to the television world, which presents the environment as more dangerous and threatening than it really is. Thus, heavy television viewers tend to see the world as a "meaner" place than do less frequent viewers. For these reasons, an argument can still be made for limiting television viewing and redirecting children toward more socially constructive activities.

6 Parental Mediation of Television Viewing

As was noted in the previous chapter, a significant amount of scholarly investigation has demonstrated that children are capable of imitating and modeling social behavior from television programs. Rather than simple or causal effects, however, various situational and personal variables that influence what and how much is learned have been identified. Among the most prominent of these variables are the family structure and the type and quantity of parent–child interaction.

Because the family environment is an important source of social information for children, it follows that family attitudes and interaction patterns should affect the acquisition of social behaviors from television. In response to this situation, the Surgeon General's Advisory Committee on Television and Social Behavior (1972) endorsed the need to guide, supervise, and control the amount and nature of children's television viewing. It suggested future investigation into the context of the "totality of environmental influences, particularly that of the home environment" (p. 187). Consequently, there is a substantial body of research indicating that direct parental mediation of television viewing (e.g., rules, restrictions, coviewing) has the potential to influence children's viewing patterns (Gunter & Svennevig, 1987; Heald, 1980; Lyle & Hoffman, 1972; Nivin, 1960; Wand, 1968), interpretation and acceptance of television content (Bryant, 1990; Chaffee & McLeod, 1972; Chaffee & Tims, 1976; Greenberg, 1972; McLeod et al., 1972), and learning of social behaviors presented in television programming (Korzenny, Greenberg, & Atkin, 1979; Leifer, Gordon, & Graves, 1974; Lull, 1988).

In general, three distinctive dimensions of direct parental mediation of television viewing have been identified in the literature (e.g., Bybee, Robinson, &

Turow, 1982; Desmond, Hirsch, Singer, & Singer, 1987; Desmond, Singer, Singer, Calam, & Colimore, 1985). The first, *restrictive* mediation, consists mostly of rule setting such as limiting viewing or controlling program choice and program type. The second, *evaluative* mediation, occurs when parents discuss and criticize programs and commercials with the child. Parents may point out "good" and "bad" things that the actors do or explain the purpose of advertisements or the reality behind television programs and their characters. Finally, *unfocused* mediation consists of more general evaluations of television and the random use of television for reward and punishment. Such guidance includes watching programs with the child, encouraging or discouraging the child to view certain programs without offering a rationale, and talking about the program that the child views in a nonevaluative manner. These discussions are less directed than the evaluative guidance.

Although parents can influence what their children learn from television by incorporating one or more of the aforementioned strategies, the literature also indicates that few parents actually become directly involved in or actively exercise control over their children's viewing, interpretation, or use of television information. Regarding nonlabeled children, Steiner (1963), McLeod et al. (1972), and Bower (1973), among others, discovered that about half of the parents in their respective samples forbade exposure to certain "adult" or "offensive" shows, set bedtime limits on viewing, or made comments on the nature of the content being viewed. However, the majority of parents did not participate in their children's television viewing. Greenberg et al. (1972) reported that the most common form of control was in reference to rules about how late to watch, but even that form of intervention was neither widespread nor consistent. Similarly, Mohr (1972) and Thompson and Slater (1983) reported that although parent–child coviewing and parental monitoring were effective in influencing children's viewing behavior, less than half of their sample engaged in either activity.

According to Rossiter and Robertson (1975), it is likely that these and other estimates of moderate parental mediation are overly optimistic because parents are most likely to exaggerate their reports on patterns, methods, and frequency of intervention. Indeed, Desmond, Singer, and Singer (1990) noted that "participant parents and children reported instances of general and television-oriented mediation with a relatively high degree of reliability, and yet we observed few instances of such activity during our home visits. . . . We were surprised to find such low frequencies of any type of family interaction" (p. 304).

The limited degree of involvement in their children's television viewing is further demonstrated by Singer, Zuckerman, and Singer (1980), who observed that parents of children who participated in their research were reluctant to attend the television workshops that they offered and were disinterested in research results concerning their own children. Similarly, Neuendorf (1979) and Cohen, Abelman, and Greenberg (1991) supplied the parents with information about the negative impact of television on children and avenues for effective parental mediation through articles in the daily newspaper, reports on local radio, and especially brochures distributed through school and by mail. The authors reported that the vast majority of parents were still unlikely to participate in their children's television viewing behavior to any significant degree after receipt of this information.

EXCEPTIONAL CHILDREN

Research also indicates that, like their nonlabeled counterparts, parents of exceptional children are infrequent mediators of television viewing. According to Abelman and Rogers (1987), there are no significant differences in the amount of mediation exercised by parents of children identified as disabled (ED, LD, MR), intellectually gifted, or nonlabeled. As can be seen in Table 6.1, a low level of mediation (based on self-reports of the frequency of 15 separate forms of intervention) is typical of parents of LD (42%), ED (43%), MR (51%), gifted (44%), and nonlabeled children (48%). Although more parents of gifted, LD, and ED children are likely to engage in a high level of mediation than are parents of nonlabeled and MR children, active and direct participation in their children's television viewing is typically a rare occurrence.

Interestingly, when direct mediation of television viewing does occur, there are significant differences in the type of mediation conducted by parents of children in the different educational categories (see Table 6.2). Parents of gifted children, for example, tend to be highly focused, purposeful, and evaluative in their mediation. They typically engage in the more participatory forms of mediation, including explaining and discussing programming with their children and encouraging informed decision making about program selection. Desmond et al. (1985) also noted that verbal IQ (a control variable in their investigation) was moderately related to parental discussion of television rather than rule making. In general, research suggests that parents of gifted children tend to allow their

TABLE 6.1
Quantity of Direct Parental Mediation

Mediation	Child Classification				
	LD	ED	MR	Gifted	Nonlabeled
Low	42%	43%	51%	44%	48%
Moderate	31	29	38	33	40
High	27	28	12	23	12

Note. Based on data reported in "From 'Plug-in Drug' to 'Magic Window': The Role of Television in Special Education" by R. Abelman and A. Rogers, 1987. Paper presented at the 7th Annual World Conference on Gifted and Talented Children, Salt Lake City, UT.

TABLE 6.2
Type of Direct Parental Mediation

Mediation	LD	ED	MR	Gifted	Nonlabeled
			Child Classification		
Restrictive					
Forbid certain programs		**	*		**
Restrict viewing		*			**
Specify viewing time	**a				*
Specify programs to watch	*				
Switch channels on					
objectionable programs					*
Evaluative					
Explain program				**	
Explain advertising				*	
Evaluate character role		*		**	
Discuss character motivations				**	
Discuss plot/story line				**	
Unfocused					
Coview with child					*
Encourage use of TV guide				*	
Use TV as reward	**	**	**		
Withhold TV as punishment	**	**	**		
Talk about characters	*	*		*	

aFrequency: * 35–50% of the sample, ** 50–75% of the sample.
Note. Based on data reported in "From 'Plug-in Drug' to 'Magic Window': The Role of Television in Special Education" by R. Abelman and A. Rogers, 1987. Paper presented at the 7th Annual World Conference on Gifted and Talented Children, Salt Lake City, UT.

children more freedom to choose their own friends and make decisions, and encourage their creative interests and activities outside the home (Clark, 1979; Colangelo & Dettman, 1983; Dewing, 1970). This philosophy and practice apparently generalizes to the child's use of television.

In contrast, Cummings and Maddux (1985) noted that "if the child is born with a handicapping condition, the difficulties, frustrations, and heartaches of parenting are multiplied and parenting may become intolerable, or nearly so" (p. 4). Yanok and Derubertis (1989) reported that it is common for parents of disabled children to believe they are "ill prepared to address the special learning need of their children. Hence, out of frustration or despair, they may have selected to relinquish any additional responsibility for their children's education" (p. 198). In addition to helplessness, the family environments of ED and LD children are characterized by instability, underorganization, and chaos (Amerikaner & Omizo, 1984; Green, 1990). Given these factors, it is not surprising that parents of children with a disabling condition engage in unfocused and/or restrictive mediation and appear to have no overriding strategy or singular approach to deal with their child's television usage (see Table 6.2). Parents of nonlabeled children, however, are overwhelmingly restrictive in their mediation, choosing to simply limit the type and quantity of viewing.

It should not be assumed that because of low levels of direct parental mediation parents are uninvolved in or fail to influence their children's television viewing. Although the aforementioned investigations examined explicitly stated rules and practices regarding television, they did not deal with other forms of social interaction that might affect children's learning from television. More implied or global forms of intervention and interaction have been found to exist in the households and have the potential to either indirectly mediate or inspire more direct mediation of what and how children learn from television.

Parental Perceptions of Television Effects

Among the most prominent factors that are likely to contribute to the amount and type of parental control of the home viewing situation are parents' perceptions of television's impact on their children. Mills and Watkins (1982), for example, discovered that one reason for the lack of parental mediation found in previous research was that many parents did not perceive television to be a harmful or beneficial force in their children's lives. According to these authors, "there was a clear relationship between parents' awareness of possible [negative] effects of televiewing and subsequent enforcement of rules at home" (p. 11). This was also found to be the case in investigations conducted by Bybee et al. (1982), Messaris (1983), and Messaris and Kerr (1983).

Abelman (1990a) reported that divergent perceptions of television's effects significantly influenced the actual quantity and form of direct parental intervention. Among his findings were that:

1. Parents who were more concerned with cognitive effects (e.g., media influences on children's thought processes and content) were more likely to discuss and criticize television content, point out "good" and "bad" things that the actors do, and explain the purpose of advertisements and the reality behind television programs and characters.

2. Parents who were more concerned with behavioral effects (e.g., media influences on children's behavior) were more likely to mediate via restrictive methods—that is, limit viewing in terms of time, programs, or program type.

3. Parents who were more concerned with behavioral effects were also more likely to engage in the mediation of their children's television viewing than other parents.

What about parents of exceptional children, who may be more or less sensitive to particular media effects based on the nature of their child's exceptionality?

Part of the KIDVID investigation conducted by Abelman and his colleagues (Abelman & Pettey, 1989; Abelman & Rogers, 1987; Abelman & Ross, 1986, 1990) sought to address this issue by determining whether cognitive, affective, or behavioral effects of television were more salient for parents of exceptional children than for parents of nonlabeled children, and whether differences in perceptions were based on the type of exceptionality of the child. Questionnaires were mailed to and completed by parents of 8-year-old LD ($N = 373$), ED ($N = 232$), MR ($N = 214$), gifted ($N = 364$), and nonlabeled ($N = 386$) children in four cities: Cleveland, OH; Hartford, CT; Austin, TX; and Washington, DC. One section of the questionnaire asked parents about their attitudes toward the likely effects of television on their own children.

Statements referring to various commonly debated positive and negative consequences of television viewing were presented. These statements were derived from the extensive literature review of mass communication research presented in Murray (1980) and discussed in Liebert, Sprafkin, and Davidson (1982). Respondents noted whether they felt that television was a "very important contributory cause," an "important contributory cause," a "somewhat important contributory cause," a "contributory cause of little importance," or "not a contributory cause at all" for each of 35 statements. Table 6.3 lists the most frequently identified positive and negative effects of television on children, as indicated by the primary caregiver (or both parents when available).

Learning Disabled Children.   According to Cummings and Maddux (1985), many physicians have a tendency to shrug off learning disabilities as a mild handicap the child will outgrow. Consequently:

> Vital treatment time is lost, inappropriate behaviors become entrenched, and the handicap causes more difficulty than necessary. A learning disability is often referred to as a mild handicap, but that is misleading, since it is mild only in comparison to more severe handicaps such as severe mental retardation. For the affected child and his family, the condition is serious indeed. (p. 19)

Thus, the family experiences all the difficulties and frustrations associated with the disorder but often receives little guidance for treatment or behavior modification upon early detection.

If this scenario is an accurate one, then it serves as a viable explanation for the highly unfocused parental mediation of television viewing demonstrated by parents of LD children, as is depicted in Table 6.2. In addition, because it is not possible to point to one specific cause of this disabling condition and it is "likely that several causative factors are responsible . . . and may interact with each other (e.g., poor environmental conditions at home and poor instructional conditions at school could worsen the effects of a neurologically based learning disorder)" (Lewis, 1988, p. 366), it is not surprising that parents believe that television has caused or significantly contributed to a wide variety of effects.

TABLE 6.3
Perceived Effects by Parents

Perceived Effect	Child Classification				
	LD	ED	MR	Gifted	Nonlabeled
Cognitive					
Decreases reading ability	** a			***	
Increases verbal ability				*	
Decreases creativity				*	
Increases knowledge and awareness of the world				***	
Decreases attention span	**	**			
Increases curiosity				*	
Affective					
Decreases desire to learn	**		*		
Increases stereotyping of roles/gender		*	*		
Decreases interest in reading	*			*	
Increases self-concept					
Decreases self-concept	*		*	*	
Behavioral					
Increases desire for immediate gratification	*				**
Increases aggressive behavior	**	***	**		**
Decreases physical activity			*		*

aFrequency: * 35–50% of the sample, ** 50–75% of the sample, *** 75–100% of the sample.

Note. Based on data reported in "From 'Plug-in Drug' to 'Magic Window': The Role of Television in Special Education" by R. Abelman and A. Rogers, 1987. Paper presented at the 7th Annual World Conference on Gifted and Talented Children, Salt Lake City, UT.

As can be seen in Table 6.3, approximately 92% of the sample of parents of LD children identified at least one significant effect of television viewing on their children; 73% identified a cognitive, affective, and behavioral effect that was attributable to television. In addition, the effects identified by parents were overwhelmingly negative: The majority (50–75%) believed that television decreases children's reading ability, attention span, and desire to learn, and increases children's aggressive behavior. Many (35–50%) believed that television decreases their children's interest in reading, diminishes their self-concept, and increases the desire for immediate gratification.

Emotionally Disturbed Children.   As noted in chapter 1, emotional disturbance is often thought of as a behavioral disorder by many parents and professionals. The importance of environmental factors in the development and maintenance of such disorders can be seen in many of the etiological theories and behavioral approaches used to treat ED children (see Doorlag, 1988). It is therefore understandable that most (75–100%) parents of ED children believed that television has a significant effect on their son's or daughter's behavior (Table 6.3), particularly with regard to aggressive activity. The parents' primary forms of mediation are punitive in nature (e.g., forbidding or restricting viewing). Although much of their mediation also tends to be unfocused (see Table 6.2), there are behavioral outcomes associated with this mediation (e.g., punishing and rewarding by allowing or withholding television viewing).

Mentally Retarded Children. The MR children that participated in the KID-VID investigation were mild-to-moderately retarded and lived in community placements. According to Lynch (1988), these children are likely to possess "reduced motivation, an external locus of control, and deficiencies in social discrimination" (p. 112; see also Schloss & Sedlak, 1982). Although parents of MR children are less likely to attribute significant effects to television viewing than other parents, Table 6.3 suggests that perceived effects are typically associated with reduced motivation (e.g., decreases desire to learn) and deficiencies in social discrimination (e.g., increases stereotyping of roles/gender, decreases self-concept). Fifty to 75% of the sample also believed that aggressive behavior could be attributed to television viewing.

Intellectually Gifted Children. Parents of gifted children have been found to be typically more conscious of their children's learning processes (Clark, 1979) and the sources of external stimuli that tend to advance or hinder their children's intellectual progression (Page, 1983) than the parents of intellectually average children. Colangelo and Dettman (1983), Gallagher, Kaplan, and Sato (1983), and others have noted that a common concern of parents of gifted children is how to better encourage and enrich their child's intellectual growth and minimize distractions. This concern clearly generalizes to their perceptions of the likely impact of television on their children; 85% of the parents identified at least one effect that was highly attributable to television. As can be seen in Table 6.3, parents of gifted children generally believe that television can have both positive (e.g., increase verbal skill, increase creativity, increase knowledge of the world, increase curiosity) and negative (e.g., decrease in reading ability) cognitive effects on their children.

Interestingly, the special affective and social needs of gifted children are also of great concern to parents (Elgersma, 1981; Richert, 1981; Vare, 1979), and may suggest to them a special vulnerability to attractive televised portrayals. Although gifted children are more intellectually sophisticated than their average counterparts, "they are still children, and their advanced mentality does little to help them through the problems of growing up" (Barbe, 1965, p. 175). This concern is evident in the research findings presented in Table 6.3. Parents perceive affective consequences of television viewing on their children, and these perceptions tend to be negative (e.g., decreased interest in reading, lower self-concept).

In general, it appears that the low level of mediation of gifted children's television viewing is more likely associated with their parents' belief that television can be a positive force in their children's lives rather than a neutral or negative force. The fact that parents of gifted children typically adopt an evaluative form of intervention when they do engage in direct mediation of television viewing also attests to their level of involvement and interest regarding their children's use of television.

Child-Rearing Practices/Communication Interaction

Numerous studies have demonstrated that the type and quantity of family interaction (Belsky, Rovine, & Taylor, 1984; Belsky, Taylor, & Rovine, 1984; Doane, 1978; Easterbrooks & Goldberg, 1984; Perkins, 1989), child-rearing practices (Osofsky & Oldfield, 1972; Sears, Maccoby, & Levin, 1957; Strommen, McKinney, & Fitzgerald, 1977; Tims & Masland, 1984), and disciplinary style (Aronfreed, 1969; Gunter & Svennevig, 1987; Hoffman, 1975; Hoffman & Salzstein, 1967) are related to children's social and moral behavior. Furthermore, parental communication style has been found to create an atmosphere that can either serve to enhance or retard emerging linguistic, comprehensional, and empathetic skills of the child (Fischer & Bullock, 1984; Luria, 1982; Maccoby, 1980; Wood, 1980). Several mass communication researchers have sought to determine whether the interaction, socialization, and disciplinary style of parents, either concurrent with or in the absence of specific household rules regarding television, are related to children's use of television information.

Two main categories of child-rearing practices have been identified by Aronfreed (1969, 1976) and Hoffman (1970, 1975) and subsequently applied to parental mediation of television viewing: induction and sensitization.[1] The main difference between these two modes of child rearing is that induction is communication oriented and sensitization is based on the exercise of actual or implied power. Inductive practices "tend to make the child's control of its behavior independent of external contingencies. In contrast, [sensitization] merely sensitizes the child to the anticipation of punishment" (Aronfreed, 1969, pp. 309–310).

---

[1]Hoffman (1970) actually differentiated among three major categories of child-rearing/disciplinary practices—induction, power assertion, and love withdrawal. The latter two categories reflect the same parental discipline patterns as Aronfreed's (1969) discussion of sensitization techniques, and were collapsed by Korzenny et al. (1979) and Abelman (1985) to form the sensitization category.

Induction techniques include the use of reasoning and explanation, and appeals to the child's pride and achievement, and they exert little external power over the child. Parents who engage in this form of child rearing typically point out to the child why one course of action may be better than another for the child's own well-being or because of its effect on others. Sensitization "includes physical punishment, deprivation of material objects or privileges, the direct application of force, or the threat of any of these" (Hoffman, 1970, p. 285). These power-assertive methods of discipline have been linked to aggressive behavior in children, and they are frequently employed with more aggressive children or by parents who perceive their children as more aggressive than others (Olweus, 1978, 1980).

Korzenny et al. (1979), as a part of the CASTLE investigation conducted at Michigan State University, explored the role of parent–child interaction in an effort to specify some of the conditions under which children's modeling of antisocial television portrayals was minimized and maximized. The authors hypothesized that enduring parental modes of discipline and interaction should directly mediate the degree to which children acquire and perform antisocial behaviors seen on television. They found that children with parents who disciplined primarily with reasoning and explanation were least affected by antisocial television content and that children with parents who disciplined primarily with actual and implied power were most affected.

Similarly, in their longitudinal investigation of families with preschool and early elementary-school children, Jerome and Dorothy Singer and their colleagues (Desmond et al., 1985, 1990; Singer, Singer, & Rapaczynski, 1984) examined child-rearing attitudes and family interaction patterns and their role in influencing children's beliefs about and comprehension of media portrayals and their television viewing habits. They found that the comprehension of television by kindergartners and first graders, as well as their beliefs regarding the reality of the medium, were reliably linked with parental mediation of television viewing and to more general patterns of discipline. In addition, it was found that "love withdrawal," a form of sensitization, was associated with low levels of rules about and heavy viewing of television by the child. In a summary of their research findings, Desmond et al. (1990) suggested that "general family communication style may have been more critical than specific TV rules and discipline for enhancing a range of cognitive skills, including television comprehension" (p. 302). Regarding the most effective form of family communication style, the authors conclude:

> It is moral judgement and explanation about issues presented on television, rather than the simple act of underlining or pointing out content in a neutral manner, that characterizes the families of children who are skillful at comprehending several aspects of the medium. Children who dwell in such a positive atmosphere of family communication are less fearful of being harmed, less aggressive, and more willing

to wait patiently than are children from families who simply comment on television's array of people and events. (p. 304)

Noting that the exploration of parents' impact on their children's learning from television has focused on antisocial behavior and tended to "exclude other forms of social behavior that might be acquired" (p. 53), Abelman (1986a) examined the child-rearing practices under which children's awareness of prosocial television portrayals was likely to be maximized and minimized. Parents were classified as primarily inductive or sensitizing based on an instrument used by Hoffman and Saltzstein (1967) and Korzenny et al. (1979). Parents were presented with hypothetical situations, each with nine possible responses that were reflective of inductive and sensitizing in each way presented. The children were assessed for their awareness of pro- and antisocial information on television and their modes of conflict resolution when placed in various hypothetical social situations (e.g., "Someone you know from school is calling your mother bad names." "Suppose your friends are going to the movies, but your parents asked you to stay home and finish your homework").

Results from this investigation indicated that children of parents who were primarily inductive in their child-rearing practices had a greater awareness of television's prosocial fare (e.g., altruism, sharing, cooperation) and demonstrated a greater propensity for prosocial solutions to conflict than did children whose parents were primarily sensitizing. Parental child-rearing practices did not necessarily influence children's program choice, which tended to be high in antisocial content (although sensitizing parents often employed deprivation of favorite television programs as a disciplinary device). However, they did influence children's perceptions of the reality of those programs and the type of social information they extracted and applied to their own life situations.

This same avenue of inquiry was applied to parents of LD, ED, and gifted children as part of the KIDVID investigation discussed earlier (Abelman, 1991a). Indices were constructed to measure children's ability to identify and label the types of prosocial behaviors—those behaviors that are generally accepted by society as constructive, appropriate, and legal (Greenberg, Atkin, Edison, & Korzenny, 1977)—that appear in commercial television programs. These behaviors included altruism, empathy, cooperation, sympathy, sharing, and reparation. After each behavior was thoroughly defined and examples were provided to and gathered from the children, each child was presented with 20 actual examples of commercial television fare ranging from 3 minutes to 15 minutes in length and instructed to say "stop" when they identified a prosocial behavior within the context of the program. The investigator noted the placement in the videotape where the child believed each prosocial act occurred. Children's ability to label prosocial behavior was assessed by having them circle the name of the behavior on a questionnaire whenever they stopped the program. The findings from this investigation are presented in Fig. 6.1.

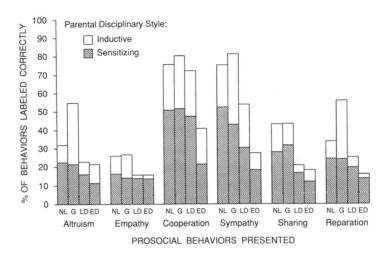

FIG. 6.1. Nonlabeled (NL), gifted (G), learning disabled (LD), and emotionally disturbed (ED) children's achievement levels in labeling prosocial behaviors by parental disciplinary style. *Note.* From data reported in "Parental Communication Style and Its Influence on Exceptional Children's Television Viewing" by R. Abelman, 1991. *Roeper Review, 14*(1), pp. 23–27.

Learning Disabled Children.   In general, achievement scores were lower for LD children with sensitizing parents than for nonlabeled children with sensitizing parents. Furthermore, scores for LD children with inductive parents were lower than those of nonlabeled children with sensitizing parents. However, LD children with inductive parents demonstrated better knowledge of prosocial behaviors (except empathy) than LD children with sensitizing parents, especially for cooperation and sympathy.

Emotionally Disturbed Children.   Similarly, achievement scores were lower for ED children with sensitizing parents than for LD children with sensitizing parents; scores of ED children with inductive parents were lower than those of nonlabeled children with sensitizing parents. However, there were significantly higher achievement scores among ED children with inductive parents than ED children with sensitizing parents with regard to the identification and labeling of altruism, cooperation, and sympathy.

Intellectually Gifted Children.   Gifted children were significantly better at identifying and labeling prosocial behavior on television if they came from households in which parents were primarily inductive as opposed to sensitizing in their child-rearing practices. In addition to higher levels of achievement for altruism, empathy, cooperation, sympathy, sharing, and reparation, gifted children with inductive parents scored higher than nonlabeled children with inductive parents on each of the prosocial behaviors. However, gifted children with sensitizing parents obtained scores comparable to intellectually average children with sensitizing parents.

In any discussion of parents' interactions with and disciplining of their children, it is important to point out that children are not mere passive recipients of parental child-rearing practices. The nature of the child often dictates or shapes the type, intensity, and regularity of parental discipline and interaction, as well as how the child is likely to react to these activities. According to Brody, Pillegrini, and Sigel (1986):

> Just as researchers realized, a decade and a half ago, the limitations of unidirectional models of socialization, they today recognize that families comprise several subsystems (i.e., spousal or marital, parent–child, and the sibling subsystem), each of which affects and is affected by events that occur in the other subsystems (Belsky, 1981). In particular, this suggests that parenting both influences and is influenced by the child. (p. 291)

Indeed, this observation serves to explain the tendency for inductive child-rearing practices to be more frequently found among parents of gifted children (Morrow & Wilson, 1961; Roedell et al., 1980), particularly when compared with other groups of exceptional children (Cummings & Maddux, 1985; Cunningham & Sloper, 1980; Farber & Jenne, 1963; Lynch & Lewis, 1988b). In general, it has been found (see Perkins & Green, 1988) that parents of high-achieving children are significantly clearer and more open in their communication with their children than parents of intellectually average children, who, in turn, were significantly clearer and more interactive than parents of LD children. This may be associated with the tendency of disabled children to be less effective in their own communication skills than nonlabeled (Knight-Arest, 1984) or gifted children (Page, 1983).

Along the same line, Ditton, Green, and Singer (1987) undertook a series of studies to determine if parental communication deviance (i.e., the inability to name, categorize, direct shared focal attention, and explain aspects of the world to children) was associated with the kind of cognitive deficits shown by children with learning disabilities. The analysis revealed that 87% of parents of LD children were rated high in communication deviance. Similarly, Owen, Adams, Forest, Stolz, and Fisher (1971) and Amerikaner and Omizo (1984) found that families of LD children scored in the chaotic (versus functional) range on family adaptability, were generally less cohesive and more disorganized and disengaged than families of nondisabled children.

The findings from the KIDVID studies suggest that any parent who regularly engages in more inductive and less sensitizing modes of discipline can indirectly influence what their child observes when watching television. Janos and Robinson's (1985) observation that "parents who spend more time with their children, facilitate their interests, answer their questions, and provide a warm supportive base for intellectual exploration are likely to foster psychological maturity and adjustment" (p. 169) is particularly applicable to children's television viewing behavior.

Gender Differences

Exceptionalities aside, one of the more salient variables influencing the type and quality of parent–child interaction is gender. That differences exist between father–child and mother–child interaction in general is well documented (e.g., Clark-Stewart, 1980; Frodi, Lamb, Hwang, & Frodi, 1982; Lamb, 1977; Pedersen, Anderson, & Cain, 1980), even when fathers assume active care-giving roles. Gender differences in disciplinary practices have also been identified. For instance, Hoffman (1970) suggests that inductive strategies are positively related to the development of children's conscience when the mother is the primary agent of discipline, but there is no evidence of any such relationship when the primary agent of discipline is the father. Baumrind (1971) noted that fathers tended to be more authoritarian or sensitizing than mothers when playing the role of disciplinarian. This raises some interesting issues in light of the limited degree of direct parental mediation of television.

Abelman (1985) examined the association between mother and father disciplinary styles and their children's behavioral predisposition and exposure to pro- and antisocial television fare. It was found that children's viewing of prosocial television portrayals increased with the salience of fathers and/or mothers engaging in inductive styles of discipline. It was also found that the viewing of antisocial behavior was greatest for children whose fathers and/or mothers engage in sensitizing styles of discipline and fathers who engaged in inductive styles, and least for children whose mothers used an inductive approach.

In addition, there was evidence that the disciplinary style employed by mothers had a greater impact on children's modes of conflict resolution and mass communication usage than the disciplinary style used by fathers. In other words, regardless of whether fathers were sensitizing or inductive, children from households whose mothers were inductive were more likely to react to conflict in a prosocial manner and expose themselves to a greater amount of prosocial television content. This was also found to be the case in the KIDVID studies, regardless of the exceptionality of the child.

Although it has been reported that mothers and fathers impact differently on family functioning, there is also evidence that the gender of the child plays an important role as well. A significant amount of research suggests that how a parent responds to a child may be largely dependent on whether the child is male or female. Margolin and Patterson (1975), for example, have demonstrated that fathers provided almost twice as many positive reactions to their sons as to their daughters. Similarly, Maccoby and Jacklin (1974) found that boys were punished more often than girls and received more praise and encouragement by mothers. This pattern also exists in the literature on exceptional children (e.g., Cummings & Maddux, 1985; Eccles, 1985; Farber & Jenne, 1963; Nihira, Meyers, & Mink, 1980; Parker & Colangelo, 1979). Interestingly, there is no evidence of signifi-cant gender differences in regard to type or frequency of direct parental media-tion of television for nonlabeled or exceptional children (Abelman, 1985; Abel-man & Pettey, 1989; Desmond et al., 1987; Singer et al., 1984).[2]

CONCLUSION

Although television has the potential to offer children both desirable and objec-tionable information in great quantities, parents have the potential to influence what and how children learn from television. A significant amount of research suggests that the most efficient way parents can exert their influence is through the purposeful and direct mediation of their children's television viewing. How-ever, there is every indication that parents of nonlabeled and exceptional children alike tend to offer only modest levels of direct intervention.

Interestingly, there exist both parent- and child-oriented variables that serve as determinants of parental mediation. It is here that significant differences emerge between households of nonlabeled and exceptional children. Although parents of nonlabeled children tend to perceive television effects as being predominantly behavioral in nature, parents of exceptional children do not. Perceived effects held by parents of gifted children, for example, tend to be predominantly cogni-tive in nature, but parents of LD children are concerned about cognitive, affec-tive, and behavioral effects. Whereas parents of nonlabeled children are largely restrictive in their mediation, parents of gifted children are more evaluative and parents of LD, ED, and MR children are largely unfocused. Additional findings suggest that any parent regularly engaging in more inductive and less sensitizing modes of general discipline can indirectly influence what their child learns when watching television. However, gifted children are found to be more responsive and disabled children less responsive to parental disciplinary style than their nonlabeled peers with regard to television viewing behavior.

The most peripheral glance through the popular periodicals and scholarly

---

[2]Abelman (1987a) notes that "the sex of the [gifted] child was, for the most part, not a significant predictor of any parental response to the television/child relationship. Sex exhibited only a weak association with a high level of mediation, suggesting that boys may be more likely to receive parental intervention than are girls" (p. 220). However, the significance of this finding was at the .05 level.

journals will reveal that there is no shortage of reports that television is capable of disrupting family life and the interactions between family members (e.g., Bryant, 1990; Gunter & Svennevig, 1987; Murray, 1980; Murray & Salomon, 1984). The information presented in this chapter suggests that the converse is also true: Family life influences how children are affected by watching television.

7 Teaching Critical Viewing Skills in School

It was not too long ago that educators cursed the day Vladimir Zworykin invented television, calling it the "plug-in drug" (Winn, 1977) and reinforcing FCC Commissioner Newton Minow's contention that the medium was a "vast wasteland." Over the years, many educators have claimed witness to television's negative impact on young children's language acquisition, reading ability, and attention span in the classroom (e.g., California State Department of Education, 1980). The National Parents and Teachers Association (PTA) has waged war on television and, beginning in the 1960s, devoted much of its time and resources to campaigns aimed at modifying children's television viewing and what they learn from television (PTA, 1977, 1978). The American Medical Association (1976, 1982), American Academy of Pediatrics (1986), American Psychological Association (1985; Abeles, 1986), American Academy of Child Psychology (1984), and National Council for Children and Television (1979, 1980), among others, have followed suit.

Educators, parents, and researchers have tried to identify ways to minimize the negative and maximize the positive influences of television by teaching children to be "literate" viewers. As was stated in the 10-year update of the Surgeon General's report on children and television (Pearl, Bouthilet, & Lazar, 1982a):

> Recognition of the importance of television as a part of a child's growing-up experience has led in recent years to the view that children need to learn something about how to watch television and how to understand it. Much as they are taught to appreciate literature, to read newspapers carefully, and so on, they need to be prepared to understand television as they view it in their homes. (p. 81)

Many funding agencies have supported this notion. In 1978 the Idaho Department of Education funded an ESEA Title IV-C Innovative Education project to promote the viewership skills of the youngsters in the third through sixth grades. Similar funding has been available through the U.S. Office of Education (Withrow, 1980), the National Education Association, the National PTA, and the American Broadcasting Companies.

Although the theoretical rationales, objectives, methods, and emphases differ from project to project, all have offered some combination of self-examination of television use and instruction in production terminology and technique, and all have been at least moderately effective in increasing knowledge about television (for reviews see Anderson, 1980; Brown, 1991; Corder-Bolz, 1982). The degree to which increased knowledge about television reduces possible adverse influences of certain types of content is not entirely clear. However, the results of one study are encouraging in that they suggest that classroom interventions designed to alter children's attitudes about aggression-laden content can reduce antisocial behavior in children who are heavy viewers of television violence (Huesmann, Eron, Klein, Brice, & Fischer, 1983).

EXCEPTIONAL CHILDREN

What has been presented so far in this book suggests strongly that ED, LD, and MR children are vulnerable with respect to the adverse effects of television viewing. Compared with their nondisabled peers, they watch more television overall and more aggression-laden programs. Their attention is drawn to the most salient features of programs, and their comprehension of the story line and presentation (e.g., special effects) are extremely limited. Not surprisingly, they perceive much of the fictional content they view as real, which increases the likelihood that they will incorporate what they watch. With regard to behavioral effects, exposure to *both* aggressive and nonaggressive television programs has been shown to induce antisocial behavior, which means that restricting their viewing of aggressive content (even if this were a practical intervention) would not be addressing the problem.

For intellectually gifted children, the regular viewing of adult-oriented fare is especially problematic because they assimilate information so rapidly (Scruggs & Cohn, 1983). Although intellectually advanced, gifted children may not have the emotional, social, or cognitive experience necessary to accurately process at least some of what they view on television. One must bear in mind that intellectual superiority does not in and of itself inoculate children against the adverse effects of television viewing.

One logical way to reduce the vulnerability of exceptional children to the medium is parental mediation of television viewing. However, as we saw in chapter 6, parents of exceptional children are unlikely to offer supervision during viewing, despite the fact that they are more aware of their children's learning processes and environmental influences on intellectual and social development. This lack of parental monitoring and mediation has the potential to amplify the impact of the medium (Desmond et al., 1990; Greenberg & Atkin, 1979; Gunter & Svennevig, 1987) and contribute to higher levels of television viewing.

Despite their long-term and overwhelmingly negative predisposition toward the medium, special educators are beginning to teach responsible and critical televiewing skills. This is due, in part, to their recognition that exceptional children spend much of their leisure time watching television, have a strong affinity for certain media characters, have the potential to learn much from the medium, and are not adequately supervised in their viewing habits (Abelman & Rogers, 1987).

Aside from reducing a child's vulnerability to the negative effects of television, special educators have recognized that bringing television into the classroom advances other educational objectives such as teaching academic skills and concepts. Chapter 8 is devoted specifically to this topic. As we discuss in that chapter, ED, LD, and MR children often have attentional and motivational deficits in most traditional learning situations. Given the inherent appeal of television for most children, the incorporation of television material into lessons presents exciting possibilities for learning. This applies to intellectually gifted children as well, for whom the regular curriculum often lacks stimulation and inhibits motivation. Television-assisted instruction is consistent with the needs of intellectually gifted children "to master basic skills and knowledge, and at the same time, deal effectively with the most contemporary developments and uses of that knowledge" (Robertson, 1984, p. 137).

The primary curricula developed for teaching viewing skills to exceptional children have addressed two general goals: (a) to make exceptional children literate consumers of television by teaching them how television programs are made, how to differentiate reality from fantasy, how special effects make the impossible appear real, and the commercial motivation underlying television advertising; and (b) to help them recognize and evaluate both the antisocial and prosocial content of programs. Implicit in the first goal is the belief that achieving a degree of television literacy reduces the viewer's vulnerability to television's untoward influences. The second goal reflects the desire to enhance television's positive potential by tuning children in to the socially desirable content.

In this chapter we describe two different curricula for enhancing television viewing skills. The first one, the Curriculum for Enhancing Social Skills Through Media Awareness (CESSMA), has been used with ED, LD, and non-labeled students. The second, KIDVID Critical Viewing Curriculum, has been used with gifted, LD, and nonlabeled children. Because the goals of these curricula are so different, each is presented separately.

CURRICULUM FOR ENHANCING SOCIAL SKILLS
THROUGH MEDIA AWARENESS

The CESSMA was developed specifically to help ED and LD children to become more literate consumers of television (Sprafkin, Watkins, & Gadow, 1986). It consists of 14 lessons that are organized around brief videotaped segments excerpted from television shows popular with young children. The CESSMA is designed to be taught in 30-minute lessons and requires minimal advance preparation. Each lesson plan provides an overview, objectives, outline, commentary for the video presentation, narrative for the lesson, and instructions for the suggested activities. The curriculum is divided into four major units.

The primary objective of the five lessons in Unit 1 ("Real and Pretend") is to develop the child's awareness of the difference between reality and fantasy on television. The unit is based on the concept of storytelling (i.e., some stories are real, some are possible but pretend, and others are pure fantasy). This concept is then elaborated by an exploration of the jobs people do when telling stories on film or television (script writers, directors, camera operators) and how the lives of actors differ from the lives of the characters they play. The unit includes a lesson on animation as a special storytelling technique.

Several videocassettes were created for this unit to illustrate the storytelling concept. One videocassette contains excerpts from 13 television shows (e.g., situation comedies, dramas, presidential address), and the children have to decide whether each segment is real, possible but pretend, or impossible. In another video, portions of programs about television production were edited together to illustrate the various jobs involved in making a television program, such as the writer, director, set designer, makeup person, camera operator, and actors/actresses. To illustrate the relationship of an actor and the role(s) he plays, a video was created to show the same actor playing several roles (e.g., Michael Landon playing Jonathan from "Highway to Heaven," Pa on "Little House on the Prairie," and Little Joe on "Bonanza"), and several actors playing the same role (such as that of Tarzan and James Bond). For the lesson on animation, several television programs dealing with how cartoons are made were edited together.

Activities for Unit 1 include the "hands on" variety as well as viewing video segments and answering questions about such things as real/possible/impossible. For example, Fig. 7.1 illustrates an activity that reinforces the concept that many jobs are involved in making a television program. Children are asked to identify the professions represented both pictorially and descriptively. To help them grasp the concept of animation, children manipulate "flip books" that illustrate how a series of pictures can be drawn such that they appear to move, and toy movie viewers that show how the rate of movement can be regulated.

In Unit 2 ("Special Effects"), five lessons introduce children to the various cinematic techniques that make television scenes appear so real. There are lessons on superpower actions, costumes and makeup, puppetry, and aggression.

Activity Sheet
Name My Job

This picture shows some of the people who help to make television programs:

Actor   Makeup Person
Acresss   Scriptwriter
Camera Operator   Set Designer
Director

Try to name the job of each of the people described below and find them in the picture.

1. I make sure that the actors and all the people who work the cameras, lights, and sound equipment are all doing their job. I try to make the TV program as interesting as I can.

2. I write the story to be used in a TV program.

3. I pretend to be one of the TV characters that the scriptwriter includes in the TV program. I dress up and put on makeup to look like the character, and I say the lines written in the script.

4. I work the camera that records the pictures and sounds that make up the TV program.

5. I use makeup and wigs to make the actors look like the characters they are pretending to be in the TV show.

6. I'm in charge of designing the place. I may have to build a room and put in furniture if the TV program takes place in a house.

FIG. 7.1. Activity, "Name My Job," from Unit 1 (Real and Pretend) of the CESSMA. *Note.* from *Curriculum for Enhancing Social Skills Through Media Awareness* (pp. 15–16) by J. Sprafkin, L. T. Watkins, and K. D. Gadow, 1986. Unpublished curriculum, State University of New York at Stony Brook. Drawing by Dr. Patrick Grim. Reprinted by permission.

The emphasis is on showing children how things are "faked" cinematically so that their awareness of how the pretend can look so real will be grounded in a detailed understanding of technique.

This unit includes video segments that both teach children how special effects techniques are executed and provide them with the opportunity to apply what they have learned. For the teaching segment, children are shown excerpts of several television shows and films that demonstrate how certain special effects (e.g., bending steel, flying, killing) are accomplished and how phenomenal characters (e.g., the werewolf from "Thriller" or Jabba from "Star Wars") are created. To get them to practice what they have learned, children are shown excerpts from actual television programs that made use of special effects and are asked to explain how the scene was accomplished.

Activities for Unit 2 are quite varied and are fun. Children are asked to act out the filming of a bionic jump, the bending of steel with bare hands, and a fight scene. They get to make a puppet, design a monster outfit, and design a set for "Superman."

The two lessons of Unit 3 ("Commercials") teach children to identify commercials as persuasive messages and to understand how advertising uses special effects techniques to make products seem more appealing. The video portion of this unit includes the "Six Billion Dollar Sell," a Consumers Union film for children that describes a variety of advertising gimmicks. The featured activity in this unit is having children plan the techniques they would use if they wanted to sell a new product. They also get to watch commercials and to identify the sales techniques used in each.

In Unit 4 ("Review"), two final lessons are used to review the entire curriculum. In one lesson, children watch videotaped excerpts and are asked to identify the cinematic techniques that were used. In the final lesson, a videocamera is brought into their classroom, and the students are taped while discussing what they know about television. The tape is replayed so that television is demystified as the children see themselves on television.

Several measures were developed to assess the impact of the CESSMA. It was reasoned that a critical viewing skills curriculum could influence children's knowledge about special effects and commercials, their perceptions of the realism of television content, their attitudes toward television, their identification with television characters, and their television viewing habits. Accordingly, the evaluation instruments tapped these areas. They are described briefly here (for a more detailed account, see Sprafkin, Watkins, & Gadow, 1990):

1. The TV Knowledge measure assesses children's perceptions about the reality of television content, the veracity of commercials, and the techniques of special effects. Two equivalent versions were developed for pretest and posttest administration. Modeled after the PORT, POC, and KATT (described in chapters 3 and 4), the measure has children view media excerpts and respond to a series of orally presented yes/no (i.e., true/false) questions. The answer sheets contain representative picture cues for each segment and geometric shape cues (e.g., circle, square, triangle) for each question to maximize adherence to the instructions (see Fig. 7.2).

2. The Follow-Up Knowledge measure evaluates children's retention of the

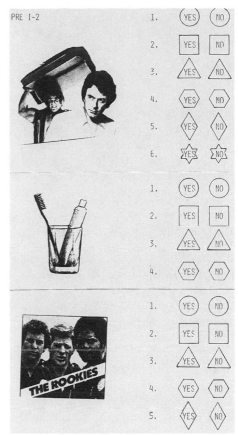

FIG. 7.2. Sample response sheet from the TV Knowledge measure. *Note.* Courtesy of Sprafkin, Watkins and Gadow.

major concepts taught in the curriculum (after 2 months) and their ability to apply that knowledge when they watch media excerpts that are longer than those used in the TV Knowledge measure.

3. The TV Attitudes instrument is a 14-item orally presented questionnaire asking children to rate on a 3-point scale (or by yes/no response) a variety of evaluative statements about television programming and commercials, such as how truthful, good, enjoyable, believable, and valuable television material seems to be.

4. The Character Identification measure assesses the degree to which children identify with seven popular television characters. Children are asked to indicate on a 3-point scale ("not at all," "a little," "a lot") how much they (a) get upset when the character is sad or in trouble on television, (b) act like the character, and (c) wish to be like the character when they grow up. Two separate indices are derived, Aggressive Character Identification and Nonaggressive Character Identification.

5. The Television Viewing Habits measure is a series of television diaries (similar to those described in chapter 2) that were used to derive estimates of the children's overall exposure to television and viewing of particular types of programs.

The efficacy of the CESSMA has been evaluated with ED, LD, and non-disabled elementary school children. As is the case for most systematic curriculum evaluations, some classes were taught the curriculum and several otherwise equivalent classes were not (to provide a control for repeated testing and the passage of time). The aforementioned outcome measures were given before (pretest) and after (posttest) the curriculum to determine the degree of effectiveness of the intervention.

Emotionally Disturbed Children

The CESSMA was field tested in a public elementary school for ED children on Long Island (Sprafkin et al., 1990). Thirteen classes of students, including 70 boys and 11 girls between 6 and 12 years of age ($M = 9.3$ years), participated in the evaluation (IQ: $M = 93$). Six of the classes ($n = 38$) received the curriculum and seven ($n = 43$) served as controls who participated in testing but did not receive any treatment.

The data were analyzed using a statistical procedure (analysis of covariance) that assessed posttest performance on the various measures adjusting for variations in pretest scores. The curriculum group (62% correct) significantly outperformed the control group (56% correct) on TV Knowledge. Follow-up testing 2 months later showed that the curriculum group maintained their lead over the control group. Another promising finding was that the ED children in the intervention group identified less with aggressive television characters than those in the control group.

This finding is important because previous research has suggested that children who identify the most with television characters are the most aggressive (Huesmann et al., 1983), and the process of identifying with television characters may catalyze the violence viewing–aggression relationship (Huesmann et al., 1984). Furthermore, Huesmann et al. (1983) found that the children who showed the greatest reduction in aggressive behavior following an intervention designed to mitigate the effects of television violence were those who also reduced their identification with television characters. In contrast, Sprafkin et al. did not find that initial identification with television characters was associated with degree of improvement from the curriculum. In fact, despite the enhanced knowledge about television and reduced identification with aggressive characters, there was no evidence that the CESSMA significantly altered either television viewing attitudes or habits.

Learning Disabled Children

A total of 62 boys and 24 girls (age: $M = 9.3$ years; IQ: $M = 86$) from a public elementary school for LD children participated in the second CESSMA study (Sprafkin et al., 1990). Eight of the classes ($n = 43$) received the CESSMA and eight ($n = 43$) served as no-treatment controls. The LD children in the curriculum group showed significantly greater television knowledge (63% correct) than those in the control group (52% correct), and these gains were still in evidence 2 months later (Follow-Up Knowledge). The knowledge domain was the only one in which the curriculum was found to have an impact. On measures of identification with television characters, attitudes toward television, and viewing habits, the CESSMA and control groups responded similarly to one another.

Specific Knowledge Gained from the CESSMA

In addition to demonstrating that the CESSMA was effective in teaching ED and LD children about television, it is also useful to know specifically what facts and concepts were successfully taught. Identifying a curriculum's strengths and weaknesses is important to curriculum development and modification, and information about what is difficult for children to learn enhances our knowledge of their acquisition of critical viewing skills.

Table 7.1 presents a sample of the questions from the TV Knowledge test and the percent of children in the CESSMA and control groups who answered them correctly. Because the ED and LD children learned to a comparable degree, the percentages for the two schools were combined.

It appears that the more concrete the concept taught and tested, the better the curriculum gain. For example, at posttest the majority of the CESSMA group knew that broken glass on television is made out of sugar, milk on commercials contains white glue, weapons on television are not real, and apparently heavy objects may actually be very light props. The control group, however, was performing at about chance level on such questions. Unfortunately, knowledge of such technical facts did not guarantee that all children would correctly reason through their implications. For example, only about 65% of the children in the CESSMA group correctly reasoned that actors have no need of medical attention after scenes involving aggression, their injuries are fake and therefore do not hurt, and cameramen are in no danger of being struck by flying bullets during the filming of a crime drama. Although not impressive, the CESSMA group's performance on these items was better than that of the control group, which performed at chance level or worse.

Knowledge of more generalized concepts concerning the reality/fantasy components of television programming also improved after CESSMA training. For example, the control group was more likely than the CESSMA group to make the

TABLE 7.1

Sample Questions from the TV Knowledge Posttest and Follow-Up
and the Percentage of Children in the Curriculum and Control
Classes Who Correctly Answered Each Question

Test Questions[a]	Curriculum	Control	p <[b]
"$6 Million Man"			
This scene shows the bionic man punching his fist through a car windshield.			
1. If a man practices real hard, he can do everything this man can do. (No)	72	51	.01
2. Most people can punch their hand through glass and not get hurt. (No)	78	57	.01
3. The man in this show was able to break away because he is very strong. (No)	63	37	.001
4. The window on the windshield broke so easily because it was made of sugar. (Yes)	85	43	.001
5. Scientists can change a person into someone as strong as the man in this program. (No)	71	44	.001
"Cinnamon Toast Crunch Cereal"			
Cereal commercial that takes place at a children's gymnastics event.			
1. Cinnamon Toast Crunch cereal makes you better at sports than other cereals can. (No)	73	65	ns
2. People who do gymnastics like Cinnamon Toast Crunch cereal best. (No)	66	60	ns
3. The milk in this commercial was probably Elmer's glue. (Yes)	66	29	.001
"Mod Squad"			
Fight scene in this crime drama showing a man breaking a chair against his opponent.			
1. The chair broke because the man was very strong. (No)	67	50	.05
2. Most chairs would break apart in a fight like we just saw. (No)	57	34	.01
3. The man who was hit with the chair was OK right away. (Yes)	69	54	.05

TABLE 7.1
(*Continued*)

Test Questions[a]	Curriculum	Control	p <[b]
"Ghostbusters"			
Scene from the movie showing the Ghostbusters fighting with Gozor on the roof of a building.			
1. The lady could jump so high because she had special powers. (No)	69	44	.01
2. When the lady did the big jump, they had to stop the camera several times. (Yes)	69	56	ns
3. The marshmallow man was probably smaller than the people. (Yes)	61	37	.01
4. The men in this movie had to be careful not to get hurt when they used the laser guns. (No)	51	40	ns
5. The lady broke out of the statue so easily because it was made of something like sugar. (Yes)	88	62	.001
6. The rocks we saw falling off the building were probably made out of styrofoam. (Yes)	86	68	.01

[a]The correct answer for each question appears in parentheses.

[b]Chi square test was performed on each item to determine whether the percentage correct score varied significantly between the Curriculum and Control groups.

Note. From data reported in "Efficacy of a Television Literacy Curriculum for Emotionally Disturbed and Learning Disabled Children" by J. Sprafkin, L. T. Watkins, and K. D. Gadow, 1990. *Journal of Applied Developmental Psychology, 11,* pp. 225–244.

mistake of attributing characteristics of the character being portrayed to the actor or actress. Furthermore, they were more likely to have the following misperceptions: (a) television police continue to work as police off screen, (b) actors who are portrayed as siblings on television are related in real life, (c) actors are selected for roles due to their possession of special powers (e.g., superhuman strength), and (d) magical powers and super strength can be cultivated through practice and continue after the show is over.

Sadly, assessments of the situational reality of television fare never rose above chance level in either curriculum or control groups. Both groups of children were equally likely to agree that police shootouts and car chases are a common occurrence in the real world. Perhaps the cues that help the viewer to distinguish between reality and fiction are much subtler in crime dramas (on which these items were based) than in other programming (e.g., superhero, commercials).

Both curriculum and control groups seemed to be more skeptical of commercials than program material. Few children claimed that using certain products makes you perform better or makes other people like you more, whether they participated in the CESSMA or not. The CESSMA group knew more about special effects techniques utilized in commercial advertising if the techniques had been explicitly described during the curriculum lessons. Unfortunately, both groups of children were duped by ambiguous premium claims (e.g., believing a premium comes in the package when it really must be sent away for). Further training in decoding such commercial claims would certainly be in order, given that premiums are a popular advertising technique and one that often results in parent–child conflict in the supermarket (Atkin, 1975).

Concepts that were presented more carefully in the CESSMA were learned better by the children. For example, the children had a good grasp of costumes, masks, puppets, breakaways, and staged flying, all of which were thoroughly covered by the curriculum. Their understanding of magical disappearances, use of miniatures, and rapidly spliced edits, all of which were mentioned only in passing, was significantly poorer. It is likely that had there been more time spent on such concepts, the children would have mastered them as well.

Summary

Despite the behavioral and cognitive differences between ED and LD children, the CESSMA had a comparable salutary effect on their knowledge and perceptions of specific television content and an equally disappointing effect on general media attitudes and television viewing habits. Knowledge gains were maintained for at least 2 months after the curriculum. The extent of the children's improvements from the CESSMA was independent of their IQ and reading level. Not surprisingly, concept acquisition was greatest for information that was elaborated on and concrete. These findings suggest that the CESSMA is quite effective in teaching a cognitively diverse group of ED and LD children how to make more accurate judgments of media content.

THE KIDVID CRITICAL VIEWING CURRICULUM

As stated earlier, television literacy has emerged largely as a defensive reaction to a recognized social problem rather than as a positive educational and instructional tool. Educators have adopted television literacy curricula with the hopes of mediating or controlling the negative impact of commercial television. Indeed, most intervention projects available on the market for the past decade reflect contemporary researchers' preoccupation with the medium's antisocial content to the exclusion of other forms of social behavior. Most curricular materials either ignore the prosocial potential of commercial television fare and produce special instructional stimuli (e.g., Blessington, 1981; Columbia Broadcasting System,

1979; Singer & Singer, 1984; Singer, Zuckerman, & Singer, 1980; Warford, 1981; Young, 1981), or address antisocial issues in popular commercial television to the exclusion of the prosocial elements contained with the same material they condemn (e.g., Anderson, 1983; Buerkel-Rothfuss, 1978; Dorr, 1986; Lloyd-Kolkin, 1981; Murray & Salomon, 1984).

With all of the criticism of the plenitude of antisocial content on television, it is often forgotten that contemporary television also contains fairly frequent displays of socially desirable or prosocial behavior on both Saturday morning and prime-time programming (Greenberg et al., 1980; Poulos et al., 1976). However, given the nature of programming, particularly that geared toward adult audiences, it is often difficult for young children to find this prosocial content:

Prosocial fare is typically not as visually and aurally explicit as antisocial fare and is usually more ingrained in the plot of the program than the often gratuitous antisocial demonstrations. Consequently, young children who do not have the cognitive sophistication to extract these behaviors from the interweaving of the plot or who are unable to link a moral with its behavioral consequences are likely to miss a good portion of available prosocial content. (Abelman, 1987b, p. 47)

One of the primary goals of the KIDVID Critical Viewing Curriculum was to facilitate children's ability to extract the prosocial content from the context of a television program. It is a 3-week curriculum that was originally developed for intellectually average and gifted children (Abelman, 1982; Abelman & Courtright, 1983) and was expanded to incorporate LD children several years later (Abelman, 1987b, 1991b). Curricular materials were developed with the assistance of special education administrators and teachers and a panel of exceptional children, and more than 100 hours were spent watching and discussing television with small groups of gifted, LD, and nonlabeled children.

Week 1 of the curriculum is designed to increase the children's awareness of their own television viewing habits and the pro- and antisocial behaviors contained within their favorite programs. The children are taught to distinguish between program types; explore the meaning of themes, plots, and conflict; and examine the quality and quantity of prosocial and antisocial behavior in various types of programs. Activities include the keeping of a daily diary of television viewing; defining and identifying various types of television programs (see Fig. 7.3); isolating conflicts, plots, and themes within programs; and learning to identify prosocial and antisocial behaviors in popular programming.

Week 2 explores the motives and consequences of behavior and the way they are portrayed on television compared with real life. Children are expected to understand that television characters behave in very predictable ways when resolving conflict and that they are predominantly prosocial or antisocial (unlike real people who exhibit both types of behavior). Activities include generating numerous motives and consequences of a behavior as depicted on television,

TV PROGRAM TYPE
WORKSHEET

DIRECTIONS

1. Work on one page at a time.
2. Read each Element List and look at each picture carefully.
3. Decide what type of TV program is being described. It will be one of the program types listed at the bottom of the page.
4. Next to "TYPE" write in the name of the type of TV program that goes with the element list and picture.
5. Next to "EXAMPLE" give an example of that type of show -- one that you watch.

Element List

a host; prizes; people do not play characters, they play themselves; some people win and some lose; lots of lights

TYPE _____

EXAMPLE_____

Element List

on TV every weekday; same people on the show everyday; stories don't end but contiune to the next day's show; takes place in hospitals or homes

TYPE _____

EXAMPLE_____

Element List

good guys and bad guys; takes place in many different locations, indoors and outdoors; crime; violence; somebody gets caught

TYPE _____

EXAMPLE_____

Element List

one or more people talk directly to you; maps, charts and graphs; pictures of people or important things that happened that day

TYPE _____

EXAMPLE_____

TV PROGRAM LIST

DRAMA   ACTION/ADVENTURE   GAME SHOWS

      NEWS   SOAP OPERAS   TALK SHOWS

             SPORTS   COMEDY

FIG. 7.3. Activity, "TV Program Type," from the KIDVID Critical Viewing Curriculum. *Note.* From *Critical Television Viewing Curriculum: A Teacher's Manual* (p. 16), by R. Abelman, 1981. Unpublished curriculum, Cleveland State University.

identifying the motive and consequence most befitting the characters, and viewing a 30-minute program to extract the main characters, plot, theme, conflict, and form of conflict resolution.

Week 3 examines alternatives to aggressive behavior. Students are expected to realize that there are several ways to resolve conflict when motives and consequences are weighed. Activities include generating both prosocial and antisocial

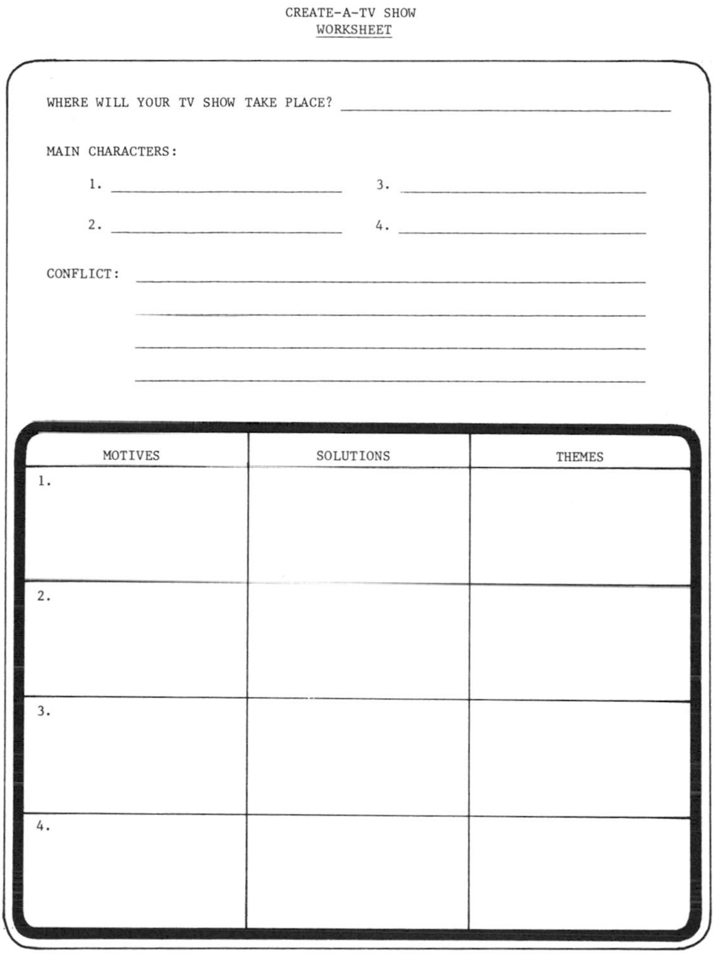

CREATE-A-TV SHOW
WORKSHEET

WHERE WILL YOUR TV SHOW TAKE PLACE? _____

MAIN CHARACTERS:

    1. _____   3. _____

    2. _____   4. _____

CONFLICT: _____

          _____

          _____

          _____

	MOTIVES	SOLUTIONS	THEMES
1.			
2.			
3.			
4.			

FIG. 7.4. Activity, "Create-A-TV Show," from the KIDVID Critical Viewing Curriculum. *Note.* From *Critical Television Viewing Curriculum: A Teacher's Manual* (p. 45), by R. Abelman, 1981. Unpublished curriculum, Cleveland State University.

solutions to problems depicted on television and creating a children's television program that includes all the components examined during the 3 weeks of the intervention (see Fig. 7.4).

The KIDVID curriculum incorporates the viewing and discussion of actual programs and excerpts from the current television season. The purpose of this is threefold:

1. To guarantee the relevancy of the instructional objectives of each activity by providing actual examples of the subject being discussed.

2. To generate a high level of interest and participation among the students by providing familiar and highly appealing stimuli.

3. To encourage the students to apply the concepts taught in the curriculum to the programs they actually watch at home, thus enhancing the generalizability of the intervention.

The selection of programs and program segments viewed in class was based on those favorite television shows and characters most commonly suggested by approximately 150 fourth-grade gifted, LD, and nonlabeled students across six elementary schools. Programs were then taped off the air. These programs plus several previously recorded episodes of favorite programs constituted the videotape materials used in the KIDVID curriculum.

Sixteen fourth-grade classrooms received the curriculum and an equal number comprised the control group. A total of 218 gifted children, 125 LD children, and 312 nonlabeled children from four schools in a medium-sized university community participated in the evaluation. Intact classrooms were assigned to either the curriculum or control condition by the respective school principals, who based their decision on scheduling and other administrative concerns and not on the ability of the students or quality of the teachers. There was no significant difference in any demographic characteristic between the conditions.

Indices were constructed to measure the children's ability to identify and label the types of prosocial behaviors portrayed on commercial television programs. As part of the KIDVID curriculum, the various prosocial behaviors were defined, discussed, and exemplified in excerpts from broadcast programming. These behaviors include:

Altruism—defined as helping behavior or giving aid to another so that the other can move toward his or her goal. It included physical assistance, instructions, helping with a task, giving advice, and giving requested or needed information. Helping behaviors aimed toward illegal acts were not considered acts of altruism.

Empathy—defined as sharing the experiences and feelings of another. The elements necessary to experience empathy included recognizing another's emotion, recognizing the other and self as separate, and feeling an emotion similar to that of the other person.

Cooperation—defined as the working together by two or more individuals to achieve interdependent goals.

Reparation—defined as behaviors intended to correct a behavior committed by the person and judged as a wrongdoing by that person. There could be several acts of reparation for a single wrongdoing, including attempts to repair physical damage, admission of a mistake, apology, attempts to ensure that the wrongdoing would be eliminated or reduced, and admission of deceit accompanied by corrective truth-telling.

Sympathy—defined as expressing positive feelings for another's plight, such as concern, compassion, pity, and caring.

Sharing—defined as the spontaneous gift or loan of one's own possessions (or anything one has) to another person.

To assess the children's ability to identify and label prosocial behavior at the termination of the curriculum intervention, they were presented with 20 actual examples of commercial television fare (ranging from 15 min to an hour in length) that were never before discussed or used in curricular activities. The children were instructed to say "stop" each time they identified a prosocial behavior. The investigator then noted the placement in the videotape where the child believed the prosocial act occurred and asked him or her to circle the label for the depicted behavior on the questionnaire. The children's responses were cross-referenced with an accurate assessment of prosocial behavior to determine the ratio of correct identification and labeling.

Finally, four questions measured children's awareness of the overall availability of prosocial and antisocial behavior on television programs. These items were:

1. How many television shows have people helping and liking each other in them?

2. How many television shows have people fighting and being mad at each other in them?

3. How many television shows that have a lot of people fighting and being mad at each other also have people helping and liking each other in them?

4. How many television shows that have a lot of people helping and liking each other also have people fighting and being mad at each other in them?

The response choices were none, few, some, many, and all (coded 1–5).

Identification of Prosocial Behaviors

Intellectually Gifted Children.   The curriculum proved to be quite effective in increasing gifted children's ability to identify prosocial behaviors within the context of commercial television programming. In particular, only 8% of the control group were able to identify more than half the prosocial behaviors in comparison with 48% of the curriculum group. Comparison of the pretest and posttest evaluations of the curriculum groups clearly shows that the intervention significantly enhanced the gifted children's ability to identify the behaviors presented to them.

Learning Disabled Children.   Much like the gifted children in the study, only 4% of the LD children in the control group were able to identify more than half of the prosocial behaviors in the sample programs. However, after the intervention, 31% of the curriculum group were able to do so. Although none of the LD children were able to identify all the behaviors (even after the 3-week curriculum), a comparison of the pretest and posttest evaluations showed a significant increase in those being able to identify more than half of the behaviors.

Nonlabeled Children.   Only 5% of the control group were able to identify more than half of the prosocial behaviors in the sample programs, which was comparable to the accuracy rate of the gifted and LD children. As a result of the intervention, 34% of the curriculum group were able to identify more than half of the behaviors. Their accuracy level was greater than that of the LD group but lower than that of the gifted children.

Awareness of Prosocial Behaviors

Intellectually Gifted Children.   A significant difference in gifted children's perception of how many television shows contain people engaging in prosocial behavior was found as a result of the curriculum. This difference was found to be based on the children's response to two of the four items. First, less than 3% of the gifted children participating in the curriculum noted that "few" or "no" television shows had prosocial behavior, compared with approximately 30% of the control group. In addition, 71% of the curriculum group indicated that "many" programs have prosocial behavior, compared with 32% of the control group. This suggests an increased awareness of prosocial behavior within programs, particularly in light of the moderate to low level of awareness revealed in the pretest.

Learning Disabled Children.   A significant difference in LD children's perception of how many television shows contain people engaging in prosocial behavior was also found. The overall significance was based on the difference in response to only one of the four items. Approximately 3% of the LD children participating in the curriculum noted that "few" television programs contained prosocial behavior, whereas 27% of the control group had a similar perception.

Nonlabeled Children.   A significant difference in nonlabeled children's perception of how many television shows contain people engaging in prosocial behavior was also found. Approximately 10% of the nonlabeled children participating in the curriculum noted that "few" television programs contained prosocial behavior, compared with 25% of the control group. Similarly, about one-third of the control group noted that "many" programs contained prosocial behavior, compared with 60% of the curriculum group.

Labeling of Prosocial Behaviors

An analysis of the pretest scores indicated no significant difference in children's ability to label prosocial behavior based on their assignment to the control or curriculum groups or their educational classification. In addition, there were no significant differences in the control groups' pretest and posttest scores. Figure 7.5 provides the summary results from the curriculum groups' pretest and posttest responses for LD, gifted, and nonlabeled children. For all children there were significant improvements in their ability to accurately label acts of altruism, empathy, cooperation, sympathy, sharing, and reparation.

Summary

The KIDVID curriculum, which was designed to teach children to recognize and understand prosocial behaviors that are portrayed on entertainment programs, has been shown to be effective with LD, gifted, and nonlabeled children. All three groups of children who participated in the 3-week curriculum were better able than controls to recognize and label prosocial behaviors presented within programs and to perceive that prosocial behaviors are commonly contained in the programs they watch.

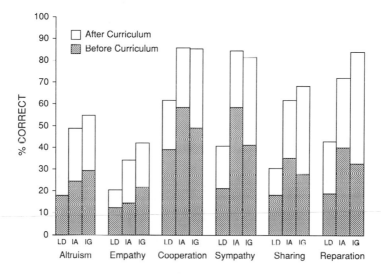

FIG. 7.5.   Percentage correct scores by learning disabled (LD), intellectually average (IA), and intellectually gifted (IG) children for labeling prosocial behaviors in television excerpts before and after exposure to the KIDVID Critical Viewing Curriculum. *Note.* Based on data reported in "TV Literacy III—The Gifted and Learning Disabled: Amplifying Prosocial Learning Through Curricular Intervention" by R. Abelman, 1991. *Journal of Research and Development in Education, 24*(4), pp. 51–60.

CONCLUSIONS

The critical viewing skills curricula discussed in this chapter were quite different in terms of their stated objectives, but both were designed to influence how children process television content. The CESSMA was found to enhance ED and LD children's knowledge about television production techniques and to sharpen their ability to discriminate between realistic and fictional content. The KIDVID curriculum improved LD and gifted children's ability to recognize and label prosocial behaviors that are contained in television fare. Unfortunately, these curriculum evaluations do not provide evidence of change in attitudes toward television or in viewing habits.

It is worth mentioning that in curriculum evaluations with regular class children, it is also common to find that knowledge gains occur in the absence of changes in attitudes (e.g., Dorr, Graves, & Phelps, 1980; Watkins, Sprafkin, Gadow, & Sadetsky, 1988) or viewing habits (e.g., Huesmann et al., 1983). Attitudes are difficult to modify and may require different methods than the acquisition of knowledge. In any case, television viewing skills curricula are valuable, even if they *only* enhance knowledge of television and the social behaviors portrayed therein. The challenge of future curriculum developers is to identify effective strategies for changing viewing habits and attitudes toward the media and for preventing undesirable reactions to television such as an antisocial behavior.

As we discussed in chapter 5, most field studies on television violence show that simply viewing television, regardless of content, can lead to increased rates of antisocial behavior compared with preexposure baseline levels. One implication of these results is that television literacy curricula should include lessons covering both aggressive and nonaggressive content, which was the case for the CESSMA curricula. However, the KIDVID curriculum takes this one step further and teaches children to recognize and evaluate specific instances of antisocial and prosocial behaviors in programs they typically view. More important, however, is the need to understand the processes involved in media reactivity so more effective television literacy curricula can be developed. As previously noted, perceptions of reality have been found to influence reactivity to aggressive media displays in laboratory settings (Feshbach, 1976; Sawin, 1981), but it remains to be shown if media literacy curricula can achieve similar outcomes in natural settings.

It is interesting to note that very few critical viewing skills curricula address social or affective learning from television. According to Dorr (1981), "television's role in affective development and functioning has not received much attention in the decade of the 1970s. Maybe its turn will come in the 1980s" (p. 344). However, this has not been the case. The majority of television literacy curricula examine the more cognitive aspects of learning from television to the exclusion of the values and social information that children can acquire from the medium.

One explanation for the emphasis on cognitive effects might be that a child's social or affective development has been traditionally reserved for family and church. The practice of providing for the social and affective needs of children in the classroom has lagged for several additional reasons (Mehrens & Lehman, 1973):

1. The post-Sputnik demand for increased intellectual competence extruded some of the school's curricular concern for student affect and social interaction. Parents prefer that the school report student progress in cognitive skills rather than in other domains.

2. Many educators believe that students who attain cognitive objectives will show a corresponding change in appropriate affective behaviors and engage in appropriate social behaviors to reach those objectives.

3. An affective response is hard to change and, even when altered, such a change is hard to measure accurately.

4. The teaching techniques for providing affective change are not nearly as well developed or successful as techniques for attaining cognitive curricular objectives.

Although these beliefs are commonly held by teachers, Mehrens and Lehman (1973) suggest that they are not necessarily true. Furthermore, other educators propose that cognitive, affective, and social skills should not be separated, but rather "approached by the classroom teacher in a concerted manner so [each dimension] is achieved by the learner as part of a unified learning situation" (Lazar, Gensley, & Gowan, 1972, p. 27).

The implementation of television literacy curricula is quite consistent with many of the criteria established for special education (Adelman & Taylor, 1986). Likewise, such curricula satisfy the guidelines set out for instructing gifted children. For example, some educators (e.g., Karnes, Shwedel, & Kemp, 1985; Karnes, Shwedel, & Williams, 1983) have suggested that a curriculum for gifted children should: (a) be based on interest and needs rather than on predetermined order or sequence of instruction; (b) access abstract and higher-level thinking processes; and (c) encourage creative and productive thinking.

There is little question that television literacy responds to these issues. Television is of interest to nearly all children and plays a significant role in their lives. Television viewing is a learned behavior (e.g., Collins, 1983; Salomon, 1981) that reinforces basic cognitive skills (e.g., determining theme, utilizing context cues, forming temporal sequences, eliciting awareness of cause and effect), requires mental energy and effort (Salomon, 1983), and provides ample avenues for abstract and critical thinking (Anderson, 1981). Furthermore, examining and evaluating social behaviors contained in television programs is an appropriate classroom activity in that the development of social skills is well ingrained in special education.

8 Instructional Applications

The use of television to educate children can be traced to the first commercial broadcasts in 1940 (see O'Bryan, 1980, for a historical perspective). However, development was slow, and it was not until 1952 that educational television (ETV) received a real boost from the federal government. In that year, the Federal Communications Commission (FCC) reserved 242 television channels (mostly UHF) for education, and the Ford Foundation of the Educational Radio and Television Center was established, which became National Educational Television (NET) in 1958. In 1953 the first ETV station was on the air, and by the end of the decade, 43 additional channels had joined its ranks. Much of the early enthusiasm for ETV was prompted by a deep concern for the quality of the American education system, and ETV was seen as a partial solution to the problem of overcrowded schools and incompetent teachers. In order to improve the efficacy of public education, it was argued that television master teachers should present the lessons, and the regular teacher should facilitate the learning process with classroom activities. In-school television instruction could be provided either by a closed-circuit system in which the central studio was located within the school (ITV) or by an ETV station. The latter is also considered ITV if the series is broadcast during school hours for in-school use (Crane, 1980; Dirr, 1980).

Early tel-lessons (ITV) were characteristically poor by commercial standards; exciting production techniques were rarely used; and many master teachers failed to come across well on television. Not surprisingly, therefore, two extensive literature reviews of research on the efficacy of ITV failed to support the superiority of television over standard classroom instruction (Kumata, 1960; Schramm, 1962). The early research also suggested that ITV was more effective with younger students (elementary school) and with certain subjects (e.g., math, science, and social studies); the same can be said to characterize the current state of the art (O'Bryan, 1980). Perhaps the most serious challenge to ITV, which also led to its ultimate demise, was from teachers. The notion that they could be replaced by a machine certainly did not sit well. "By the end of 1959, it [ITV] was falling far behind the production values of commercial broadcast television, and it is now relatively rarely used in schools" (O'Bryan, 1980, p. 9).

The early history of ETV, the other vehicle for instruction via television, was fraught with technological problems (e.g., lack of UHF receivers), scheduling difficulties, and, more importantly, an inability to generate an audience, which was true through the late 1960s. Moreover, relatively little effort had been put into children's programming. All this changed, however, with the publication of the Carnegie Commission's (1967) report, which recommended, among other things, creating a Corporation for Public Television, increasing funding for ETV, and improving the quality of children's shows to a level equivalent to that of commercial television. In 1968 the Children's Television Workshop (CTW) was formed, and its first program, "Sesame Street," which appeared in 1969, was an enormous success.[1] With adequate financial backing, state-of-the-art production techniques, quality research, educational consultants, and a professional production staff, "Sesame Street" was able to compete with commercial television programs and at the same time facilitate learning. "Sesame Street" was followed by other successes such as "The Electric Company," designed to teach beginning reading to 7- to 10-year-old children with reading problems. More recently, CTW has ventured into encouraging 8- to 12-year-olds to develop interests in science and math with series such as "3-2-1 Contact" and "Square One TV," respectively.

The way in which CTW went about planning, developing, and evaluating their shows has come to be known as "The CTW Model," which brings together expertise in "production, content, children, and pedagogy" (Mielke, 1990). Among its elements are involvement of educational experts in program development, assessment of the needs and abilities of the target audience, specification of educational goals and behavioral objectives, and empirical evaluation of production techniques and overall impact (Mates, 1980). The last element is of particular interest for the purposes of the present chapter.

The CTW model incorporates two general types of evaluations: formative and summative. Formative research is part of the process of creating a television program, and its purpose is to improve quality and effectiveness. It is conducted on a small scale, and the results are usually not published. Ideally, the program developer uses formative research to find the best match between production techniques and teaching objective. Once the content and audience have been specified, the production team can then put together rough-cut segments for in-

---

[1]"Sesame Street" is not without its critics (see, for example, Healy, 1990).

process production evaluation (see Crane, 1980). At this stage, the three priority concerns are appeal, attention, and comprehension, which can be assessed in several ways. They include eye contact with the television screen while viewing in the classroom or in a more controlled setting using a distractor method (e.g., Palmer, 1974), rating scales, selector buttons (response indicated by pressing a button), personal interviews, and stop-action or freeze-frame analyses (subject asked to recall or answer questions about a specific segment). In-process evaluations can also be conducted prior to final editing. Mates (1980) cites the making of "The Electric Company" as a good example of how formative research using eye-movement recordings was used to shape format. The data suggested that print located near the center of the screen in close proximity to dramatic action drew the greatest amount of viewer attention (O'Bryan & Silverman, 1972), as did scanning print from left to right (O'Bryan & Silverman, 1973). Formative research is an ongoing activity for long-running series such as "Sesame Street," as illustrated in Flagg's (1990) description of the research preceding the airing of the episode that explained the death of one of the characters, Mr. Hooper.

Summative research refers to the educational effectiveness of an entire series. Such research has shown, for example, that "Sesame Street" is effective in teaching preacademic skills (Ball & Bogatz, 1970; Bogatz & Ball, 1971), that "The Electric Company" teaches basic reading skills (Ball & Bogatz, 1973; Ball, Bogatz, Kazarow, & Rubin, 1974), and that "Square One TV" increases problem-solving performance (Hall, Esty, & Fisch, 1990). Unfortunately, summative research is conducted less often than formative research because program developers are more likely to direct new funds toward new productions rather than the evaluation of existing series (Crane, 1980).

When both formative and summative research is dutifully carried out and the findings are incorporated into the production process, the end product can be most satisfying, for example, "Sesame Street." However, the evaluation procedure is not without its limitations (Crane, 1980). In reality, such research is expensive and time-consuming. Moreover, the needs and demands of the funding source can clearly bias program development. There is also a built-in negative incentive in some cases to use formative research because the findings could be used by the funding source to abandon the project. Even when these evaluations are conducted, their ultimate utility often hangs on the nature of the interpersonal interactions of the production team.

Actual data on the extent to which television is used in U.S. public schools for instructional purposes are somewhat limited. The 1977 School TV Utilization Study (Dirr & Pedone, 1979) found that while 37% of all elementary and secondary school students did receive some ITV on a regular basis, the general usage pattern was limited to 1 hour per week. Elementary schools typically viewed shows directly off the air from a public television station, but secondary schools taped most of their programs for presentation at a later time. The most highly used programs were those that were also most widely broadcast on public television stations. Only 17% of the teachers surveyed had received any formal training in the use of television for instructional purposes. Another study conducted by the Corporation for Public Broadcasting (Spergel, 1979) identified more than 1,000 instructional series broadcast by public television stations. However, the basic core (i.e., broadcast by 10 or more of the 160 licensees) of instructional programs consisted of 137 series.

The early 1970s witnessed a significant increase in public attention to the ill effects of commercial television on child development and subsequent demand for more suitable programming. Because the production of appealing educational programs was extremely expensive, it was necessary for stations to pool their resources and form consortia and networks. The Agency for Instructional Television (AIT) became a pioneer in this regard by becoming a nonprofit program cooperative. AIT obtains its production funds, not from government or corporate grants, but from subscriber stations who receive free use of the programs. Programs can also be rented from AIT by nonsubscribers. AIT's mission has been to develop a variety of high-quality programs for national broadcasting and classroom use. Out of this effort came series such a "Ripples," "Inside/Out," and "Bread and Butterflies." The development of large regional networks led to a wider distribution of programs and more ambitious projects, as did the formation of the Public Broadcasting Services (PBS), which is an organization of public television stations in the United States. By 1977, PBS made 24 instructional programs available for classroom or home use with audiences ranging from preschool to college level (Carlisle, 1978).

In spite of the growth of ETV in the past three decades, O'Bryan (1980) notes that most children prefer commercial television, and the achievements of "Sesame Street" have not been equaled. Although ITV has enhanced its appeal by providing program guides for teachers (e.g., suggest ways to introduce the show and present follow-up activities to enhance learning and generalization), it is not widely used by our public schools. Nevertheless, both ETV and ITV have carved an important niche in American education as an adjunct to the learning process.

Unfortunately for the field of special education, very little has been done to meet the instructional needs of disabled children. Granted, "Sesame Street" does provide instructional segments for MR children and their parents, and "The Electric Company" is designed for poor readers; however, few programs have been developed specifically for MR, ED, or LD children. This is not so much an oversight as it is a reflection of the financial realities of producing high-quality (i.e., competitive with commercial television standards) educational programs. It is very difficult to obtain adequate financial backing for programs designed to reach small audiences; such projects are not perceived as being cost-effective (Mates, 1980).

One of the few inroads by ETV into the education of exceptional children was made by CTW with their program "Sesame Street" (see Ardi, 1977; Hayes, 1977; Kolucki, 1977). During the 1975–1976 broadcast season, CTW produced twenty-three 1- to 3-min segments designed specifically for preschool MR children, and the segments were aired during the first 20 min of each Wednesday show. The teaching segments were based upon the "Families Play to Grow" program of the Joseph P. Kennedy, Jr., Foundation and addressed motor, cognitive, and affective development. Generally, the segments showed a Down's syndrome child engaged in activities with nondisabled peers. During the early formative stages of developing these special segments, educational consultants suggested that they should be slow-paced, visually sparse (eliminate distracting stimuli), verbally succinct (avoid overload of dialogue), live action (no abstract animation), and repetitious. It was also suggested that music was helpful, as was modeling social reinforcement (i.e., nondisabled preschoolers were socially accepting of the MR child).

As is characteristic of CTW, formative research was conducted to determine if the segments for the disabled were achieving their intended objectives (Ardi, 1977). In one study, specially prepared test tapes were presented to nondisabled preschoolers attending a day-care program ($N = 45$; age: $M = 4.3$ years) and to MR children enrolled in a special school ($N = 91$; chronological age range = 4–12 years; developmental age range = 18 months to 8 years). The results showed that both groups were very attentive, regardless of the length of the segment. Interestingly, the MR group was more involved in the programs than the nonretarded children, as evidenced by moving to the music, calling out letters and numbers, and engaging in imitating the activity on the screen. Also, the most visually complex segments were also the ones that drew the most attention and participation. Comprehension was also assessed through individual interviews, and it was found that the MR group had an excellent understanding of the "Families Play to Grow" segments. In order to increase the utility of these segments, CTW also disseminates information to caregivers about how to interact with the MR child prior to, during, and following the broadcast (Kolucki, 1977).

EXCEPTIONAL CHILDREN

There are numerous explanations why television is, or should be, an effective instructional tool for ED, LD, and MR people (see, for example, Altman & Talkington, 1971; Baran, 1973; Barber-Smith & Reilly, 1977; Edwards, 1976; Elias, 1983; Goldstein, 1964; Solomon, 1976a, 1976b; Striefel, 1972). Perhaps the most common is that watching television in general is inherently motivating. Many people have commented that highly inattentive and disruptive children will sit and watch television for extended periods of time. In the special education classroom, motivation is generally inferred from the fact that television-oriented classroom fare generates higher levels of on-task behavior, less disruptiveness, greater eye contact with lesson materials, more students' participation, or some combination of these variables. Because the use of media is often a novelty or break from the standard routine, it is unclear exactly what mechanism accounts for this seemingly enhanced performance. Laboratory studies of media effects, even in severely impaired MR and ED subjects, show that disabled children are very attentive to television (e.g., Grieve & Williamson, 1977; Striefel & Smeets, 1974) even when audiovisual distractors are present (e.g., Gadberry et al., 1981). This apparent heightened state of attention is often presumed to be important because attention deficits are, or have been, etiologically linked to the learning problems of MR (e.g., Zeaman & House, 1963) and LD (e.g., Douglas & Peters, 1979) children.

An even more compelling indication of television's appeal to disabled children is its effectiveness as a reinforcer. In one study, Greene and Hoats (1969) showed that a MR child would increase his work rate to prevent distortion in a TV program. Similarly, a number of investigators have found that severely disabled children will depress keys or buttons in order to watch media material (e.g., Friedlander, Wetstone, & McPeek, 1974; Rynders & Friedlander, 1972; Striefel & Smeets, 1974). Moreover, this behavior appears to be fairly resistant to satiation (e.g., Striefel & Smeets, 1974). Perhaps the most interesting study of this aspect of television was conducted by Dorow (1976). She investigated whether televised elementary music lessons would be an effective reinforcer for completion of math problems. Seventeen nonambulatory educable mentally retarded (EMR) residents (age: $M = 20$ years) with kindergarten- to first-grade-level arithmetic skills completed arithmetic problems during 3-minute work periods. At the end of each period, those who had completed at least one problem correctly were allowed to watch a 10-minute videotape, whereas those who did not were returned to their living units. It was found that the videotapes were an effective reinforcer for arithmetic performance. Moreover, comparison between pretest and posttest Music Listening Skills Test scores showed a significant increase in correct answers.

It is clear that viewing television is a reinforcing experience for many children. However, as we all know, not all television programs are equally appreciated. For example, investigators have actually designed procedures to increase television viewing and knowledge retention for nonpreferred programs such as commercial news broadcasts (Keilitz, Tucker, & Horner, 1973; Phillips, Phillips, Fixsen, & Wolf, 1971; Wildman & Kelly, 1980).

Another major justification for the use of television with disabled children relates to the nature of their learning problems and the characteristics of the medium. In general, it is often noted that television can be used to increase the salience of important task-related stimuli, decrease or minimize distracting or task-irrelevant stimuli, and provide the necessary repetition (without fatiguing the instructor) for skill acquisition. Although this sounds very well and good, it is a fact that very little empirical research has explored these applications of television. Television is also efficient because it reduces the amount of individual student–teacher contact and is amenable to an effective teaching strategy, namely, modeling. Not surprisingly, each disability is also associated with a somewhat different rationale for media instruction. In the case of the MR children, for example, their responsiveness to modeling (Baran, 1973; Striefel, 1972), need for repetition, lack of adequate socialization, and attention deficits all have television applications. For LD children, television has appeal because it provides multisensory input (e.g., Reilly & Barber-Smith, 1982; see also Nasser & McEwen, 1976, for a review of research with nondisabled individuals), which is an important component of special education folklore. For ED children, a group that is generally unresponsive to traditional teaching methods, the use of television offers considerable potential for the teaching of social skills (Elias, 1983). This medium not only holds the child's attention, but can be used to present lessons about interpersonal relations by employing teaching dialogue similar to everyday conversations (i.e., interactions between characters). Moreover, for ED children, "environmental inputs are often inconsistent and less salient than those portrayed through television" (p. 36).

Much of the interest in instructional applications for the media can be traced directly to the research literature on modeling. Early studies showed little difference in the efficacy of film-mediated versus live model presentations (Bandura, 1969; Sarason & Ganzer, 1969), and additional research found that modeling in television presentations was an effective strategy for teaching or prompting a variety of prosocial and academic behaviors to students in regular classes. Other investigations demonstrated that exceptional children were also responsive to instruction based on modeling procedures (e.g., Altman & Talkinton, 1971; Lovaas, Berberich, Perloff, & Schaeffer, 1966; Paloutzian, Hasazi, Striefel, & Edgar, 1971; Sarason, 1968; Stephan, Stephano, & Talkington, 1973).

For these and other reasons, it is generally believed that the use of television in instructional settings is an effective teaching strategy for exceptional children. However, its use is also associated with certain disadvantages as well. The most critical flaw is that it does not interact with the learner by providing feedback about his or her behavior. The inclusion of postviewing activities, such as discussion (e.g., Baran, 1977; Elias, 1983; Sprafkin & Rubinstein, 1982; Wildman & Kelly, 1980) or supplementary academic experiences (e.g., Kolucki, 1977), may be necessary to effect behavioral change with media-oriented instruction (e.g., Mates, 1980; Parker, 1970). A second major disadvantage is the enormous cost of producing commercially comparable programs, especially for limited audiences. At the present time, it is inconceivable that there could be a commercial television-grade ETV series designed specifically for either ED, LD, or MR children. Although ITV solves some of the problems of viewer choice (e.g., because the student is required to watch, "commercially quality" may be less of an issue), it is still expensive.

Formal Characteristics

Perhaps one of the most striking ironies in the literature on the instructional uses of television with disabled children is the meager amount of research on the effects of various media production techniques, also called formal characteristics or formal features, on knowledge and skill acquisition (see chapter 4). Formal characteristics include things such as character representation (e.g., live actor, animated figure), chromatic qualities (color or black-and-white), and production techniques (e.g., close-ups, zooms, camera cuts, and so forth). Many have commented that such investigations should be conducted (e.g., Allen, 1975; DiVesta, 1975), whereas others have noted that special video techniques could be used to increase the salience of task-relevant cues (e.g., Lesser, 1972) or enhance attention to the program. Some investigators have questioned the assumption that the facilitation of attending behavior via production techniques necessarily leads to increased learning (e.g., Friedrich & Stein, 1973). For example, media techniques may actually distract the child from the educational content and inhibit comprehension. One study with nondisabled children found that recall of story content was greater for a film without camera cuts than for a film with frequent cuts (Salomon & Cohen, 1977). However, another study that investigated the effects of fast- and slow-paced humorous inserts found that humorous inserts not only increased attention but also facilitated comprehension (Bryant, Boynton, & Wolf, 1980). A computer search of the research literature identified only seven studies of media formal characteristics that involved either ED, LD, or MR individuals. Each is described here in chronological order.

Mentally Retarded Individuals. Rynders and Friedlander (1972) investigated preference for color film versus black-and-white slides versus an out-of-focus slide in institutionalized severely MR children. The slide sequence was composed of still shots from the film, which showed caregivers interacting with a young resident. Data analysis revealed that the film was clearly preferred over the slide presentation and the neutral stimulus. In fact, the response pattern of only one child failed to conform to this finding.

Striefel (1974) investigated preference for various formal characteristics in MR children in a residential facility. Subjects were separated into two groups, a higher functioning or educable mentally retarded (EMR) group and a lower functioning or trainable mentally retarded (TMR) group. During a baseline phase, subjects were exposed to episodes of "Sesame Street," "Mister Rogers' Neighborhood," and "Captain Kangaroo" (see Striefel & Smeets, 1974) to determine which show each subject favored. Four experimental conditions were generated for each show: black-and-white, color, audio only, and video only. The results showed that both groups of children enjoyed watching television. However, the higher level group clearly showed preference for specific television programs, but the lower functioning group did not. Moreover, although the EMR group preferred television shows in color, the TMR group favored black-and-white. None of the children preferred audio only or video only to audio–video presentations. Striefel and Smeets state that training tapes for the EMR students should be in color with different tapes for each session when multiple exposure to the learning activity is necessary. TMR students seem to prefer black-and-white and do not satiate with multiple presentations of the same tape.

Striefel and Eberl (1974) compared the relative efficacy of live versus videotape models to induce imitative behavior. Subjects were six MR institutionalized adolescents. The behaviors to be imitated were simple arm and hand gestures that were presented by either a live adult male model, a videotaped adult model (same person as the live model), or a videotaped child model. The findings indicated a high level of imitation with the live model for all subjects. The videotape models were also effective in inducing imitation in the female subjects, but less so for the males.

Stephens and Ludy (1975) found that a lesson using motion pictures was superior to both slides and live demonstrations in teaching institutionalized MR children action concepts. They speculated that the film instruction was superior because the film "(a) depicts the actual action in process, (b) presents the concepts in a systematic and relatively simple format, (c) effectively gains and keeps the children's attention, and (d) may be less emotionally laden, because the pictures instead of the teacher are the focus of attention" (p. 280).

Grieve and Williamson (1977) conducted two studies that involved both nonretarded and institutionalized MR children and evaluated the relative efficacy of color versus black-and-white presentations on story comprehension of nationally televised cartoon shows designed for preschool children ("Barnaby," "Joe," "Chigley," and "Camberwick Green" [British television]). In the first experiment, there were no statistically significant differences in either attention to or comprehension of television programs presented in color or black-and-white. Moreover, the degree of comprehension for both MR (high comprehension group) and nonretarded children was equivalent. Also, although the nonretarded youngsters were more attentive to the television shows than the MR youths, the latter attended from 68% (low comprehension) to 84% (high comprehension) of the total viewing time. The MR children maintained their attention throughout the 10- to 15-minute viewing period. The investigators noted that collectively these data suggest that audiovisual presentations on television monitors are a viable mode of instruction. In their second experiment, which employed a different group of subjects, they tried to determine if the superiority of mixed (auditory and visual presentations) over auditory presentations was due to redundancy or the visual aspect and concluded that the data supported the latter.

Nathanson (1977) conducted a fairly elaborate analysis of formal characteristics and attention with MR adolescents enrolled in a special day school. Subjects were randomly assigned to one of two conditions: color or black-and-white presentation. The teenagers in each condition were exposed to equivalent versions of the cartoon "Me and the Monsters" that were prepared using three different production techniques: (a) live action film with actors; (b) a pixilation film with dolls ("rapid cutting between still shots achieved by single-frame shooting," p. 26); and (c) the actual cartoon. A special effects film that served as a distractor was played simultaneously with each of the three production techniques. Nathanson found that although black-and-white presentations had greater attention value than color, differences among the three production techniques were not statistically significant. However, there was a suggestion that live action was more attention inducing.

In what is certainly one of the most exemplary studies in the area of television and exceptional individuals, Gadberry et al. (1981) examined the effects of formal characteristics (camera cuts and music) on both attention and skill acquisition (imitation) in institutionalized MR adults. They were interested in both behaviors because as Friedrich and Stein (1973) had commented, media-induced enhancement of attention does not necessarily imply a facilitation of learning. The media consisted of six films that depicted helping scenes (e.g., help carry heavy packages); the films were later transferred onto videotape and presented in black-and-white on the television monitor. Data analysis revealed that overall attention to the videotapes was high (69%), with no significant differences between media conditions. However, selective attention was affected by camera cuts (but not by music). When camera cuts occurred with high frequency, they resulted in reduced selective attention to relevant content features. Similarly, camera cuts also had an adverse effect on verbal imitation, but, interestingly, did not alter motor imitation. Based on the findings from this study, Gadberry et al. (1981) stated that:

> Television designed for retarded viewers should minimize media features, particularly those that have no inherent relevance to content. Modeling programs should emphasize clarity, comprehensibility, salience, and appeal of content rather than using media features to enhance attention artificially. The danger of disrupting selective attention to content and, therefore, the subsequent imitation of the models, is too great a risk. (p. 314)

Learning Disabled Children.   In the only study that employed exceptional children whose disability was not mental retardation, Hill (1982) investigated the effects of five television production techniques on attention (eye contact) and knowledge acquisition in LD children. Subjects ($N = 112$) were randomly assigned to experimental (9-minute science program that contained five production techniques and flat pictures) and control (9-minute science program containing flat pictures) conditions. There were two chronological age groups per condition. The results showed that for both age groups, eye contact and knowledge of science concepts was significantly greater for the experimental versus the control condition.

Summary.   It is difficult to draw very many conclusions from the research on the formal characteristics of television and exceptional children. Most of the studies have focused on MR individuals, and the evidence suggest that they: (a) like to watch television; (b) prefer black-and-white to color or show no preference (particularly the TMR group); and (c) show little or no differential reaction to mode of character representation (film with actors, animation, live demonstration). In addition to these findings, three other comments can be made about this area of research. The most obvious is that almost all of the studies have been conducted with MR people in either residential facilities or special day schools. This probably reflects the fact that the conduct of laboratory research with public school children in special education settings is a much greater hassle than with institutionalized populations. Granted, there is a compelling need to formulate effective educational procedures for these people, but the same could be said for EMR, LD, and ED children. Second, when one considers the number of relevant media, subject, task, and setting variables, one can only lament that none of the research in this area is programmatic. Third, considering the enormous brouhaha over the educational potential of television and its touted strengths, why has there been so little research on the identification of specific instructional characteristics peculiar to the media and their exploitation in classroom learning?

Academic Subjects

The basic literature on television and academic skills consists of the following types of articles: (a) discussion of why the media should be effective with exceptional students (Barber-Smith & Reilly, 1977; Goldstein, 1964; Spradlin, 1966; Striefel, 1972); (b) descriptions of academically oriented programs that used media (Barber-Smith & Reilly, 1977; Lombardi & Poole, 1968; Solomon, 1976a, 1976b); (c) reports of studies designed to evaluate the effectiveness of media in facilitating academic achievement (Hargis, Gickling, & Mahmoud, 1975; Reilly & Barber-Smith, 1982); and (d) research on procedures to increase television viewing (Keilitz et al., 1973; Phillips, Phillips, Fixsen, & Wolf, 1971; Wildman & Kelly, 1980). There are few articles on this topic, and it would be an understatement to say that the empirical base for the efficacy of media in academic instruction for exceptional children is limited.

Curriculum Suggestions.   Much of the material written on the instructional applications of the media with exceptional children consists of descriptions of activities that have apparent face validity but that are not empirically evaluated. In some cases, the investigators attempted to determine if the intended audience learned anything from the media presentation by way of pretest and posttest evaluations, but no control or comparison groups were employed. Only a few representative examples from this literature are presented here.

Solomon (1976a, 1976b) described a television-based reading program for

LD and MR students that employed videotapes and corresponding scripts from popular commercial television shows. The scripts were used to teach reading and reading-related skills, whereas television viewing was employed as a motivation device. Although Solomon described a variety of interesting activities and alluded to an evaluation of the program conducted by the Philadelphia School System (which found statistically and educationally significant gains in vocabulary, comprehension, and total reading scores on the California Achievement Test), it is very difficult to evaluate the specific effects of television because details of the study are not reported and the intervention appears to have been multifaceted.

One example of a pretest/posttest evaluation of a media program that employed no comparison or control group is a film development project by Longhi, Follett, Bloom, and Armstrong (1975). They describe the making of a film for EMR adolescents about the legal consequences of drinking alcoholic beverages when underage and the potential hazards of driving while intoxicated. This article is instructive because it implies that educational media for disabled students should be formally evaluated, and, more importantly, it shows how feedback from the film's intended audiences can improve the effectiveness of the media.

Efficacy Studies with Comparisons Groups.   Educators have discussed the educational applications of the media in teaching special education children for more than 3 decades. In view of this, it will no doubt come as a shock to some to know that a computer search of the relevant literature located only two efficacy studies that employed some type of experimental control (as compared with investigations that consist of a pretest/posttest assessment of a media presentation(s) on academic performance with an "experimental" group only). As for relative efficacy studies that compare media instruction with another intervention (other than the standard classroom fare), there are none. Moreover, because media is generally used as a component of an instructional "package," its individual contribution to the overall effectiveness of the educational program is generally unknown.

Hargis et al. (1975) evaluated the effectiveness of ITV in teaching sight words to eight school-identified LD students (7–9 years old). The children were exposed to one 30-minute period of "The Electric Company" per day for 32 consecutive school days. The sight words that comprised the dependent measure were separated into four groups: Group 1, sight words that appeared in the television shows and in the Dolch Basic Sight Words list; Group 2, sight words that appeared in the broadcast; Group 3, 15 sight words from the Dolch list that appeared in the broadcast; Group 4, 30 words of equivalent difficulty to those in Group II but not shown in the broadcast. Four weeks after the last showing of "The Electric Company," all children were tested on sight-word recognition. Comparisons between Group I and Group III and between Group II and IV were nonsignificant. In other words, sight-word acquisition from the television presentation was not markedly greater than from incidental learning. The majority of the sight words in the former two groups were identified correctly, while the majority in the latter two groups were not recognized. Interestingly, all eight students failed to recognize the word "electric," which appeared at least 64 times during the television presentation.

Based on the notion that media that present information through multiple sensory (e.g., auditory and visual) channels simultaneously increase sensory input and facilitate decoding processes, Reilly and Barber-Smith (1982) conducted a study to evaluate the utility of captioned films for the deaf as a teaching tool for LD students. They used the captioned film "Three Stone Blades," which was produced on a primary reading level. There were four conditions, one class per condition. In each class there were seven students, age 13–15 years, with second- and third-grade reading levels. Of the words presented in the story, 25 words (target words) were selected as a pretest of word recognition skills. Each class was assigned to a different treatment condition: (a) Class 1 saw the film with the teacher noting target words, which was followed by a second viewing without interruption; (b) Class 2 read the script, and the teacher had the students read each target word aloud, listen to the definition, and underline it, which was followed by a second reading without interruption; (c) Class 3 read the script with teacher instruction (same as Class 2) followed by seeing the film with teacher instruction (same as Class 1); and (d) Class 4 served as a no-treatment control. Pretest and posttest scores for each class were as follows: Class 1 (58% vs. 77%), Class 2 (21% vs. 50%), Class 3 (43% vs. 84%), and Class 4 (34% vs. 34%). In spite of obvious methodological limitations and no formal data analysis, the authors go on to suggest that the Federal Library of Captioned Films for the Deaf be made available for all disabled children, state departments of education and the Public Broadcasting Corporation develop libraries of captioned films and/or videotapes, and the Public Broadcasting Corporation provide satellite transmission of these films to public schools.

Carefully selected spots from "Sesame Street" have been effectively used to teach manual sign language concepts to MR students (Watkins, Sprafkin, & Krolikowski, 1990). A large percentage of the MR population have communicative deficits such that manual signs are taught to replace or augment oral speech. In this study 35 TMR students, ranging in age from 6 to 21 years and with an average IQ of 35, participated in a signing curriculum as part of their regular speech therapy over the course of 1 month. Some words were taught by (a) the speech therapist only (e.g., juice, lion), (b) the therapist and reinforced by "Sesame Street" spots that featured those signs (e.g., eggs, turtle), (c) the "Sesame Street" spots only (e.g., milk, spider), and (d) neither method (e.g., dog, doctor). There were 10 lessons, each about 10 minutes long. The "Sesame Street" viewing sessions lasted about 3 minutes. The children were tested before and after the curriculum on their expressive and receptive vocabulary. All three methods of teaching resulted in significant increases in both spoken and manual sign production of the targeted words compared with control items that were not taught. The therapist-only and the therapist-plus-video methods yielded significantly higher sign production scores than the video-only method. Receptive vocabulary was not significantly improved by the intervention.

These results suggest that video presentations may enhance vocabulary learning in MR individuals and may provide a useful teaching aid within the context of a comprehensive communication training program. The 10 lessons represented less than 2 hours of teaching time, more than one-third of which was television viewing. From this the average student learned to produce an additional three signs over his or her pretest performance. Viewing the "Sesame Street" spots as a review activity was equally effective as therapist-directed practice. However, whereas the video-only method resulted in some sign acquisition, it was less effective than the therapist-introduced method. These results are even more encouraging when one considers that the video materials from "Sesame Street" were not created for the MR population and were not ideal on many counts. For example, the spots contained significant background clutter; the pacing of the instruction was too rapid; the referents for what was being signed was not always shown; instructions or close-ups on how to position the hands were lacking; and audience participation was not prompted. Thus, the spots violated many of the accepted pedagogical principles for teaching MR individuals. Despite these limitations, the "Sesame Street" spots were effective with this MR population, in terms of both their educational impact and appeal.

One of the most important implications of this instructional application of television is that it provides teachers and therapists with some relief from the repetitive aspects of the instructional process, thus allowing them proportionately more time to stress the dynamic interactions that are so important to truly functional language use. An important side effect of the use of video for review is that other caregivers, such as teachers, aides, and parents who watch the video along with the students, receive instruction in basic signing, thus promoting continuity to the world outside the speech therapy session, to the classroom and home. Given that MR children are attentive to television and are slow to satiate to the same program material (Striefel & Smeets, 1974), the use of video to provide repetition and practice in language-related skills seems a promising avenue deserving additional attention by educators.

External Procedures to Enhance Television.   Some researchers have explored external procedures to enhance the educational impact of broadcast television (e.g., Keilitz et al., 1973; Phillips et al., 1971; Wildman & Kelly, 1980). In this context, "external" refers to manipulation of the learning environment compared with actual modifications of the television program per se (e.g., content, formal characteristics, and so forth). In one study, Phillips et al. (1971) used a token economy to increase both viewing and recall of information from television newscasts. Briefly, the subjects were adjudicated juvenile offenders who were wards of the county and assigned to Achievement Place, a residential facility that operated on a token economy. Youths earned and lost points (which could be exchanged for privileges) for appropriate and inappropriate behavior, respectively. In their television study, the subjects were asked questions (fill in the blank) about current events based on a particular nightly news broadcast. The results showed that earning points contingent on the number of correct answers on a news quiz significantly increased accuracy scores and television viewing. Moreover, as the value of the point system increased (i.e., larger number of points could be earned), so did television viewing. The condition that contained both gaining points for a high level of accuracy and losing points for poor performance was the most effective in enhancing accuracy and viewing (nearly 100%).

Keilitz et al. (1973) also investigated commercial television newscasts with regard to increasing the accuracy of verbal statements in three institutionalized MR adolescents. Newscasts were of two types: massed news (entire show as presented, followed by verbal discussion) and distributed news (each news item followed by verbal discussion). The investigators found that both temporal distribution of news presentations and reinforcement procedures improved verbal statements about news broadcasts.

Wildman and Kelly (1980) conducted a study to determine if television watching and television watching plus discussion increased current affairs awareness in MR adolescents in a short-term placement residential facility. The media consisted of a commercial television nightly news show. The findings indicated that although simply being required to watch newscasts in a group setting produced only slight gains in quiz performance, brief structured group discussions in conjunction with television viewing substantially increased accuracy on quiz questions.

Studies such as these suggest that although many educators consider television-presented lessons to be highly motivating, various instructional techniques commonly employed in educational settings can be used to effectively enhance learning. Although educators often preselect television programs and other media on the basis of their appeal to children, it is conceivable that heavy or repeated use could lead to a reduction in its reinforcing properties or instructional utility. Interestingly, there is little or no research on the relationship between program preference (liked vs. disliked shows) and learning or on the use of various teaching techniques (e.g., contingent reinforcement) to enhance media efficacy with exceptional children.

Other Instructional Areas

In addition to academic and social skills (see chapter 5), researchers and educators have explored the application of media in teaching a variety of skills and concepts to exceptional children. One example is vocational skills. Retzlaff (1973) described a project in which videotapes were made of actual job stations in industrial situations and distributed to classes for adolescent EMR, LD, and orthopedically impaired students. The program was described as being highly effective, but there was no formal analysis of treatment effects or the contribution of media to the total program. Ferguson and Silberberg (1979) also described a school program for ED and LD students designed to teach job-related behaviors (prevocational skills) using videotapes. In this case, however, the students themselves served as models in the media presentations. The authors noted that there was marked improvement in attendance and classroom behavior, but these were only subjective impressions.

Self-help skills and preacademic skills are other areas of media application, usually with institutionalized MR children. One residential facility used the commercial television show "Around the Bend" with apparent success with TMR adolescents (Program profits, 1971–72). This show was preferred over "Sesame Street" because the former allowed the youths to develop a continuing relationship with one specific character, and the latter's action was too rapid. Another residential facility for severely and profoundly retarded people used their own closed-circuit cable television system to develop and present a television series called "Hi Ho Time" (Haynes, 1978). The show, which relies heavily upon music, features different students in each program and teaches preacademic and self-help skills. It was deemed a success because it held attention better than network programs, the residents liked it and frequently participated in sing-along and game activities, and it raised self-esteem. No formal program evaluation was reported.

Ross (1970) conducted a sophisticated evaluation of several aspects of modeling with learning and comprehension tasks that have instructional application for MR students. She examined the effects of a valued (associated with experimenter praise) versus neutral model, individual versus group participation, and intentional (child encouraged to learn model's behavior) versus incidental (child not encouraged to learn model's behavior) learning. The results showed that EMR youngsters learned more when the model was someone they liked (i.e., model was associated with rewards). Moreover, observational data collected 1 week later indicated that generalization was also greater for children who observed the valued model. In other words, they were more likely to exhibit the model's behavior in the classroom. Ross notes that her procedure "provided considerable variety, it involved a medium that EMR children enjoy, it could serve as a supplementary device to relieve the teacher of direct teaching, and it would be particularly useful in tasks where repeated demonstrations of one set of materials are necessary" (p. 706).

In one of the few studies that sought to establish the relative efficacy of various teaching techniques, Stephan et al. (1973) assigned 33 institutionalized EMR to one of three conditions: live modeling, videotape modeling, or no-treatment control. The task involved using the telephone to include identification of the parts of a telephone, dialing the police, and taking a message for someone. The results showed that the performance of subjects in both live and videotape conditions was superior to the control group, but there was no statistically significant difference between the two treatment conditions.

Fox, Eveleigh, and Campbell (1977) demonstrated that a videotape of a child identifying numbers correctly could enhance number recognition by three female children with Down's syndrome (age 6–7 years). Each child was videotaped correctly identifying the numbers 1 through 30 with the assistance of her teacher. Each number was later superimposed on the upper right-hand quadrant of the screen. Number competency was greater for all three subjects during the latter.

A computer search located two studies that pertained to play behavior. In one investigation, Walters and Willows (1968) evaluated imitative response to aggressive and nonaggressive (i.e., socially appropriate) videotaped models in institutionalized ED and nondisabled children. An additional group watched individually a 4-minute videotape and was subsequently observed for 6 minutes in a playroom. With regard to nonaggressive solitary play behavior, the investigators found that the ED children were less likely to imitate the nonaggressive models than the nondisabled subjects. Unfortunately, because there was no ED control group (i.e., exposed to a neutral videotape) or pretape observation period, it was not possible to determine if the nonaggressive videotape actually led to an increase in appropriate imitative play or whether the two ED groups were behaviorally comparable prior to treatment. Interestingly, comparisons of the three nondisabled groups suggested that observation of the aggressive model also increased the incidence of nonaggressive behavior. The authors suggested that just watching the tape of the models interacting with the toys, regardless of how the models interacted, probably lessens inhibitions about playing with toys, which in turn leads to more activity.

In an interesting and unusual case study, Dowrick and Raeburn (1977) used a self-modeling videotape to induce appropriate play behavior in a 4-year-old hyperactive boy who was receiving haloperidol, a neuroleptic drug. The "treatment" tape was an edited version of the patient's play behavior on medication, whereas the control tape consisted of a sequence of his normal off-medication behavior. Each tape was of 6 minutes duration (a 3-minute sequence played twice). The experimental design was as follows: baseline (off medication), medication, medication plus control film, medication plus treatment film, medication plus control film, off-medication plus control film, off-medication plus treatment film, follow-up (treatment film), and follow-up (no treatment). Analysis of direct observation data suggested that both medication and the self-modeling videotape influenced play behavior positively, and the effect of the media presentation even in the off-medication condition was clinically significant.

Osborne, Kiburz, and Miller (1986) used a videotaping procedure to reduce self-injurious behavior in a 15-year-old boy who was classified as behavior disordered according to local school district criteria. Videotaping was used to show the adolescent the exact behaviors that were targeted for intervention. The simple act of viewing himself engaging in self-injurious behavior in combination with a desire to stop resulted in a marked reduction in this behavior.

Additional Applications

Media have been used in other ways that are related to instruction, a few of which are briefly noted here. One is to gauge the efficacy of treatment and monitor therapeutic progress. Evans and Clifford (1976), for example, discussed how videotapes were helpful in shaping the instructional intervention for three ED preschool children with communication deficits. Videotapes were used to make records of child behavior that were subsequently used for identifying and diagnosing specific problems, guiding treatment formulation, and evaluating response to instruction.

In a somewhat unusual study with a similar group of children (ED preschoolers with language deficits), Friedlander et al. (1974) used broadcast television sequences from "Sesame Street" to identify receptive language deficits. To do this, they formulated four conditions: (a) natural soundtrack (Channel 1 and 2); (b) natural soundtrack (Channel 1) and natural soundtrack plus low interference (Channel 2); (c) natural soundtrack (Channel 1) and natural soundtrack plus medium interference (Channel 2). The children were presented with selector buttons that allowed them to choose the soundtrack they preferred. There were three groups of subjects: nondisabled controls (N = 15), moderately disturbed (N = 7), and severely disturbed (N = 6). Friedlander et al. (1974) found that the control group clearly rejected the increasingly unintelligible soundtrack, whereas the moderately disturbed children rejected it marginally at extreme levels. The severely disturbed children, however, did not reject the garbled soundtrack at all.

Videotaping has also been used in psychotherapeutic (e.g., Mallery & Navas, 1982) and special education (e.g., Efron & Veenendaal, 1988; Ferguson & Silberberg, 1979) settings with disabled children (ED, LD, or both) to facilitate self-awareness and thus to promote more effective social interaction. This differs in a very special way from the self-modeling studies that have already been discussed (e.g., Dowrick & Raeburn, 1977; Haynes, 1978). In the latter, students model appropriate (and sometimes inappropriate) behavior to demonstrate what should be done. Self-awareness videotapes, however, seek to portray more spontaneous interactions in order to provide the student/patient with specific information about his or her behavior. This is almost always followed by some form of group discussion or group therapy session.

The last instructional application noted here pertains to the use of television to administer psychoeducational tests. Most of the research on this topic is with nondisabled children (e.g., Fargo et al., 1967; Hopkins, Lefever, & Hopkins, 1967), although some investigators have explored this procedure with MR (e.g.,

Guarnaccia, Daniels, & Sefick, 1975) and LD (e.g., Abkarian, King, & Krappes, 1987; Jacobs, 1979) children. It is noteworthy that automated or media testing was found to be equally (Guarnaccia et al., 1975) or more (Jacobs, 1979) effective than conventional testing procedures with disabled children. In spite of the obvious advantages of media-presented tests, this idea really has never caught on in a big way. The evaluation procedure for children being considered for special education services poses some unique challenges to the practicality of television testing, not the least of which is the partial or total loss of clinical impressions generated from the testing process, the management of behavior problems, and the formation of special adaptations for various disabling conditions. Nevertheless, the notion of an automated school psychologist has not been lost now that computer technology has entered the arena of educational fad and fantasy.

In one study, videotape was used to present stimulus materials as part of a psychological test of social skills development. Hughes and Hall (1985) developed a role-play test, the Behavioral Test of Interpersonal Competence for Children, to evaluate a variety of social skills, which they characterized as positive (e.g., giving a compliment) and negative (e.g., responding to unfair criticism) assertion skills.

Interactive Video

Although the primary focus of this book is broadcast and cable television, it would be an oversight not to comment on a new and exciting development, interactive video, an instructional technology that marries educational television with computer-assisted instruction. It has been defined as "a system of communication in which recorded video information is presented under computer control to active 'users,' who not only see and hear the pictures, words, and sounds, but also make choices affecting the pace and sequence of the presentation" (Hoekema, 1983, p. 4).

One such program, the Interactive Video Social Skills (IVSS) training program, was developed to teach social skills to mildly disabled children to enhance their adjustment to mainstreaming. The program taught children how to use appropriate phrasing, intonation, and body language in social exchanges. When used with ED and LD elementary school children who attended a resource room, it led to greater acceptance by nondisabled peers compared with a no-treatment control group (Thorkildsen, 1985).

Another application of interactive video technology with disabled children is Project LIVE, an acronym for Learning through Interactive Video Education. This curriculum series was developed at the University of Oregon to enhance the quality of life for disabled individuals and provide instruction on relating to others, asking for help, solving personal problems, and being responsible. Interspersed throughout the video are pauses during which the teacher reinforces the previously presented point. Project LIVE has been used extensively with MR and LD individuals and has been shown to be quite successful (Browning, Nave, White, & Barkin, 1985; Browning & White, 1986).

The strengths of interactive video for disabled children are many. One, realistic problems and solutions can be presented clearly and in a compelling manner on a video monitor. Two, reading skills are not required to learn new concepts or skills. Three, the learning is self-paced. Four, children are generally interested in watching television-presented material.

CONCLUSIONS

Although there has been an enormous growth in educational and instructional television during the past 4 decades, very little programming is designed specifically for exceptional children and the remediation of their academic cognitive, social, or motoric deficits. Granted, programs such as "Sesame Street" do periodically include segments for and with disabled children; AIT does provide media-related instructional materials for many programs to be used with disabled children; and special education personnel do use public television shows for educational purposes. Nevertheless, specific programs for exceptional children and actual use of ITV in special education classrooms are extremely limited.

In spite of numerous testimonials and discussions on why media is or should be an effective teaching tool for exceptional children, the actual database for such claims is pathetically small. Although it has been stated that television can be used to present lesson materials in such a way as to facilitate learning, few studies have investigated the relationship between various formal characteristics of media and learning. Almost all of these investigations pertain to institutionalized MR people. Even more sobering is the fact that there is even less empirical research on the efficacy of media instruction for specific academic skills. To the best of our knowledge, no one has ever conducted a well-controlled long-term media intervention study with exceptional children, established the efficacy of television instruction relative to other special-education interventions (short- or long-term), or assessed the long-term maintenance of treatment gains subsequent to the termination of the intervention. Media applications for instructional purposes include the teaching of social skills; preacademic, prevocational, and self-help skills; and appropriate play behaviors. Like many of the "good ideas" in special education, media instruction enjoys favorable testimonials and empirical obscurity. It cannot be said that it has received any real systematic study as a special education intervention, although there are several examples of exceptionally fine research in this area. The explanations for this situation are too numerous and complex to be addressed here. Suffice it to say that the literature supports the conclusion that television can be used to create enjoyable learning and participation experiences for exceptional children.

9 Practical Implications and Future Directions

This book has described much of the research pertaining to television and ED, LD, MR, and intellectually gifted children, with particular focus on viewing habits, comprehension, reactivity, and mediating environmental influences (e.g., parents and teachers). It has also discussed the rather limited attempts to use television to teach academic, language, or social skills to exceptional children. In order to provide a perspective on where this body of knowledge fits into the larger literature on children and television, brief reviews of the studies on non-labeled children were included. Although the focus throughout the book has been on empirical studies, this last chapter departs somewhat from this approach to accomplish a very different set of objectives:

1. To summarize the research findings for each group of exceptional children and offer practical suggestions for care providers.
2. To discuss the more recent television-related technologies and their implications for exceptional children.
3. To offer our ideas on future directions for research.

PRACTICAL IMPLICATIONS FOR CAREGIVERS

To help the reader gain a more coherent picture of the role of television in the lives of exceptional children, the following is a brief synopsis of the research findings for each category of exceptionality. Although researchers generally focus their attention on theoretical issues, extrapolations for clinical application can nevertheless be made from this literature. Given the limited amount of research in this area, we emphasize the tentative status of these recommendations.

Emotionally Disturbed Children

One of the most significant findings presented in this book is that elementary-school-aged ED children in self-contained special education classes watch more hours of television than any of the other groups of children studied by researchers. This is a matter for concern because they are especially attracted to crime dramas and cartoons (programs that typically contain high levels of aggressive behavior) and identify strongly with their favorite television character (who is often aggressive). Furthermore, ED children perceive much of the fictional content they view on television as real and often do not understand that special techniques are used to show people doing superhuman feats, to make cartoon characters move, and to protect actors during violent or action/adventure scenes. Commercials are also frequently misperceived by ED children. They are impressed by advertising jargon, endorsements by attractive people, and other presentation techniques and are unaware of the meaning of the disclaimers contained within the ads. Intellectual ability does not account entirely for these deficits in comprehension because the differences between ED children and nonlabeled children remain even after IQ is controlled statistically.

Attempts to correct misperceptions of television content have been very successful through the implementation of specially designed school-based critical viewing skills curricula. Significant knowledge gains have been achieved and maintained over at least several months, and identification with aggressive television characters has been diminished. However, ED children tend to learn only concrete facts from such curricula and demonstrate a very limited ability to use these facts to reason through their implications or to generalize them to other situations. It is therefore not surprising that such curricula have not been shown to influence either attitudes toward television or viewing habits. To be more effective, teachers need to enhance their students' abilities to generalize from the curriculum to their home viewing. Possible strategies might be to include in the lessons discussions of currently broadcasted programs that the youngsters typically view, role play scenes from popular programs using "scripts" that the teacher prepares, and reward children for being good "detectives" and reporting on special effects they witnessed on programs and commercials they watched the previous day.

Research examining the effects of viewing aggression-laden content on ED children has produced mixed results. Laboratory studies show that exposure to cartoons with high levels of aggressive behavior (e.g., "Tom and Jerry") increases aggressive responding in a game situation. However, field experiments show that both aggressive and nonaggressive cartoons can increase aggressive behavior and that sometimes the nonaggressive programs (e.g., "Lassie's Rescue Rangers") produce the greater effect.

Despite the fact that parents of ED children think that television decreases their children's attention span and increases antisocial behavior, they do not intervene very often to influence what their children watch. In fact, their primary intervention is to use television as a reward or withhold it as a punishment, which may only increase television's value to the child.

On the basis of the aforementioned research, the following recommendations are offered to care providers of ED children:

• Given the fact that ED children watch so much television and prefer and identify with aggressive characters, it would seem prudent to restrict their overall level of viewing, especially of aggression-laden content. However, the evidence supporting a causal link between television violence and aggressive behavior is weak (or inconclusive, at best). Further, restricting the amount of viewing without substituting socially constructive leisure activities is of questionable value. For example, if normal viewing times are replaced by activities that lead to fighting with siblings or other children, the outcomes of these experiences could be worse than those associated with watching television. The important message for caregivers is that it is unlikely that television is a primary cause of the ED child's interpersonal conflicts, and remedial efforts should be directly focused on teaching appropriate social behaviors.

• Caregivers should also be aware that viewing even nonaggressive television programs can stimulate aggressive behavior. Unfortunately, scientists have been unable to formulate satisfactory explanations for this occurrence.

• Because ED children have deficient critical viewing skills, care providers should coview programs as often as possible and discuss content that is unrealistic, upsetting, confusing, or deceptive.

• Schools should be encouraged to incorporate critical viewing skills lessons into the curriculum for ED children and to include activities to enhance generalization of skills to home viewing.

Learning Disabled Children

Elementary-school-aged LD children in self-contained special education classes typically watch more hours of television than nonlabeled peers and are fairly indiscriminant viewers. They watch whatever is on television and do not generally consult program guides. This nonselective style of viewing is consistent with the fact that LD children have very favorable and noncritical attitudes about television in general. Further, they believe that fictional content is real and do not understand that special effects are involved in scenes of violence, superhuman acts, and animated programs. They are also limited in their comprehension and recognition of commercial disclaimers, product endorsements, and exaggerated product performance, which may render them more vulnerable to what they view.

Some LD children have poor visual perceptual skills, which may limit their ability to comprehend camera techniques (e.g., zooming). They may also have difficulty temporally sequencing the events in a television program and drawing inferences about what took place over time leaps. Thus, comprehension of story line and the connection between motive and consequences are potentially sacrificed. Consequently, LD children who watch television very often do not seem to have any advantage in understanding these aspects of television better than those who are more infrequent viewers.

Attempts to improve LD children's comprehension of television through school-based critical viewing skills curricula have yielded positive results in the knowledge domain. They learn concrete facts about special effects and production techniques but demonstrate a limited ability to reason through the implications of these techniques. Unfortunately, such curricula have not been found to be effective in modifying identification with television characters, attitudes toward television, or viewing habits. It may be that effecting changes in attitude and behavior is a far more complex process and one that requires input from parents, who can reinforce key concepts at home when watching television with their children.

It is interesting that although television has been touted to be an effective medium to teach academic skills, there have been no controlled studies demonstrating this potential. With regard to using television to influence LD children's social behavior, it is discouraging that the one attempt to enhance their social problem-solving skills with a television-oriented curriculum was not successful. On a positive note, another curriculum (KIDVID) increased their ability to identify and label prosocial behaviors. The recognition of prosocial behaviors is an important first step in learning how to respond to social situations. The KIDVID curriculum could be used as the initial segment of a school-based curriculum to enhance LD children's social skills.

In the one study of how LD children react to watching aggressive and nonaggressive programs, it was found that the less intellectually able children became more aggressive following the viewing of nonaggressive cartoons. As is the case for ED children, LD children have not been found to behave more aggressively in response to aggressive versus nonaggressive cartoons. Therefore, the therapeutic value of steering LD children away from aggressive programs to seemingly innocuous programs is suspect.

Despite the fact that parents of LD children believe that television increases their children's aggressive behavior (and decreases their reading and attention span), they rarely mediate their children's television viewing. What mediation does occur tends to involve access to television as a reward or punishment or merely specifying viewing times without restricting viewing in terms of number of hours or specific programs. Such practices can increase the importance and salience of television to the child, and should therefore be used with discretion.

Given the limited research on television and LD children, we offer the following as a tentative list of recommendations:

• Many LD children have social deficits, and it would be undesirable if they substituted the less threatening television viewing for actual social interaction. However, if viewing time is not replaced with a socially valued activity, one has to question what is being gained by restricting amount of television viewing.

• LD children can benefit from having care providers watch television with them to assist them to understand what is real versus fictional, when special effects are used, and how commercials are constructed to influence their behavior. Caregivers can also review the story line, and in the process exercise the child's sequencing and recall abilities, correct misinterpretation of events, and highlight important social relationships such as motivations, actions, and consequences.

• Teachers should be encouraged to adopt a critical viewing skills curriculum and to include parent participation by sending home information and activity sheets.

Mentally Retarded Children

MR children also watch a lot of television, and they readily identify with their favorite television character, which suggests that they perceive television as realistic. It is likely that many MR children have difficulty understanding many of television's production techniques and special effects, although this has never been studied. Their comprehension of television programs has been inferred primarily from modeling studies, which show that MR people imitate aggressive and prosocial behaviors from specially prepared videos. Parents of MR children believe that television increases their children's aggressive behavior, but mediate primarily by using television as a reward or restricting its use as a punishment. The limited research on formal features suggests that programs geared to MR individuals should minimize media features (particularly if they are irrelevant to what is being taught) and maximize clarity, comprehensibility, and appealing content. Television's potential to review or reinforce what the teacher has taught in the classroom is suggested by at least one study of learning manual sign language. This seems to be one of the most promising uses of television for MR people.

The paucity of research on the reactivity of MR individuals to broadcast television makes it difficult to prescribe specific mediation guidelines for care providers. However, we offer the following as a sensible perspective on television and MR individuals:

• Television viewing should not be a substitute for education, habilitation, or socialization. However, instructional media appear to hold great educational promise, especially to reinforce academic skills and concepts.

• MR individuals are likely to misperceive many realistic versus fantasy portrayals, special effects, and the persuasive intent underlying commercials, which could result in inappropriate (and potentially harmful) instances of imitation or unfair influence on purchasing decisions. Care providers can reduce these untoward effects on MR viewers by teaching them basic critical viewing skills in the context of regular home viewing.

Intellectually Gifted Children

Gifted children watch fewer hours of television than their intellectually average peers during the elementary-school years, and are generally more accurate in their assessments of reality versus pretend on television. They are, however, likely to watch more television during both the preschool years and early adolescence, stages when they are arguably most vulnerable to social influences (see Colangelo & Kelly, 1983; Janos, Fung, & Robinson, 1985). Gifted preschoolers are more likely to watch educational programming targeted at older audiences, and to start viewing adult-oriented commercial programs at an earlier age than their peers. The seemingly "age-inappropriate" content of these programs would certainly be considered problematic for nonlabeled and disabled children, and raises concerns about gifted children's possible misinterpretation of televised messages. Such concerns are reinforced by research suggesting that young gifted children are likely to (a) perceive many of the fictional characters found in the more sophisticated adult-oriented genre, such as soap operas and episodic dramas, as real, and (b) fail to accurately comprehend many of the complex visual techniques employed as narrative devices in these programs.

Although the natural inclination of caregivers would be to curtail the viewing of these programs or limit viewership to familiar, less complex content, this would not necessarily be the most appropriate prescription for gifted children. Many aspects of comprehension of television information actually improve with exposure. In particular, gifted children's comprehension of editing techniques employed to manipulate projective size and their ability to temporally integrate story line increase dramatically with higher levels of exposure. Viewership gives gifted children the opportunity to observe and familiarize themselves with advanced or abstract concepts and relationships that are normally learned at an older age. In other words, it allows them to practice their perceptual abilities and puts their knowledge of the real and televised worlds to the test.

This is not to suggest that excessive television viewing should be endorsed or permitted. Rather, young intellectually gifted children's natural attraction to television may be indicative of their natural curiosity and urge to learn, and should be encouraged. Furthermore, although stimulus properties such as novelty and complexity may arouse cognitive uncertainty or generate confusion and misperceptions, the resolution of this uncertainty requires a form of mindful processing that in itself is stimulating to gifted children. Consequently, the viewing of novel television programming should also be encouraged. The new technologies discussed in the next section provide an ample supply of alternative fare to that provided by traditional broadcast outlets.

"Encouragement" is the operative word in the parenting of gifted children, particularly with regard to the mediation of their television usage. Research suggests that parental communication and disciplinary styles that offer encouragement (i.e., inductive strategies) result in greater learning of prosocial behavior and less learning of antisocial behavior from television. Similarly, more constructive or evaluative forms of direct parental intervention of television viewing have been found to yield greater results. Fortunately, the vast majority of parental mediation of gifted children's television is of an encouraging nature. More restrictive methods of mediation are rarely employed. Parents are most likely to discuss and evaluate programs, story line, and character roles and motivations, and to stimulate critical thinking about these factors. This strategy has been linked to parents' awareness of possible negative effects (decreases reading ability), but general belief that television has positive effects (increases knowledge and awareness of the world) as well. Evaluative mediation that encourages positive learning from television and places viewing into proper perspective with regard to other media (e.g., books) and other activities (e.g., school) is clearly the most appropriate method of intervention and direction for gifted children.

It should be noted, however, that certain forms of encouragement may actually be dysfunctional. Salomon's (1984) work on the amount of invested mental energy high-ability children put into processing television programming revealed that they tend to expend less effort if they believe that: (a) the task of viewing is simple, (b) the material can be attended to and processed automatically or without any particular skill or ability, or (c) the skills or abilities required for viewership are already mastered. Evaluative statements by parents, albeit positive and constructive (i.e., "You are such a good televiewer"), may prove to be counterproductive. When such statements are made, "children adopt the label, increasing their perceived self efficacy as televiewers even more, and thus come to expend less effort on TV than before" (p. 63).

Despite the overwhelmingly encouraging and constructive nature of parental mediation cited in the literature, the fact remains that few parents of gifted children actually participate in any form of direct television intervention. Approximately 77% of the parents of gifted children engage in either no or low/moderate levels of mediation. Although this rate of involvement actually eclipses that of parents with nonlabeled children, it falls short of those parents with LD or ED children. Suggest Davis and Rimm (1989):

It sometimes happens that devoted parents, intent on providing an ideal climate for their gifted children, fall into the trap of believing that these little beings, by virtue of their extensive vocabularies and impressive speech and logic, are capable very early of making complex decisions and setting their own goals and directions. Their interests and concerns, of course, should be considered, but parents and teachers must not abdicate responsibility for guidance. . . . If God had meant gifted children to run their houses, She would have created them bigger. (p. 388)

The purposeful use of television is a parental responsibility and should be taken seriously by all parents, particularly those with gifted children.

Mediation and intervention can also be an assumed responsibility of the classroom teacher. As special educators are well aware, gifted children have well-integrated perceptual strengths and can learn through varied sensory channels, including visual. The use of television for instruction, the incorporation of television content into an existing lesson plan, or the implementation of television literacy into a curriculum is appropriate.

It is also quite consistent with many of the educational criteria established by special educators. One approach has suggested that a curriculum for young gifted children should: (a) be based on interest and needs rather than on predetermined order or sequence of instruction, (b) access abstract and higher level thinking processes, and (c) encourage creative and productive thinking (Karnes, Shwedel, & Kemp, 1985). The use of television in the gifted classroom does this and has proven to be effective, particularly as a tool to instill and inspire critical thinking skills. In addition, school-based television curricula have increased gifted children's ability to isolate, identify, and label prosocial behaviors presented in programming, among other goals. The use of television in the classroom is further encouraged by the previously cited observation that high-ability children tend to expend more effort on television viewing if they believe that television warrants that consideration. Teachers can easily instill that perception, and are encouraged to do so.

In light of the body of information presented in this book and summarized in this chapter, the following recommendations serve as a viable prescription for the caregivers of intellectually gifted children:

• The natural attraction to television, particularly during preschool and early adolescence, may be indicative of natural curiosity and an urge to learn, and should be encouraged.

• Higher levels of viewership may actually facilitate positive learning. If viewing appears to be mindful and stimulating, setting arbitrary time limitations or program/genre preferences may be unwarranted and unwise.

• Novel and complex programming generates more thoughtful processing and cognitively stimulating activity. Familiar TV characters, predictable plots, tried-

and-true genre, and reruns should be supplemented or replaced by new shows that stretch the imagination and offer new information about television and the real world.

• Television should be treated as any potential learning tool. Its use needs to be more purposefully employed, its materials need to be selectively chosen, and it requires monitoring by an adult familiar with its functions.

• Evaluative mediation (discussing and explaining programs, storyline, character roles and motivations, and encouraging critical thinking about these factors) is clearly the most appropriate method of parental intervention and guidance.

• If parents perceive television as a medium requiring little thought or mental energy, children will treat it accordingly. Conversely, if television is perceived as effort-deserving, it will be given more thoughtful treatment by children.

• Television has a place in the classroom. The mindful treatment of the medium in school transfers to its treatment at home.

FUTURE DIRECTIONS

New Technologies

There are a number of practical implications suggested by the research presented in this book that pertain to exceptional children. The scientific literature demonstrates clearly that exceptional children have unique needs with regard to suitable television content, and existing programs offer very little for them. Given the cognitive, behavioral, and social deficits or capabilities of exceptional children, there is a need for television programs that are tailor-made for them. Chapter 8 showed how such efforts, although limited in scope, have been very successful with disabled children. More programs are needed, but until recently, there was no financially feasible way to produce programs for specialized audiences. The for-profit economics of commercial broadcast television dictate that programs reach the widest possible audience. Providing special programming for specific age groups has been the demand of child advocacy groups for years, but this has been considered by broadcasters to be economically untenable. Sadly, arguing for a further splintering of the child audience by offering programs for exceptional children would fall on "deafer" ears. However, much like the children of the 1950s, today's youth are also being exposed to significant changes in technology that will no doubt affect their daily lives. Cable services, satellite dish antennas, VCRs, personal computers, and home videogames now compete with broadcast television for their attention. Technology capable of true interaction with its user promises to change the very nature of media use. Thus, narrowcasting and direct-relay technologies may open up the children's television market in a manner most conducive to the needs and capabilities of exceptional children.

Over 60% of the households in the United States receive cable services. In order to attract subscribers, cable companies have offered a variety of channels and programs that are designed to appeal to specialized audiences. For example, many cable systems have entire channels devoted to news, music videos, health information, and congressional hearings, and programs targeted for audiences of specific racial, ethnic, and language backgrounds. At least one channel (Nickelodeon) is devoted entirely to children and, unlike broadcast television, presents programs that are designed for children of specific age groups. By targeting MR, ED, LD, or intellectually gifted children, an audience could be developed on the basis of capability and need rather than age. Pay cable channels such as Disney, HBO, Showtime, and Cinemax also offer quality programs for children. It appears that the technology and economic structure exist, and the time has come for innovative approaches to reach the specialized audiences of exceptional children.

Another new technology well suited for this purpose is the videocassette recorder (VCR). Approximately 70% of the households in the United States own at least one VCR. Videocassettes can be produced to teach and entertain special audiences. Chapter 8 showed how manual sign language can be taught to MR children using videocassette lessons. Imagine how the educational potential could be enhanced further if the cassettes were available for the child to watch at home and for the parent to learn and reinforce the signs! People who work with exceptional children could suggest a variety of training tapes (e.g., how to perform a variety of jobs, interview for a job, handle common problematic social situations) that would benefit large numbers of children. The economic feasibility arises out of the fact that cassettes aimed at children are extremely marketable. They often view the same videocassettes repeatedly, and the cassettes become part of the family's "library" (Growing avenues, 1985).

A common expectation with the introduction of appealing new communication technologies is that children's use of their leisure time will change to incorporate the novel media. Research with nonlabeled children has shown that newer technologies are used, but "in some respects the changes in children's overall media usage patterns were much less than expected" (Dorr & Kunkel, 1990, p. 12). In one survey, about one-third of the children did not use the VCR at all during the study period (Wartella, Heintz, Aidman, & Mazzarella, 1990). In another study, VCR viewing accounted for less than 2% of all media time, videogame playing for 3%, and music video viewing for less than 2%, with standard television viewing still accounting for almost three-quarters of all media time (Kubey & Larson, 1990).

There are, however, a few age-related variables that might offer some insight into the use of the new media technology by exceptional children. First, it has been found that having access to a cable system does tend to increase television viewing among preschoolers, although it does not do so for older children. Also, homes with preschoolers are more likely to have videocassettes than homes with older children (Wartella et al., 1990). Because disabled children's overall televi-

sion viewing exceeds that of nonlabeled children at all ages, and gifted preschoolers' viewing exceeds that of their nonlabeled same-aged peers, cable and
VCR access may prove problematic if this pattern of media use generalizes to the
new alternatives. Considering that parents of exceptional children have very few
household rules and regulations about television usage (particularly with regard
to time limitations and program selection), access to the new technologies may
increase overall time devoted to media rather than replace existing commercial
television use.

A second concern regarding the new technologies is whether its availability
will be equitable. Because cable television and VCRs (in fact, virtually all
nonbroadcast media) require some form of direct payment to obtain the programs
provided, individuals in the lower socioeconomic strata are less likely to make
use of the new technologies than children from more affluent families. Although
the exceptionalities considered in this book cut across socioeconomic levels,
there is a disproportionate representation of economically disadvantaged youngsters in groups of ED, LD, and MR children (Kavale, 1980; Lynch, 1988;
Tarjan, Wright, Eyman, & Keeran, 1973). Furthermore, children most likely to
be tested and identified as gifted at an early age belong to communities that
supply school districts with sufficient funds for such activities. Consequently, it
is likely that those who are disabled will have less access and those who are
gifted will have greater access to the new technologies. This poses to promote
inequity of access and create a greater distance between exceptional and nonlabeled children and among divergent exceptional populations.

There have been some developments in the regulation of the television industry that carry the potential to worsen this inequity. The Federal Communications
Commission (FCC) issued nonmandatory guidelines governing programming
obligations for children's television fare in 1974 (Docket No. 19142) and 1975
(FCC, Memorandum Opinion and Order, Docket No., 19142). In the mid 1980s,
the FCC (1984) "deregulated" these long-standing guidelines, despite the fact
that the U.S. House of Representatives' Subcommittee on Telecommunications,
Consumer Protection, and Finance (1983) reported that the quantity of weekday
children's programming supplied by broadcasters was nearly half that offered a
decade earlier. As Huston, Watkins, and Kunkel (1989) have noted, the 1984
order fundamentally changed every broadcaster's obligation to program for children:

> The FCC declared that although it expected the child audience to be served by
> broadcasters, stations might take into account other sources of children's content in
> their markets. The responsibility to serve children's interests was to be shared by all
> broadcasters in a particular market rather than required of each individual licensee.
> Content available on public television, cable, pay television, satellite and even on
> commercial videocassettes could relieve individual stations of any responsibility to
> program for children. (p. 428)

Have the new technologies picked up the slack created by the commercial broadcasters? Wartella et al. (1990) suggest that only for those households with cable are children offered both variety and diversity of children's programming. Children who are poor and/or live in many rural and urban areas do not have access to cable. Furthermore, the availability of cable and videocassettes to those who can afford them may satisfy the broadcasters' obligation to serve children and result in a further decrease in the broadcast programs that are available to less economically advantaged children, many of whom have learning and behavior disorders.

Aside from the ability to pay for the services, a certain degree of "literacy" is also required for many of the new technologies. Personal computers and videogame players in particular are much different from broadcast television because they do not deliver content in the traditional fashion or require the same skills. Indeed, they "promote interactions in which the information-processing activities are quite different from those with television" (Dorr & Kunkel, 1990, p. 6).

According to Gavriel Salomon (1990), however, the skills gained from computer use far outweigh those required for usage, leaving what he calls durable and generalizable "cognitive residue":

> One way of obtaining lasting cognitive residue from use of a computer program is through the repeated exercise of particular thought processes and strategies that the partnership requires. The program can be said to cultivate skills or strategies by activating them repeatedly, by stretching at abilities' boundaries . . . provided that the activity is mindfully carried out. (p. 35)

Thus, the potential of the new technologies to facilitate the development of information-processing skills of disabled children and further develop or fine-tune these skills in gifted children is great, *if* the child applies the necessary mental energy required of the task. It is this "if" that renders the impact of new technology similar to broadcast media—"some children under some conditions." With specific reference to computers, Salomon (1990) offers the following rendition of this much cited summary statement: "Children's cognitions . . . are affected by specific kinds of programs with which they carry out specific kinds of activities, under specific kinds of external and internal conditions for specific kinds of goals" (p. 27). In other words, the nature of the child's exceptionality is likely to influence what the child obtains from his or her interaction with new technology.

A final concern that warrants consideration is whether the increase in quantity and availability of programming provided by the new media affects parental mediation of television. As noted earlier in this book, parental mediation of television viewing is an infrequent occurrence, regardless of whether the child is nonlabeled, disabled, or gifted. Mediation further declines with the rise of multiple television sets in the household (Gross & Walsh, 1980), the result of more fragmentary viewing and the removal of the parents from the child viewing situation. Homes receiving new technologies have proven to be no different. There are only minimal levels of parental guidance with regard to the use of home computers, basic cable services, and home videogames (Haefner, Hunter, & Wartella, 1986). Similarly, there are strikingly few differences in mediation behaviors across basic, pay, and noncable households (Atkin, Greenberg, & Baldwin, 1991; Atkin, Heeter, & Baldwin, 1989).

Empirical Research

One of the major goals of this book is to stimulate interest in professionals from both communication and special education to conduct research on various aspects of television and exceptional children. It is therefore fitting that we end our discussion with important and interesting issues to be addressed in future research.

Television Viewing Habits. One of the most interesting unanswered questions about viewing habits is: Are the consequences of heavy television viewing by exceptional children the same as for nonlabeled children? Data reported in chapter 2 showed that children in self-contained special education classes watch more television than youngsters in regular classes. It was hypothesized that this put them at increased risk for its adverse effects. However, this is not necessarily the case. It is possible that children in special classes and schools are already isolated from social interation (due to rejection) and information (due to reading deficits), and television provides stimulation that they would not otherwise receive. This is analogous to the relationship between television exposure and academic achievement; heavy television use is correlated with lower academic achievement, but *not* for children from the lower socioeconomic strata, for whom television offers enriching experiences (California Assessment Program, 1982). The competing hypothesis is that the easy availability of television discourages children and their parents from seeking out more appropriate social and intellectual experiences.

Although gifted children typically watch less television than their intellectually average peers, they are extremely capable of processing and retaining information to which they are exposed. Considering that television presents information in such attractive and stimulating ways, do gifted children retain more of its messages than those from other sources? Another unanswered question is whether their intellectual capabilities put them at greater risk than their peers of learning television's undesirable content (e.g., aggression, stereotypes, materialism).

In addition to answering these questions, a more careful assessment of the reliability and validity of measures of viewing habits is warranted. None of the studies of the viewing habits of exceptional children addressed the issue of the accuracy of their data, with the exception of one study (Ahrens, 1977), which pointed out that caregiver reports of children's favorite television programs were discrepant with those of the children. Part of the problem may stem from what is meant by "favorite" program. For example, an adult may surmise that a program is a child's favorite because he or she watches it often; however, the child may watch it often only because it is aired several times a week.

The accuracy of estimates of total hours of television viewing have also been called into question (e.g., Anderson, Field, Collins, Lorch, & Nathan, 1985; Stipp, 1975). For example, parental estimates of the amount of time their child spends watching television are not particularly accurate. However, television diaries completed by parents that attempt to record how often the television is on and who is present in the room are fairly accurate estimates of the amount of time a child spends in front of a television set. However, what diaries and interviews do not do well is to estimate the amount of time the child is actually attending to the television. Some so-called "heavy television users" actually pay very little attention to the television set, and instead play with toys or games or interact with family members when the television set is on.

There is also relatively little research on the accuracy and validity of child self-reports of the total number of hours of television viewing or estimates based on reports of programs they viewed. Children are not particularly good at estimating the amount of time they actually spend watching television. Nevertheless, research on the questionnaire recall method (i.e., asking children to indicate what they watch during specific time periods) does show that this procedure yields accurate information on the relative amount of television viewing and that other methods (e.g., parent diaries, parent questionnaires) are not superior (Stipp, 1975).

Reality Perception of Television.   Research shows that ED and LD children perceive fictional television as more real than do their nonlabeled peers, which suggests that this might heighten their risk of behaving aggressively after viewing aggression-laden programs. However, the link between reality perceptions and aggressive behavior has been examined exclusively in nondisabled youths and only in laboratory studies. In other words, there is a need for experimental studies to be conducted in which the reality perceptions of ED and LD children are manipulated and behavioral effects are monitored to examine the generalizability of findings to disabled populations. Furthermore, it is important to follow up laboratory experiments with field studies to evaluate the social significance (or ecological validity) of the findings.

Comprehension of Television.   More research is needed to examine the relationship between comprehension and overt behavior (i.e., the role of comprehension in influencing children's reactivity to programs and commercials). For example, we do not know the significance of ED and LD children's lack of understanding of special effects. Further, it is unknown whether teaching children with learning and behavior disorders about special effects will change their reactions to various types of content. This has clear implications for the importance of adopting critical viewing skills curricula.

Research is also needed to determine why ED, LD, and MR children fail to adequately comprehend television content. Studies have shown that they do not understand special effects, animation, and so forth, but there has been virtually no research on the cognitive processes (e.g., attention, comprehension of central/peripheral content, sequencing story, drawing inferences) that facilitate comprehension. There has been some research on LD children's perception of projective size, but information is totally lacking on ED and MR children and on other perceptual tasks. The language of television is complex and full of symbols unique to the medium. Thus far, researchers have barely scratched the surface.

Antisocial Content.   Many care providers are concerned about the increased vulnerability of ED, LD, and MR children to the adverse effects of viewing aggressive television content. However, although the studies presented in chapter 5 show a media effect, they do not support a uniquely bad reaction to aggressive content. More research is needed to directly compare disabled and nonlabeled children to determine if the former are at greater risk with regard to behavioral effects of viewing violence-laden content. (This is difficult to accomplish, however, because the natural environments [schools, homes] of the two groups of children are often so different [i.e., special education vs. regular class, socioeconomic status, familial stress]). Similarly, are aggressive cues more salient to gifted than intellectually average children, and if so, does this produce heightened reactivity to such content?

Enhancing Prosocial Behavior and Academic Skills.   One of the most promising areas of television research is trying to enhance prosocial behaviors and improve academic skills. As previously noted, Hearold (1986), who conducted a meta-analysis of research on television, reported that the effect size was greater for viewing pro- than antisocial media material. Chapter 5 described several studies demonstrating that there were prosocial effects on both ED and MR children who viewed positive social models on television. Television offers a promising way to teach social skills. However, most of the research has involved severely disabled or institutionalized children, educational or instructional (i.e., noncommercial) television programs, and laboratory settings. To develop prosocial programs for exceptional children (whether the medium is videocassettes or broadcast television), more needs to be known about how to capture their attention and maximize learning. Current formal features research has focused exclusively on MR people and on only a handful of features. There is a need for more programmatic research and multivariable studies in this area (such as those of Gadberry et al., 1981).

It is also important to explore the use of television to teach academic skills. Sadly, this potential of television has not been demonstrated in adequately controlled studies (e.g., comparisons with no treatment and traditional teaching methods). Other interesting comparisons include assessing the effectiveness of the television lesson alone versus television plus the rest of the educational package. Television appears to be particularly useful for reinforcing what teachers introduce in class, and this potential should be explored further.

Critical Viewing Skills.   As noted previously, it is important to determine the role of critical viewing skills in mediating the influences of television. Regardless of its specific role, it is clear that exceptional children watch a lot of television and they need assistance to understand the presentation techniques and commercial aspects of the medium. There needs to be more intensive effort to enhance the efficacy of viewing skills curricula (especially in changing viewing habits and reducing reactivity to antisocial content). Future efforts should coordinate lessons between school and home so that parents can reinforce concepts and facilitate generalization to the relevant environment.

Methodological Issues.   Much of the research on children with learning and behavior problems pertains to youngsters in self-contained classes in elementary schools for disabled students. However, as pointed out in chapter 1, only a small percentage of ED and LD students are educated in such restricted environments. Therefore, many of the findings might only generalize to the more severe and socially restricted ED and LD individuals. Similarly, most of the research on MR individuals has focused exclusively on people in residential settings or special schools. It remains for future research to study less severely disabled students and/or individuals who are educated in more mainstreamed settings.

Finally and most importantly, as stated in chapter 1, there is a need to examine more homogeneous subgroups of ED, LD, and MR children and to generate theory-driven research focusing on specific aspects of these disabilities (e.g., attention, memory, or perceptual deficits). For example, it is clear from the findings reported in chapter 3 that variables other than IQ account for the distorted reality perceptions of ED and LD children. It is only through an examination of more carefully selected subgroups of exceptional children that one can begin to even hypothesize about what cognitive factor(s) underlie their perceptions of television content.

References

Abeles, N. (1986). Proceedings of the American Psychological Association, Incorporated for the year 1985. *American Psychologist, 41*, 633–647.

Abelman, R. (1981). *Critical television viewing curriculum: A teacher's manual.* Unpublished curriculum, Cleveland State University.

Abelman, R. (1982). *Amplifying the effects of television's prosocial fare through curriculum intervention.* Unpublished doctoral dissertation, The University of Texas–Austin.

Abelman, R. (1984). Television and the gifted child. *Roeper Review, 7*, 115–118.

Abelman, R. (1985). Sex differences in parental disciplinary practices: An antecedent of television's impact on children. *Women's Studies in Communication, 8*, 51–61.

Abelman, R. (1986a). Children's awareness of television's prosocial fare: Parental discipline as an antecedent. *Journal of Family Issues, 7*(1), 51–61.

Abelman, R. (1986b). Television and the exceptional child. *G/T/C, 9*(4), 26–28.

Abelman, R. (1986c). What about the exceptional child? *Television and Families, 9*(2), 36–41.

Abelman, R. (1987a). Parental mediation of television viewing. *Roeper Review, 9*(4), 217–220, 246.

Abelman, R. (1987b). TV literacy II: Amplifying the affective level effects of television's prosocial fare through curriculum intervention. *Journal of Research and Development in Education, 20*, 40–49.

Abelman, R. (1989). From here to eternity: Children's acquisition of understanding of projective size on television. *Human Communication Research, 15*, 463–481.

Abelman, R. (1990a). Determinants of parental mediation of children's television viewing. In J. Bryant (Ed.), *Television and the American family* (pp. 311–328). Hillsdale, NJ: Lawrence Erlbaum Associates.

Abelman, R. (1990b). You can't get there from here: Children's understanding of "time-leaps" on television. *Journal of Broadcasting & Electronic Media, 34*, 469–476.

Abelman, R. (1991a). Parental communication style and its influence on exceptional children's television viewing. *Roeper Review, 14*(1), 23–27.

Abelman, R. (1991b). TV literacy III—The gifted and learning disabled: Amplifying prosocial learning through curricular intervention. *Journal of Research and Development in Education, 24*(4), 51–60.

Abelman, R. (1992a, May). *Putting the cart before the horse: Exceptional children's comprehension of temporal sequencing on television.* Paper presented at the International Communication Association Conference, Miami, FL.

Abelman, R. (1992b, October). *Exceptional children's understanding of projective size on television.* Paper presented at the Speech Communication Association Conference, Chicago, IL.

Abelman, R., & Courtright, J. (1983). Television literacy: Amplifying the cognitive level effects of television's prosocial fare through curriculum intervention. *Journal of Research and Development in Education, 17,* 46–57.

Abelman, R., & Pettey, G. R. (1989). Child attributes as determinants of parental television-viewing mediation: The role of child giftedness. *Journal of Family Issues, 10*(2), 251–266.

Abelman, R., & Rogers, A. (1987). *From "plug-in drug" to "magic window": The role of television in special education.* Paper presented at the 7th Annual World Conference on Gifted Education, Salt Lake City, UT.

Abelman, R., & Ross, R. (1986). Children, television and families: An evolution in understanding. *Television and Families, 9*(1), 1–64.

Abelman, R., & Ross, R. (1990). *Mass communication: Issues and perspectives.* Needham Heights, MA: Simon & Schuster.

Abelman, R., & Sparks, G. C. (1985). How to tell the good guys from the bad guys. *Television & Families, 8*(4), 21–24.

Abkarian, G. G., King, P., & Krappes, T. L. (1987). Enhancing interaction in a difficult-to-test child: The PPVT-TV technique. *Journal of Learning Disabilities, 20,* 268–269.

Abroms, K. I., & Gollin, J. B. (1980). Developmental study of gifted preschool children and measures of psychosocial giftedness. *Exceptional Children, 46,* 334–341.

Acker, S. R. (1983). Viewers' perceptions of velocity and distance in televised events. *Human Communication Research, 9,* 335–348.

Acker, S. R., & Tiemens, R. K. (1981). Children's perceptions of changes in size of televised images. *Human Communication Research, 7,* 340–346.

Adelman, H. S., & Taylor, L. (1986). *An introduction to learning disabilities.* Glenview, IL: Scott, Foresman and Company.

Agency for Instructional Television. (1973). *Inside/Out: A guide for teachers.* Bloomington, IN: Author.

Ahrens, M. G. (1977). Television viewing habits of mentally retarded children. *Australian Journal of Mental Retardation, 4,* 1–3.

Algozzine, B. (1977). The emotionally disturbed child: Disturbed or disturbing. *Journal of Abnormal Child Psychology, 5,* 205–211.

Allen, W. H. (1975). Intellectual abilities and instructional media design. *Audio Visual Communication Review, 23,* 139–170.

Altman, R., & Talkington, L. W. (1971). Modeling: An alternative behavior modification approach for retardates. *Mental Retardation, 9*(3), 20–23.

American Academy of Child Psychology. (1984, November 28). *Draft of final report of the task force on violence and the media.* Washington, DC: Author.

American Academy of Pediatrics. (1986). *Television and the family.* Elk Grove Village, IL: Author.

American Medical Association. (1976, July). *Resolution No. 38 of the House of Delegates: Violence on TV: An environmental hazard* (Reference Committee E, p. 367). Chicago: Author.

American Medical Association. (1982, December). Resolution no. 19 of the House of Delegates. *Proceedings of the House of Delegates: 36th Interim Meeting.* Chicago: Author.

American Psychiatric Association. (1987). *Diagnostic and statistical manual of mental disorders* (3rd ed., rev.). Washington, DC: Author.

American Psychological Association. (1985, February 22). *Resolution passed by the APA Council of Representatives.* Washington, DC: Public Information Office.

Amerikaner, M. J., & Omizo, M. M. (1984). Family interaction and learning disabilities. *Journal of Learning Disabilities, 17,* 540–543.

Anderson, D. R., Alwitt, L. F., Lorch, E. P., & Levin, S. R. (1979). Watching children watch television. In G. Hale & M. Lewis (Eds.), *Attention and the development of cognitive skills.* New York: Plenum.

Anderson, D. R., Field, D. E., Collins, P. A., Lorch, E. P., & Nathan, J. G. (1985). Estimates of young children's time with television: A methodological comparison of parent reports with time-lapse video home observation. *Child Development, 56,* 1345–1357.

Anderson, D. R., & Levin, S. R. (1976). Young children's attention to "Sesame Street." *Child Development, 47,* 806–811.

Anderson, D. R., & Lorch, E. P. (1983). Looking at television: Action or reaction? In J. Bryant & D. R. Anderson (Eds.), *Children's understanding of television: Research on attention and comprehension* (pp. 1–34). New York: Academic Press.

Anderson, J. A. (1980). The theoretical lineage of critical viewing curricula. *Journal of Communication, 30,* 64–70.

Anderson, J. A. (1981). Receivership skills: An educational response. In M. E. Ploghoft & J. A. Anderson (Eds.), *Education for the television age* (pp. 19–27). Athens, OH: The Cooperative Center for Social Science Education.

Anderson, J. A. (1983). Television literacy and the critical viewer. In J. Bryant & D. R. Anderson (Eds.), *Children's understanding of television: Research on attention and comprehension* (pp. 297–330). New York: Academic Press.

Ardi, D. B. (1977, April). *New avenues of teaching resources: Sesame Street programs for the mentally retarded child.* Paper presented at the annual meeting of the Council for Exceptional Children, Atlanta. (ERIC Document Reproduction Service No. ED 139 197)

Aronfreed, J. (1969). The concept of internalization. In S. A. Goslin (Ed.), *Handbook of socialization theory and research.* Chicago: Rand McNally.

Aronfreed, J. (1976). Moral development from the standpoint of a general psychological theory. In T. Lickona (Ed.), *Moral development and behavior theory, research and social issues.* New York: Holt, Rinehart & Winston.

Atkin, C. (1975). *Effects of television advertising on children—Parent child communication in supermarket breakfast selection* (Report 7). East Lansing: Michigan State University.

Atkin, C. (1983). Effects of realistic TV violence vs. fictional violence on aggression. *Journalism Quarterly, 60,* 615–621.

Atkin, D., Greenberg, B. S., & Baldwin, T. (1991). *The home ecology of children's television viewing: Parental mediation and the new video environment. Journal of Communication, 41*(3), 40–52.

Atkin, D., Heeter, C., & Baldwin, T. (1989). How presence of cable affects parental mediation of TV viewing. *Journalism Quarterly, 66*(3), 557–563.

Bachara, G. H. (1976). Empathy in learning disabled children. *Perceptual and Motor Skills, 43,* 541–542.

Badzinski, D. M. (1991). Children's cognitive representations of discourse: Effects of vocal cues on text comprehension. *Communication Research, 18,* 715–736.

Baker, R. K., & Ball, S. J. (1969). *Mass media and violence. Staff report to the National Commission on the causes and prevention of violence* (Vol. 9). Washington, DC: U.S. Government Printing Office.

Ball, S., & Bogatz, G. A. (1970). *The first year of Sesame Street: An evaluation.* Princeton, NJ: Educational Testing Service.

Ball, S., & Bogatz, G. A. (1973). *Reading with television: An evaluation of the Electric Company.* Princeton, NJ: Educational Testing Service.

Ball, S., Bogatz, G. A., Kazarow, K., & Rubin, D. (1974). *Reading with television: A followup evaluation of the Electric Company.* Princeton, NJ: Educational Testing Service.

Bandura, A. (1963, October 22). What TV violence can do to your child. *Look,* pp. 46–52.

Bandura, A. (1965). Influence of models' reinforcement contingencies on the acquisition of imitative responses. *Journal of Personality and Social Psychology, 1,* 589–595.

Bandura, A. (1969). *Principles of behavior modification.* New York: Holt, Rinehart and Winston.

Bandura, A., Ross, D., & Ross, S. A. (1961). Transmission of aggression through imitation of aggressive models. *Journal of Abnormal and Social Psychology, 63,* 575–582.

Bandura, A., Ross, D., & Ross, S. A. (1963). Imitation of film-mediated aggressive models. *Journal of Abnormal and Social Psychology, 66,* 3–11.

Bandura, A., & Walters, R. H. (1963). *Social learning and personality development.* New York: Holt, Rinehart & Winston.

Baran, S. J. (1973). TV and social learning in the institutionalized MR. *Mental Retardation, 11*(3), 36–38.

Baran, S. J. (1977). Television programs as socializing agents for mentally retarded children. *Audio Visual Communication Review, 25,* 281–289.

Baran, S. J., Chase, L. J., & Courtright, J. A. (1979). Television drama as a facilitator of prosocial behavior: "The Waltons." *Journal of Broadcasting, 23*(3), 277–284.

Baran, S. J., & Meyer, T. P. (1975). Retarded children's perceptions of favorite television characters as behavioral models. *Mental Retardation, 13*(4), 28–31.

Barbe, W. (1965). *Psychology and education of the gifted: Selected readings.* New York: Appleton-Century-Crofts.

Barbe, W., & Renzulli, J. (1981). *Psychology and education of the gifted* (3rd ed.). New York: Irvington.

Barber-Smith, D., & Reilly, S. (1977). Use media to motivate reading. *Audiovisual Instruction, 22*(10), 33–34.

Barker, D. (1988). "It's been real": Forms of television representation. *Critical Studies in Mass Communication, 5*(1), 42–56.

Barton, J. N., & Starnes, W. T. (1989). Identifying distinguishing characteristics of gifted and talented/learning disabled students. *Roeper Review, 12,* 23–28.

Baumrind, D. (1971). Current patterns of parental authority. *Developmental Psychology Monographs, 4*(1), 2.

Becker, G. (1978). *The mad genius controversy.* Beverly Hills, CA: Sage.

Beery, V. W. (1967). Matching auditory and visual stimuli by average and retarded readers. *Child Development, 18,* 827–833.

Belsky, J. (1981). Early human experience: A family perspective. *Developmental Psychology, 17,* 2–23.

Belsky, J., Rovine, M., & Taylor, D. G. (1984). The Pennsylvania infant and family project, III: The origins of individual differences in infant-mother attachment: Maternal and infant contributions. *Child Development, 55,* 718–728.

Belsky, J., Taylor, D. G., & Rovine, M. (1984). The Pennsylvania infant and family project, II: The development of reciprocal interaction in the mother-infant dyad. *Child Development, 55,* 706–717.

Birch, H. G., & Belmont, L. (1964). Auditory-visual integration in normal and retarded readers. *American Journal of Orthopsychiatry, 34,* 852–861.

Birch, H. G., & Belmont, L. (1965). Auditory-visual integration, intelligence, and reading ability in school children. *Perceptual and Motor Skill, 20,* 205–305.

Blessington, J. (1981). What the TV industry is doing to help youth. In M. E. Ploghoft and J. A. Anderson (Eds.), *Education for the television age* (pp. 116–122). Athens, OH: The Cooperative Center for Social Science Education.

Bogatz, G. A., & Ball, S. (1971). *The second year of Sesame Street: A continuing evaluation* (Vols. 1 and 2). Princeton, NJ: Educational Testing Service.

Borkowski, J. G., Peck, V. A., & Damberg, P. R. (1983). Attention, memory, and cognition. In J. L. Matson & J. A. Mulich (Eds.), *Handbook of mental retardation* (pp. 479–497). New York: Pergamon.

Bower, R. T. (1973). *Television and the public.* New York: Rinehart and Winston.

Bretherton, I., O'Connell, B., Shore, C., & Bates, E. (1984). The effect of contextual variation on symbolic play: Development from 20 to 28 months. In I. Bretherton (Ed.), *Symbolic play: The development of social understanding* (pp. 271–298). New York: Academic Press.

Bricklin, P. M., & Gallico, R. (1984). Learning disabilities and emotional disturbance: Critical issues in definition, assessment, and service delivery. *Learning Disabilities, 3,* 141–156.

Brody, G., Pillegrini, A., & Sigel, I. (1986). Marital quality and mother-child and father-child interactions with school-aged children. *Developmental Psychology, 22,* 291–296.

Brotman, S. N. (1990). *Extending telecommunications service to Americans with disabilities: A report on telecommunications services mandated under the Americans with Disabilities Act of 1990.* Washington, DC: Northwestern University.

Brown, A. L. (1976). The construction of temporal sequences by preoperational children. In A. D. Pick (Ed.), *Minnesota symposia on child psychology* (pp. 28–83). Minneapolis, MN: University of Minnesota Press.

Brown, A. L., & Murphy, M. (1975). Reconconstruction of arbitrary versus meaningful sequences by preschool children. *Journal of Experimental Child Psychology, 20,* 307–326.

Brown, J. A. (1991). *Television "critical viewing skills" education.* Hillsdale, NJ: Lawrence Erlbaum Associates.

Browning, P., Nave, G., White, W. A. T., & Barkin, P. Z. (1985). Interactive video as an instructional technology for handicapped learners: A development and research program. *Australia and New Zealand Journal of Developmental Disabilities, 11,* 123–128.

Browning, P., & White, W. A. T. (1986). Teaching life enhancement skills with interactive video-based curricula. *Education and Training of the Mentally Retarded, 21,* 236–244.

Bryan, T. (1976). Peer popularity of learning disabled children: A replication. *Journal of Learning Disabilities, 9,* 307–311.

Bryan, T. H. (1977). Children's comprehension of nonverbal communication. *Journal of Learning Disabilities, 10,* 501–506.

Bryan, T. H. (1979). *Social skills and social relationships of learning disabled children.* Chicago: Chicago Institute for Learning Disabilities, University of Illinois.

Bryant, J. (Ed.). (1990). *Television and the American family.* Hillsdale, NJ: Lawrence Erlbaum Associates.

Bryant, J., & Anderson, D. R. (Eds.). (1983). *Children's understanding of television: Research on attention and comprehension.* New York: Academic Press.

Bryant, J., Boynton, K. R., & Wolf, M. A. (1980). Acquisition of information from educational television programs as a function of differently paced humorous inserts. *Journal of Educational Psychology, 72,* 170–180.

Buerkel-Rothfuss, N. (1978). *Mediating effects of television violence through curriculum intervention.* Unpublished doctoral dissertation, Michigan State University, East Lansing.

Bybee, C., Robinson, D., & Turow, J. (1982). Determinants of parental guidance of children's television viewing for a special subgroup: Mass media scholars. *Journal of Broadcasting, 16,* 697–710.

California Assessment Program. (1982). *Survey of sixth grade school achievement and television viewing habits.* Sacramento, CA: California State Department of Education.

California State Department of Education. (1980). *Student achievement in California schools, 1979–1980 annual report—Television and student achievement.* Sacramento, CA: Author.

Calvert, S. L., & Gersh, T. L. (1985, May). *Developmental differences in children's television story comprehension: Effects of content cues and auditory formal production features.* Paper presented at the International Communication Association Conference, Honolulu, Hawaii.

Calvert, S. L., Watkins, B. A., Wright, J. C., & Huston-Stein, A. (1979). *Recall of television content as a function of content type and level of production feature use.* Paper presented at the meeting of the Society of Research in Child Development, San Francisco.

Carlisle, R. (Ed.). (1978). *Patterns of performance: Public broadcasting and education, 1974–1976.* Washington, DC: Office of Educational Activities, Corporation for Public Broadcasting.

Carnegie Commission. (1967). *Public television: A program for action.* New York: Harper & Row.

Case, R. (1984). The process of stage transition: A neo-Piagetian view. In R. J. Sternberg (Ed.), *Mechanisms of cognitive development* (pp. 19–44). New York: W. H. Freeman.

Case, R., & Khanna, F. (1981). The missing links: Stages in children's progression from sensorimotor to logical thought. In W. Fischer (Ed.), *New directions for child development* (pp. 19–44). San Francisco: Jossey-Bass.

Chaffee, S. H., & McLeod, J. M. (1971, September). *Adolescents, parents, and television violence.* Paper presented at American Psychology Association meeting, Washington, DC.

Chaffee, S. H., & McLeod, J. M. (1972). Adolescent television use in the family context. In G. A. Comstock & E. A. Rubinstein (Eds.), *Television and social behavior: Television and adolescent aggressiveness* (Vol. 3, pp. 149–172) (DHEW Publication No. HSM 72-9058). Washington, DC: U.S. Government Printing Office.

Chaffee, S. H., & Tims, A. R. (1976). Interpersonal factors in adolescent TV use. *Journal of Social Issues, 32,* 98–115.

Children's Television Workshop. (1990). *Sesame Street research: A 20th anniversary symposium.* New York: Author.

Choate, R. B. (1980). The politics of change. In E. L. Palmer & A. Dorr (Eds.), *Children and the faces of television* (pp. 323–338). New York: Academic Press.

Clark, B. (1979). *Growing up gifted.* Los Angeles, CA: Charles E. Merrill.

Clark-Stewart, K. A. (1980). The father's contribution to children's cognitive and social development in early childhood. In F. A. Pedersen (Ed.), *The father-infant relationship: Observational studies in the father-infant relationship: Observational studies in the family setting.* New York: Praeger.

Cohen, A., Abelman, R., & Greenberg, B. S. (1990). Telling children not to watch. In R. J. Kinkle (Ed.), *Television and violence* (pp. 2–22). Detroit, MI: Mental Health Association of Michigan.

Cohn, S. J. (1981). What is giftedness? A multidimensional approach. In A. H. Kramer (Ed.), *Gifted children: Challenging their potential* (pp. 33–45). New York: Trillium Press.

Cohn, S. J., Cohn, C. M. G., & Kanevsky, L. S. (1988). Giftedness and talent. In E. W. Lynch & R. B. Lewis (Eds.), *Exceptional children and adults: An introduction to special education* (pp. 456–501). Glenview, IL: Scott, Foresman.

Colangelo, N., & Dettmann, D. F. (1983). A review of research on parents and families of gifted children. *Exceptional Children, 50*(1), 20–27.

Colangelo, N., & Kelly, K. R. (1983). A study of student, parent, and teacher attitudes toward gifted programs and gifted students. *Gifted Child Quarterly, 27,* 107–110.

Coleman, J. M., & Fults, B. A. (1982). Self-concept and the gifted classroom: The role of social comparisons. *Gifted Child Quarterly, 26,* 116–120.

Collins, W. A. (1979). Children's comprehension of television content. In E. Wartella (Ed.), *Children communicating: Media and development of thought, speech, understanding* (pp. 21–52). Beverly Hills, CA: Sage.

Collins, W. A. (1982). Cognitive processing in television viewing. In D. Pearl, L. Bouthilet, & J. Lazar (Eds.), *Television and behavior: Ten years of scientific progress and implications for the eighties* (Vol. 2, pp. 9–23) (DHHS Publication No. ADM 82-1196). Washington, DC: U.S. Government Printing Office.

Collins, W. A. (1983). Interpretation and inference in children's understanding of television. In J. Bryant & D. Anderson (Eds.), *Children's understanding of television: Research on attention and comprehension* (pp. 125–150). New York: Academic Press.

Collins, W. A., & Getz, S. K. (1976). Children's social responses following modeled reactions to provocation: Prosocial effects of a television drama. *Journal of Personality, 44,* 488–500.

Collins, W. A., Wellman, H., Keniston, A., & Westby, S. (1978). Age-related aspects of comprehension and inferences from a televised dramatic narrative. *Child Development, 49,* 389–399.

Columbia Broadcasting System, Office of Social Research. (1979). *A study of the CBS television reading program.* New York: Author.

Comstock, G., Chaffee, S., Katzman, N., McCombs, M., & Roberts, D. (1978). *Television and human behavior.* New York: Columbia University Press.

Comstock, G. A., & Rubinstein, E. A. (Eds.). (1971). *Television and social behavior, Vol. 1, Content and control.* Washington, DC: Government Printing Office.

Conti-Ramsden, G., & Snow, C. E. (Eds.). (1990). *Children's language* (Vol. 7). Hillsdale, NJ: Lawrence Erlbaum Associates.

Cook, T. D., Kendzierski, D. A., & Thomas, S. V. (1983). The implicit assumptions of television research: An analysis of the 1982 NIMH report on *Television and behavior. Public Opinion Quarterly, 47,* 161–201.

Corder-Bolz, C. R. (1982). Television literacy and critical television viewing skills. In D. Pearl, L. Bouthilet, & J. Lazar (Eds.), *Television and behavior: Ten years of scientific progress and implications for the eighties* (Vol. 2, pp. 91–101). Washington, DC: U.S. Government Printing Office.

Crane, V. (1980). Content development for children's television programs. In E. Palmer & A. Dorr (Eds.), *Children and the faces of television: Teaching, violence, selling* (pp. 33–48). New York: Academic Press.

Cullinan, D., Epstein, M. H., & Kauffman, J. M. (1984). Teachers' ratings of students' behaviors: What constitutes behavior disorder in school? *Behavioral Disorders, 10,* 9–19.

Cummings, R. H., & Maddux, C. D. (1985). *Parenting the learning disabled.* Springfield, IL: Charles C. Thomas.

Cunningham, C. E., & Barkley, R. A. (1978). The role of academic failure in hyperactive behavior. *Journal of Learning Disabilities, 11,* 274–280.

Cunningham, C., & Sloper, P. (1980). *Helping your exceptional baby: A practical and honest guide to raising a mentally handicapped child.* New York: Pantheon.

Daniels, P. R. (1983). *Teaching the gifted/learning disabled child.* Rockville, MD: Aspen Systems Corporation.

Davis, G. A., & Rimm, S. B. (1989). *Education of the gifted and talented.* Englewood, NJ: Prentice-Hall.

Davis, H., & Walton, P. (1983). *Language, image, media.* Oxford: Blackwell Scientific.

DeKoning, T. L., Conradie, D. P., & Nel, E. M. (1980). *The effect of different kinds of television programming on the youth.* Pretoria, Republic of South Africa: Human Sciences Research Council.

DeKoning, T. L., Conradie, D. P., & Nel, E. M. (1990). The effect of different kinds of television programs on South African youth. In K. D. Gadow (Ed.), *Advances in learning and behavioral disabilities* (pp. 79–101). Greenwich, CT: JAI Press.

Desmond, R. J., Hirsch, B., Singer, D. G., & Singer, J. L. (1987). Gender differences, mediation, and disciplinary styles in children's responses to television. *Sex Roles: A Journal of Research, 16,* 375–389.

Desmond, R. J., Singer, J. L., Singer, D. G., Calam, R., & Colimore, K. (1985). Family mediation patterns and television viewing: Young children's use and grasp of the medium. *Human Communication Research, 11*(4), 461–480.

Desmond, R. J., Singer, J. L., & Singer, D. G. (1990). Family mediation: Parental communication patterns and the influence of television on children. In J. Bryant (Ed.), *Television and the American family* (pp. 293–309). Hillsdale, NJ: Lawrence Erlbaum Associates.

Dewing, K. (1970). The reliability and validity of selected tests on creative thinking in a sample of seventh grade West Australian children. *British Journal of Educational Psychology, 40,* 35–42.

Dirr, P. J. (1980). The future of television's teaching face. In E. Palmer & A. Dorr (Eds.), *Children and the faces of television: Teaching, violence, selling* (pp. 99–108). New York: Academic Press.

Dirr, P. J., & Pedone, R. J. (1979). *Uses of television for instruction, 1976–77.* Washington, DC: Corporation for Public Broadcasting.

Ditton, P., Green, R. J., & Singer, M. T. (1987). Communication deviances: A comparison between parents of learning disabled and normally achieving students. *Family Process, 26,* 75–87.

DiVesta, F. (1975). Trait–treatment interactions, cognitive processes, and research on communication media. *Audio Visual Communication Review, 23,* 185–196.

Doane, J. A. (1978). Family interaction and communication deviance in disturbed and normal families: A review of research. *Family Process, 17,* 357–376.

Dodge, K. A. (1980). Social cognition and children's aggressive behavior. *Child Development, 51,* 162–170.

Dodge, K. A., & Newman, J. P. (1981). Biased decision making processes in aggressive boys. *Journal of Abnormal Psychology, 90,* 375–379.

Dominick, J. R., & Greenberg, B. S. (1972). Attitudes toward violence: The interaction of television exposure, family attitudes, and social class. In G. A. Comstock & E. A. Rubinstein (Eds.), *Television and social behavior. Vol. III: Television and adolescent aggressiveness* (pp. 314–335). Washington, DC: U.S. Government Printing Office.

Donahue, M., Pearl, R., & Bryan, T. (1983). Communicative competence in learning disabled children. In K. D. Gadow & I. Bialer (Eds.), *Advances in learning and behavioral disabilities* (Vol. 2, pp. 49–84). Greenwich, CT: JAI Press.

Donahue, T. R. (1978). Television's impact on emotionally disturbed children's value systems. *Child Study Journal, 8,* 187–201.

Donahue, W. A., & Donahue, T. R. (1977). Black, white, and white gifted and emotionally disturbed children's perceptions of the reality in television programming. *Human Relations, 30,* 609–621.

Doorlag, D. H. (1988). Behavioral disorders. In E. W. Lynch & R. B. Lewis (Eds.), *Exceptional children and adults: An introduction to special education* (pp. 407–455). Glenview, IL: Scott, Foresman.

Dorow, I. G. (1976). Televised music lessons as educational reinforcement for correct mathematical responses with the educable mentally retarded. *Journal of Music Therapy, 13,* 77–86.

Dorr, A. (1981). Television and affective development and functioning: Maybe this decade. *Journal of Broadcasting, 25,* 335–346.

Dorr, A. (1986). *Television and children: A special medium for a special audience.* Beverly Hills, CA: Sage.

Dorr, A., Graves, S. B., & Phelps, E. (1980). Television literacy for young children. *Journal of Communication, 30,* 71–83.

Dorr, A., & Kovaric, P. (1980). Some of the people some of the time—But which people? Televised violence and its effects. In E. L. Palmer & A. Dorr (Eds.), *Children and the faces of television: Teaching, violence, selling* (pp. 183–199). New York: Academic Press.

Dorr, A., & Kunkel, D. (1990). Children and the media environment: Change and constancy amid change. *Communication Research, 17*(1), 5–25.

Douglas, V. I., & Peters, K. G. (1979). Toward a clearer definition of the attentional deficit of hyperactive children. In G. A. Hale & M. Lewis (Eds.), *Attention and the development of cognitive skills.* New York: Plenum.

Dowrick, P. W., & Raeburn, J. M. (1977). Video editing and medication to produce a therapeutic self model. *Journal of Consulting and Clinical Psychology, 45,* 1156–1158.

Drabman, R. S., & Thomas, M. H. (1974). Does media violence increase children's toleration of real-life aggression? *Developmental Psychology, 10,* 418–421.

Drabman, R. S., & Thomas, M. H. (1976). Does watching violence on television cause apathy? *Pediatrics, 57,* 329–331.

Easterbrooks, M. A., & Goldberg, W. A. (1984). Toddler development in the family: Impact of father involvement and parenting characteristics. *Child Development, 55,* 740–752.

Eccles, J. S. (1985). Why doesn't Jane run? Sex differences in educational and occupational patterns. In F. D. Horowitz & M. O'Brien (Eds.), *The gifted and talented: Developmental perspectives* (pp. 251–295). Washington, DC: American Psychological Association.

Edwards, R. (1976). ETV and the handicapped child. *Special Education Forward Trends, 3*(1), 17–19.

Efron, D., & Veenendaal, K. (1988). Videotaping in groups for children of substance abusers: A strategy for emotionally disturbed, acting out children. *Alcoholism Treatment Quarterly, 4,* 71–85.

Elgersma, E. (1981). Providing for affective growth in gifted education. *Roeper Review, 3*(4), 6–8.

Elias, M. J. (1979). Helping emotionally disturbed children through prosocial television. *Exceptional Children, 46,* 217–218.

Elias, M. (1982). Using programs for emotionally disturbed children in mainstreamed or special class settings. In B. Baskin & K. Harris (Eds.), *The mainstreamed library* (pp. 178–186). Chicago: American Library Association.

Elias, M. J. (1983). Improving coping skills of emotionally disturbed boys through television-based social problem solving. *American Journal of Orthopsychiatry, 53,* 61–72.

Elias, M. J., Larcen, S. W., Zlottow, S. F., & Chinsky, J. M. (1978). *An innovative measure of children's cognitions in problematic interpersonal situations.* New Brunswick, NJ: Rutgers University. (ERIC Document Reproduction Service No. ED 178-181).

Elias, M. J., & Maher, C. A. (1983). Social and affective development of children: A programmatic perspective. *Exceptional Children, 49,* 339–346.

Elias, M., & Salvador, C. (1980). *Using "Inside/Out" as an affective education and social problem solving thinking program* (rev. ed.). New Brunswick, NJ: Department of Psychology.

Elliot, N. (1979). Language and cognition in the developing child. In E. Wartella (Ed.), *Children communicating: Media and development of thought, speech, understanding* (pp. 187–214). Beverly Hills, CA: Sage.

Emery, M., & Emery, F. (1980). The vacuous vision: The TV medium. *Journal of University of Film Association, 32* (1,2), 27–31.

Eron, L. D. (1982). Parent–child interaction, television violence, and aggression of children. *American Psychologist, 37,* 197–211.

Evans, R., & Clifford, A. (1976). Captured for consideration-using videotape as a aim to the treatment of the disturbed child. *Child: Care, Health, and Development, 2,* 129–137.

Eyman, R. K., & Call, T. (1977). Maladaptive behavior and community placement of mentally retarded persons. *American Journal of Mental Deficiency, 82,* 137–144.

Farber, B., & Jenne, W. C. (1963). Family organization and parent-child communication: Parents and siblings of a retarded child. *Monograph of the Society for Research in Child Development,* 7(28).

Fargo, G. A., Crowell, D. C., Noyes, M. H., Fuchigami, R. Y., Gordon, J. M., & Dunn-Rankin, P. (1967). Comparability of group television and individual administration of the Peabody Picture Vocabulary Test: Implications for screening. *Journal of Educational Psychology, 58,* 137–140.

Fechter, J. V., Jr. (1971). Modeling and environment generalization by mentally retarded subjects of televised aggressive or friendly behavior. *American Journal of Mental Deficiency, 76,* 266–267.

Federal Communications Commission. (1984, January 13). Children's television programming and advertising practices: Report and order. *Federal Register, 49,* 1704–1727.

Ferguson, B., & Silberberg, S. (1979). A video program for special adolescents. *Journal of Learning Disabilities, 12,* 508–511.

Feshbach, S. (1955). The drive-reducing function of fantasy behavior. *Journal of Abnormal and Social Psychology, 50,* 3–11.

Feshbach, S. (1972). Reality and fantasy in filmed violence. In J. P. Murray, E. A. Rubinstein, & G. A. Comstock (Eds.), *Television and social behavior. Vol. 2. Television and social learning* (pp. 318–345). Washington, DC: U.S. Government Printing Office.

Feshbach, S. (1976). The role of fantasy in the response to television. *Journal of Social Issues, 32*(4), 71–85.

Feshbach, S., & Singer, R. (1971). *Television and aggression.* San Francisco: Jossey-Bass.

Fischer, K. W., & Bullock, D. (1984). Cognitive development in school-age children: Conclusions and a new direction. In W. A. Collins (Ed.), *The elementary school years: Understanding development in middle childhood* (pp. 76–146). Washington, DC: National Academic Press.

Fivush, R., & Mandler, J. (1984). *Developmental changes in the understanding of temporal order.* Unpublished manuscript.

Flagg, B. N. (1990). *Formative evaluation for educational technologies.* Hillsdale, NJ: Lawrence Erlbaum Associates.

Flavell, J. H. (1978). The development of knowledge about visual perception. In C. B. Keasey (Ed.), *Nebraska symposium on motivation* (pp. 43–77). Lincoln: University of Nebraska Press.

Flavell, J. H. (1986). The development of children's knowledge about appearance-reality distinction. *American Psychologist, 41,* 418–425.

Flavell, J. H., Everett, B. A., Croft, K., & Flavell, E. R. (1981). Young children's knowledge about visual perception: Further evidence for the Level 1–Level 2 distinction. *Developmental Psychology, 17,* 99–103.

Flavell, J. H., Flavell, E. R., & Green, F. L. (1987). Young children's knowledge about the apparent–real and pretend–real distinctions. *Developmental Psychology, 23,* 816–822.

Flavell, J. H., Flavell, E. R., Green, F. L., & Korfmacher, J. E. (1990). Do young children think of television images as pictures or real objects? *Journal of Broadcasting and Electronic Media, 34*(4), 399–419.

Flavell, J. H., Flavell, E. R., Green, F. L., & Wilcox, S. A. (1980). Young children's knowledge about visual perception: Effect of observer's distance from target on perceptual clarity of target. *Developmental Psychology, 16,* 10–12.

Flessati, E., & Fouts, G. (1985, May). *Effects of time-compressed television and children's activity level on observational learning.* Paper presented at the International Communication Association conference, Honolulu, Hawaii.

Fox, L. H., Brody, L., & Tobin, D. (1983). *Learning disabled/gifted children.* Baltimore, MD: University Park Press.

Fox, P., Eveleigh, B., & Campbell, J. (1977). Effects of videotape recordings on learning characteristics. *Pointer, 22*(1), 42–47.

Franks, B., & Dolan, L. (1982). Affective characteristics of gifted children: Educational implications. *Gifted Child Quarterly, 26,* 172–178.

Freedman, J. L. (1984). Effect of television violence on aggressiveness. *Psychological Bulletin, 96,* 227–246.

Freedman, J. L. (1986). Television violence and aggression: A rejoinder. *Psychological Bulletin, 100,* 372–378.

Friedlander, B. Z., Wetstone, H. S., & McPeek, D. L. (1974). Systematic assessment of selective language listening deficit in emotionally disturbed pre-school children. *Journal of Child Psychology and Psychiatry, 15,* 1–12.

Friedrich, L. K., & Stein, A. H. (1973). Aggressive and prosocial television programs and the natural behavior of preschool children. *Monographs of the Society for Research in Child Development, 38*(4) (Serial No. 151).

Friedrich, L. K., & Stein, A. H. (1975). Prosocial television and young children: The effects of verbal labeling and role playing on learning and behavior. *Child Development, 46,* 27–38.

Friedrich-Cofer, L., & Huston, A. C. (1986). Television violence and aggression: The debate continues. *Psychological Bulletin, 100,* 364–371.

Friedrich-Cofer, L. K., Huston-Stein, A., Kipnis, D. M., Susman, E. J., & Clewett, A. S. (1979). Environmental enhancement of prosocial television content: Effects on interpersonal behavior, imaginative play, and self-regulation in a natural setting. *Developmental Psychology, 15*, 637–646.

Frodi, A. M., Lamb, M. E., Hwang, C. P., & Frodi, M. E. (1982, March). *Increased paternal involvement and family relationships.* Paper presented at the International Conference on Infant Studies, Austin, TX.

Gadberry, S., Barroni, A., & Brown, W. (1981). Effects of camera cuts and music on selective attention and verbal and motor imitation by mentally retarded adults. *American Journal of Mental Deficiency, 86*, 309–316.

Gadow, K. D., & Sprafkin, J. (1987). Effects of viewing high versus low aggression cartoons on emotionally disturbed children. *Journal of Pediatric Psychology, 12*, 413–427.

Gadow, K. D., & Sprafkin, J. (1989). Field experiments of television violence with children: Evidence for an environmental hazard? *Pediatrics, 83*, 399–405.

Gadow, K. D., Sprafkin, J., & Ficarrotto, T. (1987). Effects of viewing aggression-laden cartoons on preschool-aged emotionally disturbed children. *Child Psychiatry and Human Development, 17*, 257–274.

Gadow, K. D., Sprafkin, J., & Grayson, P. (1990). The Help–Hurt game as a measure of aggression in children with learning and behavior disorders. *Learning and Individual Differences, 2*, 337–351.

Gadow, K. D., Sprafkin, J., Kelly, E., & Ficarrotto, T. (1988). Reality perceptions of television: A comparison of school-labeled learning disabled and nonhandicapped children. *Journal of Clinical Child Psychology, 17*, 25–33.

Gallagher, J. J., Kaplan, S. N., & Sato, I. S. (1983). *Promoting the education of the gifted/talented: Strategies for advocacy.* Ventura, GA: National/State Leadership Training Institute on the Gifted and Talented.

Geen, R. G. (1975). The meaning of observed violence: Real vs. fictional violence and consequent effects on aggression and emotional arousal. *Journal of Research in Personality, 9*, 270–281.

Gelman, R., Bullock, M., & Meck, E. (1980). Preschoolers' understanding of simple object transformation. *Child Development, 51*, 691–699.

Gerbner, G. (1972). Violence in television drama: Trends in symbolic functions. In G. A. Comstock & E. A. Rubinstein (Eds.), *Television and social behavior (Vol. 1): Media content and control* (pp. 28–187). Washington, DC: U.S. Government Printing Office.

Gerbner, G., Gross, L., Signorielli, N., & Morgan, M. (1986). *Television's mean world: Violence Profile No. 14-15.* Philadelphia: University of Pennsylvania, Annenberg School of Communications.

Gerbner, G., Gross, L., Signorielli, N., Morgan, M., & Jackson-Beeck, M. (1979). The demonstration of power: Violence Profile No. 10. *Journal of Communication, 29*, 177–195.

Glasser, R. (1985). Cognitive structure and process in highly competent performance. In F. D. Horowitz & M. O'Brien (Eds.), *The gifted and talented: Developmental perspectives* (pp. 75–98). Washington, DC: American Psychological Association.

Goldstein, E. (1964). *Selective audio-visual instruction for mentally retarded pupils.* Springfield, IL: Charles C. Thomas.

Gould, J. (1972, January 11). TV violence held unharmful to youth. *The New York Times*, p. 1.

Grayson, P., Gadow, K. D., & Sprafkin, J. (1989, April). *Evaluation of a television-based social problem solving curriculum for learning disabled children.* Paper presented at the Society for Research in Child Development, Baltimore, MD. (ERIC Document Reproduction Service No. ED 304 861)

Green, R. J. (1990). Family communication and children's learning disabilities: Evidence for Cole's theory of interactivity. *Journal of Learning Disabilities, 23*(3), 145–148.

Greenberg, B. S. (1972). Children's reactions to television blacks. *Journalism Quarterly, 49*(1), 5–14.

Greenberg, B. S., & Atkin, C. K. (1979). *Parental mediation of children's social learning from television.* Report submitted to the Office of Child Development, Washington, DC.

Greenberg, B. S., Atkin, C. K., Edison, N. G., & Korzenny, F. (1977). *Prosocial and antisocial behaviors on commercial television in 1975–76. Report by Department of Communication, Michigan State University.* Washington, DC: Office of Child Development, Health, Education, and Welfare.

Greenberg, B. S., & Dominick, J. (1970). Television behavior among disadvantaged children. In B. S. Greenberg & B. Dervin (Eds.), *Use of the mass media by the urban poor.* New York: Praeger.

Greenberg, B. S., Edison, N., Korzenny, F., Fernandez-Collado, C., & Atkin, C. K. (1980). Antisocial and prosocial behaviors on television. In B. S. Greenberg (Ed.), *Life on television: Content analysis of U.S. TV drama* (pp. 99–128). Norwood, NJ: Ablex.

Greenberg, B. S., Ericson, P. M., & Vlahos, M. (1972). Children's television behaviors as perceived by mother and child. In E. A. Rubinstein, G. A. Comstock, & J. P. Murray (Eds.), *Television and social behavior: Television in day-to-day patterns of use (Vol. 4)* (DHEW Publication No. HSM 72-9059). Washington, DC: U.S. Government Printing Office.

Greenberg, B., & Reeves, B. (1976). Children and the perceived reality of television. *Journal of Social Issues, 32*(4), 86–97.

Greene, J. O., & Sparks, G. G. (1983). Explication and test of a cognitive model of communication apprehension: A new look at an old construct. *Human Communication Research, 9,* 349–366.

Greene, R. J., & Hoats, D. L. (1969). Reinforcing capabilities of television distortion. *Journal of Applied Behavior Analysis, 2,* 139–141.

Grieve, R., & Williamson, K. (1977). Aspects of auditory and visual attention to narrative material in normal and mentally handicapped children. *Journal of Child Psychology and Psychiatry, 18,* 251–262.

Griggs, S., & Dunn, R. (1984). Selected case studies of the learning style preferences of gifted students. *Gifted Child Quarterly, 28,* 115–119.

Gross, L. S., & Walsh, R. P. (1980). Factors affecting parental control over children's television viewing: A pilot study. *Journal of Broadcasting, 24,* 411–419.

Growing avenues for children's TV programming. (1985, December 30). *Broadcasting,* p. 27.

Guarnaccia, V. J., Daniels, L. K., & Sefick, W. J. (1975). Comparison of automated and standard administration of the Purdue Pegboard with mentally retarded adults. *Perceptual Motor Skills, 40,* 371–374.

Gunter, B., & Svennevig, M. (1987). *Behind and in front of the screen: Television's involvement with family life.* London: John Libbey.

Hackett, M. S. (1977). *Developmental trends in the learning of central and peripheral televised material presented verbally or in action.* Unpublished manuscript, State University of New York at Stony Brook.

Hackett, M. S., & Sprafkin, J. (1982). *Developmental trends in the comprehension of televised social behaviors.* Paper presented at the meeting of the American Psychological Association, Washington, DC.

Haefner, M. J., Hunter, L. S., & Wartella, E. A. (1986, May). *Parents, children and new media: Expectations, attitudes, and use.* Paper presented at the International Communication Association Conference, Chicago.

Hall, E. R., Esty, E. T., & Fisch, S. M. (1990). Television and children's problem-solving behavior: A synopsis of an evaluation of the effects of Square One TV. *Journal of Mathematical Behavior, 9,* 161–174.

Hall, S. (1980). Encoding/decoding. In S. Hall, D. Hobson, A. Lowe, & P. Willis (Eds.), *Culture, media, language* (pp. 128–138). London: Hutchinson.

Hallahan, D. P., & Kauffman, J. M. (1977). Labels, categories, behaviors: ED, LD, and EMR reconsidered. *Journal of Special Education, 11,* 139–149.

Hallahan, D. P., & Kauffman, J. M. (1991). *Exceptional children: Introduction to special education.* Englewood Cliffs, NJ: Prentice-Hall.

Hanratty, M. A., Liebert, R. M., Morris, L. W., & Fernandez, L. E. (1969). Imitation of film-mediated aggression against live and inanimate victims. *Proceedings for the 77th Annual Convention of the American Psychological Association,* pp. 457–458.

Hargis, C. H., Gickling, E. E., & Mahmoud, C. C. (1975). The effectiveness of TV in teaching sight words to students with learning disabilities. *Journal of Learning Disabilities, 8,* 44–46.

Harmonay, M. (Ed.). (1977). *Promise and performance: Children with special needs.* Cambridge, MA: Ballinger.

Harris, S. J. (1988). Sociolinguistic approaches to media language. *Critical Studies in Mass Communication, 5*(1), 72–82.

Hartmann, D. P. (1969). Influence of symbolically modelled instrumental aggression and pain cues on aggressive behavior. *Journal of Personality and Social Psychology, 11,* 280–288.

Hartmann, D. P., & Gelfand, D. M. (1969, June). *Motivational variables affecting performance of vicariously learned responses.* Paper presented at Western Psychological Association Meeting, Vancouver, British Columbia.

Harvey, S. E., Sprafkin, J. N., & Rubinstein, E. (1979). Prime time television: A profile of aggressive and prosocial behaviors. *Journal of Broadcasting, 23,* 179–189.

Hawkins, R. P. (1977). The dimensional structure of children's perceptions of television reality. *Communication Research, 4,* 299–320.

Hawkins, R. P., & Pingree, S. (1982). Television's influence on social reality. In D. Pearl, L. Bouthilet, & J. Lazar (Eds.), *Television and behavior: Ten years of scientific progress and implications for the eighties* (Vol. 2, pp. 224–247) (DHHS Publication No. ADM 82-1196). Washington, DC: U.S. Government Printing Office.

Hayes, L. (1977, April). *New avenues of special education resources: Sesame Street programming for the exceptional child.* Paper presented at the annual meeting of The Council for Exceptional Children, Atlanta. (ERIC Document Reproduction Service No. ED 139 198)

Haynes, R. L. (1978). 'HiHo Time!' Educational TV for the retarded. *Audiovisual Instruction, 23,* 36–39.

Heald, G. R. (1980). Television viewing guides and parental recommendations. *Journalism Quarterly, 57*(1), 141–144.

Healy, J. M. (1990). *Endangered minds: Why our children don't think.* New York: Simon & Schuster.

Hearold, S. (1986). A synthesis of 1043 effects of television on social behavior. In G. Comstock (Ed.), *Public communications and behavior: Volume I* (pp. 65–133). New York: Academic Press.

Hill, I. J. (1982). The relative effectiveness of select television production techniques on the attention and comprehension of learning disabled children (Doctoral dissertation, University of Virginia, 1981). *Dissertation Abstracts International, 42,* 2984A. (University Microfilms No. 8129308).

Himmelweit, H., Oppenheim, A. N., & Vince, P. (1958). *Television and the child: An empirical study of the effects of television on the young.* London: Oxford University Press.

Hoekema, J. (1983). Interactive video: An elephant in search of a definition. *Performance and Instruction Journal, 22*(9), 4–5.

Hoffman, M. L. (1970). Moral development. In P. H. Mussen (Ed.), *Carmichael's manual of child psychology.* New York: John Wiley.

Hoffman, M. L. (1975). Moral internalization, parental power, and the nature of parent–child interaction. *Developmental Psychology, 11,* 228–239.

Hoffman, M. L., & Salzstein, H. S. (1967). Parent discipline and the child's moral development. *Journal of Personality and Social Psychology, 5,* 45–57.

Hoffner, C., & Cantor, J. (1985). Developmental differences in responses to a television character's appearance and behavior. *Developmental Psychology, 21,* 1065–1074.

Hoffner, C., Cantor, J., & Thorson, E. (1988). Children's understanding of a televised narrative: Developmental differences in processing of audio and video content. *Communication Research, 15,* 227–245.

Hoffner, C., Cantor, J., & Thorson, E. (1989). Children's responses to conflicting auditory and visual features of a televised narrative. *Human Communication Research, 16*(2), 256–278.

Hollenbeck, A. R., & Slaby, R. G. (1979). Infant visual and vocal responses to television. *Child Development, 50,* 41–45.

Hollingworth, L. S. (1929). *Gifted children: Their nature and nurture.* New York: Macmillan.

Hollingworth, L. S. (1942). *Children above 180 IQ, Stanford–Binet: Origin and development.* New York: World Book Company.

Hopkins, K. D., Lefever, D. W., & Hopkins, B. R. (1967). TV vs. teacher administration of standardized tests: Comparability of scores. *Journal of Educational Measurement, 4,* 35–40.

Howitt, D., & Cumberbatch, G. (1976). The parameters of attraction to mass media figures. In R. Brown (Ed.), *Children and television* (pp. 167–183). Beverly Hills, CA: Sage.

Huesmann, L. R., Eron, L. D., Klein, R., Brice, P., & Fischer, P. (1983). Mitigating the imitation of aggressive behaviors by changing children's attitudes about media violence. *Journal of Personality and Social Psychology, 44,* 899–910.

Huesmann, L. R., Lagerspetz, K., & Eron, L. D. (1984). Intervening variables in the TV-violence–aggression relation: Evidence from two countries. *Developmental Psychology, 20,* 746–775.

Hughes, J. N., & Hall, D. M. (1985). Performance of disturbed and nondisturbed boys on a role play test of social competence. *Behavioral Disorders, 11,* 24–29.

Huston, A., Watkins, B., & Kunkel, D. (1989). Public policy and children's television. *American Psychologist, 44,* 424–433.

Huston, A. C., & Wright, J. C. (1983). Children's processing of television: The informative functions of formal features. In J. Bryant & D. R. Anderson (Eds.), *Children's understanding of television: Research on attention and comprehension* (pp. 35–68). New York: Academic Press.

Huston-Stein, A., Fox, S., Greer, D., Watkins, B. A., & Whitaker, J. (1981). The effects of TV action and violence on children's social behavior. *Journal of Genetic Psychology, 138,* 183–191.

Jacobs, W. R. (1979). *Television diagnosis: Futurism in psychometrics.* (ERIC Document Reproduction Service No. ED 171 004)

Janos, P. M., Fung, H. C., & Robinson, N. M. (1985). Self-concepts, self-esteem, and peer relations among gifted children who feel "different." *Gifted Child Quarterly, 29,* 78–82.

Janos, P. M., Kristi, A. M., & Robinson, N. M. (1985). Friendship patterns in highly intelligent children. *Roeper Review, 8*(1), 46–49.

Janos, P. M., & Robinson, N. M. (1985). Psychosocial development in intellectually gifted children. In F. D. Horowitz & M. O'Brien (Eds.), *The gifted and talented: Developmental perspectives* (pp. 149–195). Washington, DC: American Psychological Association.

Johnsen, S. K., & Corn, A. L. (1989). Past, present, and future of education for gifted children with sensory and/or physical disabilities. *Roeper Review, 12,* 13–22.

Justice, E. M. (1985). Metamemory: An aspect of metacognition in the mentally retarded. In N. R. Ellis (Ed.), *International review of research in mental retardation* (Vol. 13, pp. 79–107). New York: Academic Press.

Kaplan, R. M., & Singer, R. D. (1976). Television violence and viewer aggression: A reexamination of the evidence. *Journal of Social Issues, 32,* 35–70.

Karnes, M. B., Shwedel, A. M., & Kemp, P. B. (1985). Maximizing the potential of the young gifted child. *Roeper Review, 7,* 204–209.

Karnes, M. B., Shwedel, A. M., & Williams, M. (1983). Combining instructional models to develop differentiated curriculum for young gifted children. *Teaching Exceptional Children.* Reston, VA: Spring.

Kassier, M. R. (1979). The effects of televised modeling on selected pro-social behaviors of severely withdrawn children (Doctoral dissertation, Columbia University Teachers College, 1979). *Dissertation Abstracts International*, 7212A-7213A. (University Microfilms No. 7913202)

Kavale, K. A. (1980). Learning disability and cultural-economic disadvantage: The case for a relationship. *Learning Disability Quarterly, 3*(3), 97–112.

Kavanagh, J. F., & Truss, T. J. (1988). Revised definition of learning disabilities. In J. F. Kavanagh & T. J. Truss (Ed.), *Learning disabilities: Proceedings of the national conference* (pp. 549–551). Parkton, MD: York Press.

Keilitz, I., Tucker, D. J., & Horner, R. D. (1973). Increasing mentally retarded adolescents verbalizations about current events. *Journal of Applied Behavior Analysis, 6*, 621–630.

Kelly, E. (1986). *Perception of reality on television: A comparison of emotionally disturbed, learning disabled, and nonhandicapped children*. Unpublished doctoral dissertation, State University of New York at Stony Brook.

Kelly, E., Sprafkin, J., & Gadow, K. D. (1986). *A comparative study of television viewing habits in special education and regular classroom students*. Unpublished manuscript, State University of New York at Stony Brook.

Kelly, K. R., & Colangelo, N. (1984). Academic and social self concepts of gifted, general, and special students. *Exceptional Children, 50*, 551–554.

Klapper, J. T. (1960). *The effects of mass communication*. New York: The Free Press.

Knight-Arest, I. (1984). Communicative effectiveness of learning disabled and normally achieving 10- to 13-year-old boys. *Learning Disability Quarterly, 7*, 237–245.

Kolucki, B. (1977, April). *New avenues of special education resources: Sesame Street programming for the exceptional child*. Paper presented at the annual meeting of The Council for Exceptional Children, Atlanta. (ERIC Document Reproduction Service No. ED 139 199)

Korzenny, F., Greenberg, B. S., & Atkin, C. K. (1979). Styles of parental disciplinary practices as a mediator of children's learning from antisocial television portrayals. In D. Nimmo (Ed.), *Communication yearbook 3* (pp. 283–293). New Brunswick, NJ: Transaction.

Krull, R. (1983). Children learning to watch television. In J. Bryant, & D. R. Anderson (Eds.), *Children's understanding of television: Research on attention and comprehension* (pp. 103–124). New York: Academic Press.

Krull, R., & Husson, W. (1979). Children's attention: The case of TV viewing. In E. Wartella (Ed.), *Children communicating: Media and development of thought, speech, understanding* (pp. 83–114). Beverly Hills, CA: Sage.

Krupski, A. (1986). Attention problems in youngsters with learning handicaps. In J. K. Torgesen & B. Y. L. Wong (Eds.), *Psychological and educational perspectives on learning disabilities*. New York: Academic Press.

Kubey, R., & Larson, R. (1990). The use and experience of the new video media among children and adolescents. *Communication Research, 17*(1), 107–130.

Kumata, H. (1960). A decade of teaching by television. In W. Schramm (Ed.), *The impact of educational television*. Urbana: University of Illinois.

Kunkel, D., & Watkins, B. (1986, May). *Children's television regulatory policy: Where we are and how we got there*. Paper presented at the meeting of the International Communication Association, Chicago.

Kysela, G. M. (1973). The isolate child. *Deficience Mentale/Mental Retardation, 23*(4), 15–16.

Lamb, M. E. (1977). The development of parent-infant attachments in the first two years of life. In F. A. Pedersen (Ed.), *The family system: Networks of interactions among mother, father, and infant*. New York: Praeger.

Lazar, A. L., Gensley, J., & Gowan, J. (1972). Developing positive attitudes through curriculum planning for young gifted children. *The Gifted Child Quarterly, 26*, 27–31.

Lefkowitz, M. M., Eron, L. D., Walder, L. O., & Huesmann, L. R. (1972). Television violence and child aggression: A followup study. In G. A. Comstock & E. A. Rubinstein (Eds.), *Television and social behavior, Vol. III: Television and adolescent aggressiveness* (pp. 35–135). Washington, DC: U.S. Government Printing Office.

Leifer, A. D., Gordon, N. J., & Graves, S. B. (1974). Children's television: More than mere entertainment. *Harvard Education Review, 44,* 213–245.

Leifer, A. D., & Roberts, D. F. (1972). Children's response to television violence. In J. P. Murray, E. A. Rubinstein, & G. A. Comstock (Eds.), *Television and social behavior, Vol. 2: Television and social learning.* Washington, DC: U.S. Government Printing Office.

Lesser, G. S. (1972). Learning, teaching, and television production for children: The experience of "Sesame Street." *Harvard Educational Review, 42,* 232–272.

Levin, S. R., & Anderson, D. R. (1976). The development of attention. *Journal of Communication, 26*(2), 126–135.

Lewis, R. B. (1988). Learning disabilities. In E. W. Lynch, & R. B. Lewis (Eds.), *Exceptional children and adults: An introduction to special education* (pp. 352–406). Glenview, IL: Scott, Foresman.

Leyens, J. P., Camino, L., Parke, R. D., & Berkowitz, L. (1975). Effects of movie violence on aggression in a field setting as a function of group dominance and cohension. *Journal of Personality and Social Psychology, 32,* 346–360.

Liebert, R. M., & Baron, R. A. (1972). Short-term effects of televised aggression on children's aggressive behavior. In J. P. Murray, E. A. Rubinstein, & G. A. Comstock (Eds.), *Television and social behavior (Vol. 2): Television and social learning* (pp. 181–201). Washington, DC: U.S. Government Printing Office.

Liebert, R. M., Neale, J. M., & Davidson, E. S. (1973). *The early window: Effects of television on children and youth.* New York: Pergamon.

Liebert, R. M., & Sprafkin, J. (1988). *The early window: Effects of television on children and youth* (3rd ed.). New York: Pergamon.

Liebert, R. M., Sprafkin, J. N., & Davidson, E. S. (1982). *The early window: Effects of television on children and youth* (2nd ed.). New York: Pergamon.

Liss, M. A., Reinhardt, L. C., & Fredriksen, S. (1983). TV heroes: The impact of rhetoric and deeds. *Journal of Applied Developmental Psychology, 4*(2), 175–187.

Lloyd-Kolkin, D. (1981). The critical television viewing project for high school students. In M. E. Ploghoft & J. A. Anderson (Eds.), *Education for the television age* (pp. 91–98). Athens, OH: The Cooperative Center for Social Science Foundation.

Lombardi, T. P., & Poole, R. G. (1968). Utilization of videosonic equipment with mentally retarded. *Mental Retardation, 6*(5), 7–9.

Longhi, P., Follett, R., Bloom, B., & Armstrong, J. R. (1975). A program for adolescent educable mentally retarded. *Education and Training of the Mentally Retarded, 100,* 104–109.

Lottan, S. (1967). The ability of children to distinguish between the "make believe" and the "real" in children's literature. *Journal of Educational Thought, 1,* 25–33.

Lovaas, O. I. (1961). Effect of exposure to symbolic aggression on aggressive behavior. *Child Development, 32,* 37–44.

Lovaas, O. I., Berberich, J. P., Perloff, B. F., & Schaeffer, B. (1966). Acquisition of imitative speech in schizophrenic children. *Science, 151,* 705–707.

Luke, C. (1985). Television discourse processing: A schema theoretic approach. *Communication Education, 34,* 91–105.

Lull, J. (Ed.). (1988). *World families watch television.* Beverly Hills, CA: Sage.

Luria, A. R. (1982). *Language and cognition.* New York: Wiley Interscience.

Lyle, J. (1972). Television in daily life: Patterns of use. In E. A. Rubinstein, G. A. Comstock, & J. P. Murray (Eds.), *Television and social behavior* (Vol. 4, pp. 1–32) (DHEW Publication No. HSM 72-9059). Washington, DC: U.S. Government Printing Office.

Lyle, J., & Hoffman, H. R. (1972). Children's use of television and other media. In E. A. Rubinstein, G. A. Comstock, & J. P. Murray (Eds.), *Television and social behavior (Vol. 4): Television in day-to-day life* (pp. 129–256). Washington, DC: Government Printing Office.

Lynch, E. W. (1988). Mental retardation. In E. W. Lynch & R. B. Lewis, (Eds.), *Exceptional children and adults: An introduction to special education* (pp. 96–135). Glenview, IL: Scott, Foresman.

Lynch, E. W., & Lewis, R. B. (Eds.). (1988a). *Exceptional children and adults: An introduction to special education.* Glenview, IL: Scott, Foresman.

Lynch, E. W., & Lewis, R. B. (1988b). The nature and needs of exceptional people. In E. W. Lynch and R. B. Lewis (Eds.), *Exceptional children and adults* (pp. 4–45). Glenview, IL: Scott, Foresman.

Maccoby, E. E. (1980). *Social development.* New York: Harcourt, Brace, Jovanovich.

Maccoby, E. E., & Jacklin, C. N. (1974). *The psychology of sex difference.* Stanford, CA: Stanford University Press.

Maccoby, E. E., & Wilson, W. C. (1957). Identification and observational learning from films. *Journal of Abnormal and Social Psychology, 55,* 76–87.

MacMillan, D. L. (1988). Issues in mild mental retardation. *Education and Training in Mental Retardation, 23,* 273–284.

MacMillan, D. L., & Borthwick, S. (1980). The new educable mentally retarded population: Can they be mainstreamed? *Mental Retardation, 18,* 155–158.

Mallery, B., & Navas, M. (1982). Engagement of preadolescent boys in group therapy: Videotape as a tool. *International Journal of Group Psychotherapy, 32,* 453–467.

Margolin, G., & Patterson, G. R. (1975). Differential consequences provided by mothers and fathers for their sons and daughters. *Developmental Psychology, 11,* 537–538.

Marland, S. P. (1972). *Education of the gifted and talented: Report to the Congress of the United States by the Commissioner of Education.* Washington, DC: U.S. Government Printing Office.

Mates, B. F. (1980). Current emphases and issues on planned programming for children. In E. Palmer & A. Dorr (Eds.), *Children and the faces of television: Teaching, violence, selling* (pp. 19–32). New York: Academic Press.

McCarthy, J. M., & Paraskevopoulos, J. (1969). Behavior patterns of learning disabled, emotionally disturbed, and average children. *Exceptional Children, 36,* 69–74.

McConaughty, S. H., & Ritter, D. R. (1985). Social competence and behavioral problems of learning disabled boys aged 6–11. *Journal of Learning Disabilities, 18,* 547–553.

McIntyre, J. J., & Teevan, J. J., Jr. (1972). Television and violence and deviant behavior. In G. A. Comstock & E. A. Rubinstein (Eds.), *Television and social behavior. Vol. III: Television and adolescent aggressiveness* (pp. 383–435). Washington, DC: U.S. Government Printing Office.

McKinney, J. D., & Feagans, L. (1983). Adaptive classroom behavior of learning disabled students. *Journal of Learning Disabilities, 16,* 360–367.

McLeod, J., Atkin, C., & Chaffee, S. (1972). Adolescents, parents, and television use: Adolescent self-report measures from Maryland and Wisconsin samples. In G. A. Comstock & E. A. Rubinstein (Eds.), *Television and social behavior. Vol. III: Television and adolescent aggressiveness* (pp. 383–435). Washington, DC: U.S. Government Printing Office.

Mehrens, W. A., & Lehman, I. J. (1973). *Measurement and evaluation in education and psychology.* New York: Holt, Rinehart and Winston.

Messaris, P. (1983). Family conversations about television. *Journal of Family Issues, 4,* 293–308.

Messaris, P., & Kerr, D. (1983). Mothers' comments about television: Relation to family communication patterns. *Communication Research, 10,* 175–194.

Meyer, T. P. (1973). Children's perceptions of their favorite TV characters as behavioral models. *Educational Broadcasting Review, 7,* 25–33.

Mielke, K. W. (1990). Research and development at the Children's Television Workshop. *Educational Technology Research and Development, 38*(4), 7–16.

Milich, R., & Landau, S. (1982). Socialization and peer relations in hyperactive children. In K. D. Gadow & I. Bialer (Eds.), *Advances in learning and behavioral disabilities* (pp. 283–339). Greenwich, CT: JAI Press.

Mills, S., & Watkins, B. (1982, November). *Parents' perception of television effects and its relationship to televiewing restrictions.* Paper presented at the Midwestern Association for Public Opinion Research Conference, Chicago.

Mohr, P. J. (1972). Parental guidance of children's viewing of evening television programs. *Journal of Broadcasting, 23,* 213–228.

Morison, P., Kelly, H., & Gardner, H. (1981). Reasoning about the realities on television: A developmental study. *Journal of Broadcasting, 25*(3), 229–242.

Morrow, W. R., & Wilson, R. C. (1964). Family relations of bright high-achieving and underachieving high school boys. *Child Development, 35,* 1041–1049.

Morse, W. C., Cutler, R. L., & Fink, A. H. (1964). *Public school classes for the emotionally handicapped: A research analysis.* Washington, DC: Council for Exceptional Children.

Murray, J. P. (Ed.). (1980). *Television and youth: 25 years of research and controversy.* Boys Town, NE: Boys Town Center.

Murray, J. P., & Salomon, G. (1984). *The future of children's television.* Boys Town, NE: Boys Town Center.

Mussen, P., & Rutherford, E. (1961). Effects of aggressive cartoons on children's aggressive play. *Journal of Abnormal and Social Psychology, 62,* 461–464.

Naremore, R. C., & Hopper, R. (1990). *Children learning language: A practical introduction to communication development.* New York: Harper & Row.

Nasser, D. L., & McEwen, W. J. (1976). The impact of alternative media channels: Recall and innovation with messages. *Audio Visual Communication Review, 24,* 263–272.

Nathanson, D. E. (1977). *Designing instructional media* for severely retarded adolescents: A theoretical approach to trait-treatment interaction research. *American Journal of Mental Deficiency, 82,* 26–32.

National Council for Children and Television. (1979). Television and learning. *NCCT Forum, 2,* 1–42.

National Council for Children and Television. (1980). Critical television viewing. *Television and Children, 3,* 2–75.

Nelson, J. P., Gelfand, D. M., & Hartmann, D. P. (1969). Children's aggression following competition and exposure to an aggressive model. *Child Development, 40,* 1085–1097.

Nelson, K. (1978). How young children represent knowledge of their world in and out of language. In R. S. Siegler (Ed.), *Children's thinking: What develops?* (pp. 255–274). Hillsdale, NJ: Lawrence Erlbaum Associates.

Nelson, K., & Gruendel, J. (1981). Generalized event representations: Basic building blocks of cognitive development. In M. E. Lamb & A. L. Brown (Eds.), *Advances in developmental psychology* (Vol. 1, pp. 131–158). Hillsdale, NJ: Lawrence Erlbaum Associates.

Nelson, R., Gibson, F., & Cutting, D. S. (1973). Video taped modeling. The development of three appropriate social responses in a mildly retarded child. *Mental Retardation, 11*(6), 24–27.

Neuendorf, K. A. (1979). *Parental knowledge, parental mediation and perceptions of television.* Unpublished master's thesis, Department of Communication, Michigan State University.

Newcomb, H. (1979). *Television: The critical view* (2nd ed.). NY: Oxford University Press.

Newcomb, H., & Alley, R. S. (1983). *The producer's medium: Conversations with creators of American TV.* New York: Oxford University Press.

Nihira, K., Meyers, C. E., & Mink, I. (1980). Home environment, family adjustment and the development of mentally retarded children. *Applied Research in Mental Retardation, 1,* 5–24.

Nivin, H. (1960). Who in the family selects the TV program? *Journalism Quarterly, 37,* 110–111.

Nodine, B. F., Barenbaum, E., & Newcomer, P. L. (1985). Story composition by learning disabled, reading disabled, and normal children. *Learning Disabled Quarterly, 8*(3), 167–179.

O'Bryan, K. G. (1980). The teaching face: A historical perspective. In E. Palmer & A. Dorr (Eds.),

Children and the faces of television: Teaching, violence, selling (pp. 5–17). New York: Academic Press.

O'Bryan, K. G., & Silverman, H. (1972). *Report on children's television viewing strategies.* New York: Children's Television Workshop. (ERIC Document Reproduction Service No. ED 126 871)

O'Bryan, K. G., & Silverman, H. (1973). *Research report: Experimental program eye-movement study.* New York: Children's Television Workshop. (ERIC Document Reproduction Service No. ED 126 870)

O'Connell, B. G., & Gerard, A. B. (1985). Scripts and scraps: The development of sequential understanding. *Child Development, 56,* 671–681.

Olweus, D. (1978). *Aggression in the schools: Bullies and whipping boys.* Washington, DC: Hemisphere.

Olweus, D. (1980). Familial and development determinants of aggressive behavior in boys: A casual analysis. *Developmental Psychology, 16,* 644–669.

Osborn, D. K., & Endsley, R. C. (1971). Emotional reactions of young children to TV violence. *Child Development, 42,* 321–331.

Osborne, S. S., Kiburz, C. S., & Miller, S. R. (1986). Treatment of self-injurious behavior using self-control techniques with a severe behaviorally disordered adolescent. *Behavioral Disorders, 12,* 60–67.

Osofsky, J. D., & Oldfield, S. (1972). Parent–child interaction: Daughters' effect upon mothers' and fathers' behaviors. *Developmental Psychology, 7,* 157–168.

Owen, F. W., Adams, P. A., Forrest, T., Stolz, L. M., & Fisher, S. (1971). Learning disorders in children: Sibling studies. *Monographs of the Society for Research in Child Development, 36* (4, Serial No. 144).

Page, B. A. (1983). A parents' guide to understanding the behavior of gifted children. *Roeper Review, 5*(4), 39–42.

Palmer, E. L. (1974). Formative research in the production of television for children. In D. Olson (Ed.), *Media and symbols: The forms of expression, communication and education.* (The seventy-third yearbook of the National Society for the Study of Education.) Chicago: University of Chicago Press.

Paloutzian, R. F., Hasazi, J., Streifel, J., & Edgar, C. L. (1971). Promotion of positive social interaction in severely retarded young children. *American Journal of Mental Deficiency, 75,* 519–524.

Parents and Teachers Association. (1977). *Violence on TV: The effects of television on children and youth.* Chicago: National Congress of Parents and Teachers.

Parents and Teachers Association. (1978). *National PTA names best and worst TV shows with new program guide.* (Press Release.) Chicago: Author.

Parker, H. S. (1970). Is film a significant instructional resource? *Audiovisual Instruction, 15,* 47–48.

Parker, M., & Colangelo, N. (1979). An assessment of values of gifted students and their parents. In N. Colangelo & R. T. Zaffrann (Eds.), *New voices in counseling the gifted.* Dubuque, IA: Kendal/Hunt.

Pearl, D., Bouthilet, L., & Lazar, J. (1982a). *Television and behavior: Ten years of scientific progress and implications for the eighties.* (Vol. 1). Washington, DC: U.S. Government Printing Office.

Pearl, D., Bouthilet, L., & Lazar, J. (1982b). *Television and behavior: Ten years of scientific progress and implications for the eighties (Vol. 2).* Washington, DC: U.S. Government Printing Office.

Pearl, R., & Cosden, M. (1982). Sizing up a situation: LD children's understanding of social interactions. *Learning Disability Quarterly, 5,* 371–373.

Pedersen, F. A., Anderson, B. J., & Cain, R. L. (1980). Parent–infant and husband–wife interactions observed at five months. In F. A. Pedersen (Ed.), *The father–infant relationship: Observational studies in the family setting* (pp. 71–86). New York: Praeger.

Pennington, B. F. (1990). The genetics of dyslexia. *Journal of Child Psychology and Psychiatry, 31*, 193–201.

Perkins, R. P. (1989). *Communication deviances and clarity among the parents of high achieving, average, and learning disabled adolescents.* Unpublished doctoral dissertation, California School of Professional Psychology, Alameda.

Perkins, R. P., & Green, R. J. (1988). *The clear communication scale.* Unpublished manuscript, California School of Professional Psychology, Alameda.

Phillips, E. L., Phillips, E. A., Fixsen, D. L., & Wolf, M. M. (1971). Achievement Place: Modification of the behaviors of pre-delinquent boys within a token economy. *Journal of Applied Behavior Analysis, 4*, 45–59.

Piaget, J. (1969). *The child's conception of time.* London: Routledge & Kegan Paul.

Piaget, J., & Inhelder, B. (1956). *The child's conception of space.* London: Routledge & Kegan Paul.

Pillow, B. H., & Flavell, J. H. (1986). Young children's knowledge about visual perception: Projective size and shape. *Child Development, 57*, 125–135.

Polloway, E. A. (1985). Identification and placement in mild retardation programs: Recommendations for professional practice. *Education and Training of the Mentally Retarded, 20*, 218–221.

Potter, W. J. (1986). Perceived reality and the cultivation hypothesis. *Journal of Broadcasting & Electronic Media, 30*, 159–174.

Potter, W. J. (1988). Perceived reality in television effects research. *Journal of Broadcasting & Electronic Media, 32*, 23–41.

Poulos, R. W., Harvey, S. E., & Liebert, R. M. (1976). Saturday morning television: A profile of the 1974–75 children's season. *Psychological Reports, 39*, 1047–1057.

Program profits special education pupils. (1971–72). *Appalachian Advance, 6*(1), 21–24.

Quay, H. C., Morse, W. C., & Cutler, R. I. (1966). Personality patterns of pupils in special classes for the emotionally disturbed. *Exceptional Children, 32*, 297–301.

Rabinovitch, M. S., McLean, M. S., Jr., Markham, J. W., & Talbott, A. D. (1972). Children's violence perception as a function of television violence. In G. A. Comstock, E. A. Rubinstein, & J. P. Murray (Eds.), *Television and social behavior, Vol. 5, Television's effects: Further explorations* (pp. 231–252). Washington, DC: U.S. Government Printing Office.

Reeves, B., & Garramone, G. (1982). Children's person perception: The generalization from television people to real people. *Human Communication Research, 8*, 317–326.

Reeves, B., & Garramone, G. (1983). Television's influence on children's encoding of person information. *Human Communication Research, 10*, 257–268.

Reeves, B., Thorson, E., Rothschild, M. L., McDonald, D., Hirsch, J., & Goldstein, R. (1984, May). *Attention to television: Intrastimulus effects of movement and scene changes on alpha variation over time.* Paper presented at the International Communication Association Conference, San Francisco, California.

Reilly, S. S., & Barber-Smith, D. (1982). Expanded use of captioned films for learning disabled students. *Exceptional Children, 48*, 361–363.

Renzulli, J. S., Smith, L. H., White, A. J., Callahan, C. M., & Hartman, R. K. (1976). *Scales for rating the behavior characteristics of superior students.* Mansfield Center, CT: Creative Learning Press.

Retzlaff, W. F. (1973). Project worker: Videotaping work stations in industry. *Teaching Exceptional Children, 5*, 135–137.

Rice, M. L. (1983). The role of television in language acquisition. *Developmental Review, 3*, 211–224.

Rice, M. L. (1984). The words of television. *Journal of Broadcasting, 28*, 445–461.

Rice, M. L. (1990). Preschoolers' QUIL: Quick incidental learning of words. In G. Conti-Ramsden & C. E. Snow (Eds.), *Children's language* (Vol. 7, pp. 171–195). Hillsdale, NJ: Lawrence Erlbaum Associates.

Rice, M. L., Huston, A. C., & Wright, J. C. (1982). The forms of television: Effects on children's attention, comprehension, and social behavior. In D. Pearl, L. Bouthilet, & J. Lazar (Eds.), *Television and behavior: Ten years of scientific progress and implications for the eighties* (Vol. 2, pp. 24–38). Washington, DC: U.S. Government Printing Office.

Richards, G. P., Samuels, S. J., Turnure, J. E., & Ysseldyke, J. E. (1990). Sustained and selective attention in children with learning disabilities. *Journal of Learning Disabilities, 23,* 129–136.

Richert, S. (1981). Television for the gifted: A double-edge sword. *Roeper Review, 3*(4), 17–20.

Robertson, T. G. (1984). Determining curriculum content for the gifted. *Roeper Review, 6*(3), 137–138.

Robinson, J. P., & Bachman, J. G. (1972). Television viewing habits and aggression. In G. A. Comstock & E. A. Rubinstein (Eds.), *Television and social behavior. Vol. III: Television and adolescent aggressiveness* (pp. 372–382). Washington, DC: U.S. Government Printing Office.

Roedell, W. C. (1978, August). *Social development in intellectually advanced children.* Paper presented at the Annual Convention of the American Psychological Association, Toronto, Canada.

Roedell, W. C., Jackson, N. E., & Robinson, H. B. (1980). *Gifted young children.* New York: Teachers College Press.

Rolandelli, D. R., Wright, J. C., & Huston, A. C. (1985, May). *Children's auditory and visual processing of narrated and nonnarrated television programming.* Paper presented at the International Communication Association conference, Honolulu, Hawaii.

Rosengren, K. E., Wenner, L. A., & Palmgren, P. (Eds.). (1985). *Media gratifications research: Current perspectives.* Beverly Hills, CA: Sage.

Rosenkrans, M. A. (1967). Imitation in children as a function of perceived similarity to a social model and vicarious reinforcement. *Journal of Personality and Social Psychology, 7,* 307–315.

Rosenkrans, M. A., & Hartup, W. W. (1967). Imitative influences of consistent and inconsistent response consequences of a model on aggressive behavior in children. *Journal of Personality and Social Psychology, 7,* 429–434.

Ross, A. O. (1976). *Psychological aspects of learning disabilities and reading disorders.* New York: McGraw-Hill.

Ross, D. (1970). Effect on learning of psychological attachment to a film model. *American Journal of Mental Deficiency, 74,* 701–707.

Rossiter, J., & Robertson, T. S. (1975). Children's television viewing: An examination of parent-child consensus. *Sociometry, 38,* 308–326.

Routh, D. K. (1979). Activity, attention, and aggression in learning disabled children. *Journal of Clinical Child Psychology, 8,* 183–187.

Rubinstein, E. A., Fracchia, J. F., Kochnower, J. M., & Sprafkin, J. N. (1977). *Television viewing behaviors of mental patients: A survey of psychiatric centers in New York State.* New York: Brookdale International Institute.

Rubinstein, E. A., & Sprafkin, J. N. (1982). Television and persons in institutions. In D. Pearl, L. Bouthilet, & J. Lazar (Eds.), *Television and behavior: Ten years of scientific progress and implications for the 1980's* (pp. 322–330). Washington, DC: U.S. Government Printing Office.

Rushton, J. P. (1979). Effects of prosocial television and film material on the behavior of viewers. In L. Berkowitz (Ed.), *Advances in experimental social psychology* (pp. 321–351). New York: Academic Press.

Rutter, M., Tizard, J., & Whitmore, K. (Eds.). (1970). *Education, health, and behavior.* London: Longmans.

Rynders, J. E., & Friedlander, B. Z. (1972). Preference in institutionalized severely retarded children for selected visual stimulus material presented as operant reinforcement. *American Journal of Mental Deficiency, 76,* 568–573.

Salomon, G. (1979a). *Interaction of media, cognition, and learning: An exploration of how symbolic forms cultivate mental skills and affect knowledge acquisition.* San Francisco, CA: Joss-Bass.

Salomon, G. (1979b). Shape, not only content: How media symbols partake in the development of abilities. In E. Wartella (Ed.), *Children communicating: Media and development of thought, speech, understanding* (pp. 53–82). Beverly Hills, CA: Sage.

Salomon, G. (1981). Introducing AIME: The assessment of children's mental involvement with television. In H. Gardner & H. Kelly (Eds.), *Children and the world of television* (pp. 89–102). San Francisco, CA: Jossey-Bass.

Salomon, G. (1983). Television watching and mental effort: A social psychological view. In J. Bryant & D. R. Anderson (Eds.), *Children's understanding of television: Research on attention and comprehension* (pp. 181–220). New York: Academic Press.

Salomon, G. (1984). Investing effort in television viewing. In J. P. Murray & G. Salomon (Eds.), *The future of children's television* (pp. 59–64). Boys Town, NE: The Boys Town Center.

Salomon, G. (1990). Cognitive effects with and of computer technology. *Communication Research, 17*(1), 26–44.

Salomon, G., & Cohen, A. A. (1977). Television format, mastery of mental skills and the acquisition of knowledge. *Journal of Educational Psychology, 69,* 612–619.

Salvador, C. A. (1982). A formative evaluation of a social problem solving program which utilized television and group discussions in a children's residential treatment setting: A study in the dynamics of program evaluation (Doctoral dissertation, Rutgers University, 1982). *Dissertation Abstracts International, 43,* 885B. (University Microfilms No. DA8219041)

Sarason, I. G. (1968). Verbal learning, modeling, and juvenile delinquency. *American Psychologist, 23,* 254–266.

Sarason, I. G., & Ganzer, V. J. (1969). Social influence techniques in clinical and community psychology. In C. D. Spielberger (Ed.), *Current topics in clinical community psychology.* New York: Academic Press.

Sawin, D. B. (1975). Aggressive behavior among children in small playgroup settings with violent television. *Dissertation Abstracts International, 35,* 3565-B. (University Microfilms No. 75-185).

Sawin, D. B. (1981). The fantasy–reality distinction in televised violence: Modifying influences on children's aggression. *Journal of Research in Personality, 15,* 323–330.

Sawin, D. B. (1990). Aggressive behavior among children in small playgroup settings with violent television. In K. D. Gadow (Ed.), *Advances in learning and behavioral disabilities* (pp. 157–177). Greenwich, CT: JAI Press.

Scardamalia, M., & Bereiter, C. (1984). Development of strategies in text processing. In H. Mandl, N. L. Stein, & T. Trabasso (Eds.), *Learning and comprehension of text* (pp. 379–406). Hillsdale, NJ: Lawrence Erlbaum Associates.

Schloss, P. J., & Sedlak, R. (1982). Behavioral features of the mentally retarded adolescent: Implications for mainstream educators. *Psychology in the Schools, 19,* 98–105.

Schramm, W. (1962). What we know about learning from instructional television. In *Educational television: The next ten years.* Stanford, CA: Institute for Communication Research.

Schramm, W., Lyle, J., & Parker, E. B. (1961). *Television in the lives of our children.* Stanford, CA: Stanford University Press.

Schumaker, J. B., & Hazel, J. S. (1988). Social skills training. In K. A. Kavale, S. R. Forness, & M. Bender (Eds.), *Handbook of learning disabilities* (pp. 111–153). Austin, TX: PRO-ED.

Scott, E., & Bryant, B. (1978). Social interactions of early-reading and non-reading kindergarten students with high intellectual ability. *Catalog of Selected Documents in Psychology, 8,* 95.

Scruggs, T. E., & Cohn, S. J. (1983). Learning characteristics of verbally gifted students. *Gifted Child Quarterly, 27*(4), 169–172.

Sears, R. R., Maccoby, E. E., & Levin, H. (1975). *Patterns of child rearing.* Evanston, IL: Peterson.

Simon, H. (1976). Cognition and social behavior. In J. Carroll & J. Payne (Eds.), *Cognition and social behavior.* Hillsdale, NJ: Lawrence Erlbaum Associates.

Singer, D., Singer, J., & Zuckerman, D. (1981). *Getting the most out of TV.* Santa Monica, CA: Goodyear.

Singer, D. G., Zuckerman, D. M., & Singer, J. L. (1980). Helping elementary children learn about television. *Journal of Communication, 30*(3), 84–93.

Singer, J. L., & Singer, D. G. (1984). Intervention strategies for children's television. In J. P. Murray & G. Salomon (Eds.), *The future of children's television* (pp. 93–102). Boys Town, NE: The Boys Town Center.

Singer, J. L., Singer, D. G., & Rapaczynski, W. S. (1984). Family patterns and television viewing as predictors of children's beliefs and aggression. *Journal of Communication, 34*(2), 73–89.

Skeen, P., Brown, M., & Osborn, D. (1982). Young children's perception of "real" and "pretend" on television. *Journal of Perceptual and Motor Skills, 54,* 883–887.

Smith, R., Anderson, D. R., & Fischer, C. (1985). Young children's comprehension of montage. *Child Development, 56,* 962–971.

Solomon, B. (1976a). Using videotape to motivate the LD student. *Academic Therapy, 11,* 271–274.

Solomon, B. (1976b). Using entertainment television shows on videotape to teach the retarded. *Reading Improvement, 13,* 180–181.

Sparks, G. G., & Abelman, R. (1985). Can TV really frighten children? *Television & Families, 8*(1), 27–30.

Spergel, H. K. (1979). *A listing of educational series broadcast by public television licensees, 1978–1979.* Washington, DC: Corporation for Public Broadcasting.

Spradlin, J. E. (1966). Environmental factors and the language development of retarded children. In S. Rosenberg (Ed.), *Developments in applied psycholinguistic research.* Riverside, NJ: Macmillan.

Sprafkin, J., & Gadow, K. D. (1986). Television viewing habits of emotionally disturbed, learning disabled, and mentally retarded children. *Journal of Applied Developmental Psychology, 7,* 45–59.

Sprafkin, J., & Gadow, K. D. (1987). An observational study of emotionally disturbed and learning disabled children in school settings. *Journal of Abnormal Child Psychology, 15,* 393–408.

Sprafkin, J., & Gadow, K. D. (1988). The immediate impact of aggressive cartoons on emotionally disturbed and learning disabled children. *Journal of Genetic Psychology, 149,* 35–44.

Sprafkin, J., Gadow, K. D., & Dussault, M. (1986). Reality perceptions of television: A preliminary comparison of emotionally disturbed and nonhandicapped children. *American Journal of Orthopsychiatry, 56,* 147–152.

Sprafkin, J., Gadow, K. D., & Grayson, P. (1984). Television and the emotionally disturbed, learning disabled, and mentally retarded child: A review. In K. D. Gadow (Ed.), *Advances in learning and behavioral disabilities* (pp. 151–213). Greenwich, CT: JAI Press.

Sprafkin, J., Gadow, K. D., & Grayson, P. (1987). Effects of viewing aggressive cartoons on the behavior of learning disabled children. *Journal of Child Psychology and Psychiatry, 28,* 387–398.

Sprafkin, J., Gadow, K. D., & Grayson, P. (1988). The effects of cartoons on emotionally disturbed children's social behavior in school settings. *Journal of Child Psychology and Psychiatry, 29,* 91–99.

Sprafkin, J., Kelly, E., & Gadow, K. D. (1987). Reality perceptions of television: A comparison of emotionally disturbed, learning disabled, and nonhandicapped children. *Journal of Developmental and Behavioral Pediatrics, 8*(3), 149–153.

Sprafkin, J. N., Liebert, R. M., & Poulos, R. W. (1975). Effects of a prosocial televised example on children's helping. *Journal of Experimental Child Psychology, 20,* 119–126.

Sprafkin, J., & Rubinstein, E. A. (1982). Using television to improve the social behavior of institutionalized children. *Prevention in Human Services, 2,* 107–114.

Sprafkin, J. N., Rubinstein, E. A., & Stone, A. (1977). *A content analysis of four television diets.* New York: Brookdale International Institute.

Sprafkin, J., Watkins, L. T., & Gadow, K. D. (1986). *Curriculum for enhancing social skills through media awareness.* Unpublished curriculum, State University of New York at Stony Brook.

Sprafkin, J., Watkins, L. T., & Gadow, K. D. (1990). Efficacy of a television literacy curriculum for emotionally disturbed and learning disabled children. *Journal of Applied Developmental Psychology, 11,* 225–244.

Stein, A. H., & Friedrich, L. K. (1972). Television content and young children's behavior. In J. P. Murray, E. A. Rubinstein, & G. A. Comstock (Eds.), *Television and social behavior. Vol. II: Television and social learning* (pp. 202–317). Washington, DC: U.S. Government Printing Office.

Steiner, G. (1963). *The people look at television.* New York: Knopf.

Stephan, C., Stephano, S., & Talkington, L. (1973). Use of modeling in survival skill training with educable mentally retarded. *Training School Bulletin, 70,* 63–68.

Stephens, W. E., & Ludy, I. E. (1975). Action-concept learning in retarded children using photographic slides, motion picture sequences, and live demonstrations. *American Journal of Mental Deficiency, 80,* 277–280.

Sternberg, R. (1982). A componential approach to intellectual development. In R. Sternberg (Ed.), *Advances in the psychology of human intelligence* (Vol. 1, pp. 413–463). Hillsdale, NJ: Lawrence Erlbaum Associates.

Sternberg, R. J., & Spear, L. C. (1985). A triarchic theory of mental retardation. In N. R. Ellis (Ed.), *International review of research in mental retardation* (Vol. 13, pp. 301–326). New York: Academic Press.

Sternberg, R. J. (1985). *Beyond IQ: A triarchic theory of human intelligence* New York: Cambridge University Press.

Sternberg, R., & Davidson, J. E. (1985). Cognitive development in the gifted and talented. In F. D. Horowitz, & M. O'Brien (Eds.), *The gifted and talented: Developmental perspectives* (pp. 37–74). Hyattsville, MD: American Psychological Association.

Sternberg, R. J., & Davidson, J. E. (Eds.) (1986). *Conceptions of giftedness.* Cambridge, MA: Cambridge University Press.

Stipp, H. (1975). *Validity in social research: Measuring children's television exposure.* Unpublished doctoral dissertation, Columbia University, New York.

Stone, W. L., & La Greca, A. M. (1990). The social status of children with learning disabilities: A re-examination. *Journal of Learning Disabilities, 23,* 32–37.

Striefel, S. (1972). Television as a language training medium with retarded children. *Mental Retardation, 10*(2), 27–29.

Striefel, S. (1974). Isolating variables which affect TV preferences of retarded children. *Psychological Reports, 35,* 115–122.

Striefel, S., & Eberl, D. (1974). Imitation of live and videotaped models. *Education and Training of the Mentally Retarded, 9,* 83–88.

Striefel, S., & Smeets, P. M. (1974). TV preference as a technique for selection of reinforcers. *Psychological Reports, 35,* 107–113.

Strommen, E. A., McKinney, J. P., & Fitzgerald, H. E. (1977). *Developmental psychology: The school-aged child.* Homewood, IL: Dorsey Press.

Surgeon General's Scientific Advisory Committee on Television and Social Behavior. (1972). *Television and growing up: The impact of televised violence* (Report to the Surgeon General). Rockville, MD: National Institute of Mental Health.

Swanson, H. L. (Ed.). (1987). *Advances in learning and behavioral disabilities (Suppl. 1): Memory and learning disabilities.* Greenwich, CT: JAI Press.

Talkington, L. W., & Altman, R. (1973). Effects of film-mediated aggressive and affectual models on behavior. *American Journal of Mental Deficiency, 77,* 420–425.

Tannenbaum, A. J. (1979). Pre-Sputnik post-Watergate concern about the gifted. In A. H. Passow (Ed.), *The gifted and the talented: Their education and development* (pp. 5–27). Chicago: University of Chicago Press.

Tannenbaum, P. H. (1971). Emotional arousal as a mediator of communication effects. *Technical reports of the Commission on Obscenity and Pornography* (Vol. 8). Washington, DC: U.S. Government Printing Office.

Tarjan, G., Wright, S. W., Eyman, R. K., & Keeran, D. V. (1973). Natural history of mental retardation: Some aspects of epidemiology. *American Journal of Mental Deficiency, 77,* 369–379.

Taylor, B., & Howell, R. (1973). The ability of three, four and five year old children to distinguish fantasy from reality. *Journal of Genetic Psychology, 122,* 315–318.

Terman, L. M., & Oden, M. II. (1947). *Genetic studies of genius: Vol. 4, The gifted child grows up: Twenty-five years' follow-up of a superior group.* Stanford, CA: Stanford University Press.

Terman, L. M., & Oden, M. H. (1959). *Genetic studies of genius: Vol. 5, The gifted group at mid-life: Thirty-five years' follow-up of the superior child.* Stanford, CA: Stanford University Press.

Thompson, T. L., & Slater, D. (1983, November). *Parent-child co-viewing and parental monitoring of television: Their impacts and interaction.* Paper presented at the Speech Communication Association Conference, Washington, DC.

Thorkildsen, R. (1985). Using an interactive videodisc program to teach social skills to handicapped children. *A.A.D.,* November, 383–385.

Thorson, E., Reeves, B., & Schleuder, J. (1985). Message complexity and attention to television. *Communication Research, 12,* 427–454.

Tims, A. R., & Masland, J. L. (1984, June). *Political socialization processes: The linkage between parental social value priorities and the family communication environment.* Paper presented at the International Communication Association Conference, San Francisco, California.

U.S. House of Representatives Subcommittee on Telecommunications, Consumer Protection, and Finance. (1983). *Summary of children's programing on commercial television.* Washington, DC: Author.

U.S. Office of Education. (1977). *Federal Register, 42,* 42478.

U.S. Department of Education. (1989). *Twelfth annual report to Congress on the implementation of the Education of the Handicapped Act.* Washington, DC.

U.S. Senate, Subcommittee on Communication. (1969). *Federal Communications Commission policy matters and television programming (Part 2).* Washington, DC: U.S. Government Printing Office.

Vallecorsa, A. L., & Garriss, E. (1990). Story comprehension skills of middle-grade students with learning disabilities. *Exceptional Children, 57*(1), 48–54.

Vande Voort, L., Senf, G. M., & Benton, A. L. (1972). Development of audiovisual integration in normal and retarded readers. *Child Development, 43,* 1260–1272.

Van Evra, J. (1990). *Television and child development.* Hillsdale, NJ: Lawrence Erlbaum Associates.

Vare, J. Q. (1979). Moral education for the gifted: A confluent model. *Gifted Child Quarterly, 23,* 487–499.

Vellutino, F. R. (1987). Dyslexia. *Scientific American, 256,* 34–41.

Vurpillot, E. (1964). Perception et representation dans la constance de la forme. *Psychologique, 64,* 61–82.

Wagner, R. K., & Torgesen, J. K. (1987). The nature of phonological processing and its causal role in the acquisition of reading skills. *Psychological Bulletin, 101,* 192–212.

Wakshlag, J. J., Reitz, R. J., & Zillmann, D. (1982). Selective exposure to and acquisition of information from educational television programs as a function of appeal and tempo of background music. *Journal of Educational Psychology, 74,* 666–677.

Wales, R. (1979). Deixis. In P. Fletcher, & M. Garman (Eds.), *Language acquisition* (pp. 241–260). New York: Cambridge University Press.

Walters, R. H., & Willows, D. C. (1968). Imitative behavior of disturbed and nondisturbed children following exposure to aggressive and nonaggressive models. *Child Development, 39,* 79–89.

Wand, B. (1968). Television viewing and family differences. *Public Opinion Quarterly, 32,* 84–94.

Warford, P. (1981). Educational projects at ABC television. In M. E. Ploghoft & J. A. Anderson (Eds.), *Education for the television age* (pp. 101–105). Athens, OH: The Cooperative Center for Social Science Education.

Wartella, E. (Ed.). (1979). *Children communicating: Media and development of thought, speech, understanding.* Beverly Hills, CA: Sage Publications.

Wartella, E. (1981). The child as viewer. In M. E. Ploghoft & J. A. Anderson (Eds.), *Education for the television age* (pp. 28–34). Athens, OH: The Cooperative Center for Social Science Education.

Wartella, E., Heintz, K. E., Aidman, A. J., & Mazzarella, S. R. (1990). Television and beyond: Children's video media in one community. *Communication Research, 17*(1), 45–64.

Watkins, L. T., Sprafkin, J., Gadow, K. D., & Sadetsky, I. (1988). Effects of a critical viewing skills curriculum on elementary school children's knowledge and attitudes about television. *Journal of Educational Research, 81,* 165–170.

Watkins, L. T., Sprafkin, J., & Krolikowski, D. M. (1990). Effects of video based training on spoken and signed language acquisition by students with mental retardation. *Research in Developmental Disabilities, 11,* 273–288.

Weener, R. D., & Senf, G. M. (1982). Learning disabilities. In H. E. Mitzel (Ed.), *Encyclopedia of educational research* (5th ed., pp. 1059–1068). New York: The Free Press.

Welch, A., & Watt, J. (1982). Visual complexity and young children's learning of TV. *Human Communication Research, 8,* 133–145.

Wells, W. D. (1973). *Television and aggression: Replication of an experimental field study.* Unpublished manuscript, Graduate School of Business, University of Chicago.

Whitmore, J. R., & Maker, C. J. (1985). *Intellectual giftedness in disabled persons.* Rockville, MD: Aspen Systems Corporation.

Wiig, E. H., & Semel, E. M. (1976). *Language disabilities in children and adolescents.* Columbus, OH: Merrill.

Wiig, E. H., & Semel, E. M. (1984). *Language assessment and intervention of learning disability.* Columbus, OH: Merrill.

Wildman, B. G., & Kelly, J. A. (1980). Group news watching and discussion to increase the current affairs awareness of retarded adolescents. *Child Behavior Therapy, 2,* 25–36.

Wildmon, D. E. (1985). *The home invaders.* Wheaton, IL: Victor Books.

Winn, M. (1977). *The plug-in drug.* New York: Bantam Books.

Withrow, F. B. (1980). Objectives for critical television viewing skills curricula. *Television and Children, 3,* 32–33.

Wolf, M. A., Abelman, R., & Hexamer, A. (1982). Children's understanding of television: Some methodological considerations and a question-asking model for receivership skills. In M. Burgoon (Ed.), *Communication Yearbook 5* (pp. 405–431). New Brunswick, NJ: Transaction Press.

Wood, D. J. (1980). Teaching the young child: Some relationships between social interaction, language, and thought. In D. R. Olson (Ed.), *The social foundations of language and thought* (pp. 280–296). New York: Norman.

Wright, J. C., & Huston, A. C. (1983). A matter of form: Potentials of television for young viewers. *American Psychologist, 38,* 835–843.

Wright, J. C., Huston, A. C., Ross, R. P., Calvert, S. L., Rolandelli, D., Weeks, L. A., Raeissi, P.,

& Potts, R. (1984). Pace and continuity of television programs: Effects on children's attention and comprehension. *Developmental Psychology, 20,* 653–666.

Yanok, J., & Derubertis, D. (1989). Comparative study of parental participation in regular and special education programs. *Exceptional Children, 56,* 195–199.

Young, M. R. (1981). The P.T.A. Project. In M. E. Ploghoft & J. A. Anderson (Eds.), *Education for the television age* (pp. 111–115). Athens, OH: The Cooperative Center for Social Science Education.

Zeaman, D., & House, B. J. (1963). The role of attention in retardate discrimination learning. In N. R. Ellis (Ed.), *Handbook of mental deficiency.* New York: McGraw-Hill.

Zeaman, D., & House, B. J. (1979). A review of attention theory. In N. R. Ellis (Ed.), *Handbook of mental deficiency* (2nd ed., pp. 63–120). Hillsdale, NJ: Lawrence Erlbaum Associates.

Zendel, I. H., & Pihl, R. O. (1983). Visual and auditory matching in learning disabled and normal children. *Journal of Learning Disabilities, 16*(3), 158–160.

Zigler, E., & Farber, E. A. (1985). Commonalities between the intellectual extremes: Giftedness and mental retardation. In F. D. Horowitz & M. O'Brien (Ed.), *The gifted and talented: Developmental perspectives* (pp. 387–408). Washington, DC: American Psychological Association.

Zillmann, D. (1969). *Emotional arousal as a factor in communication-mediated aggressive behavior.* Unpublished doctoral dissertation, University of Pennsylvania, Philadelphia.

Author Index

Subject Index